I've often told friends, "If you can find God in Hollywood, you can find him anywhere." Lee Stanley not only found the Lord; he went to work for him. This moving book is clearly the work of an award-winning filmmaker, full of vivid scenes, memorable images, and dialogue that'll make you laugh one moment and cry the next, all contributing to an uplifting sense of divine promise fulfilled.

Jeff Maguire, Academy Award – nominated screenwriter and
the screenwriter for the motion picture *Gridiron Gang*

A truly superb memoir that inspires as it informs about neglected juveniles and what it takes for the human heart to change. Stanley's style is as compelling as his story—vigorous and sensuous, with a filmmaker's gift for drama and pacing. I did not want to put it down.

Robert Siegel, professor emeritus of English,
University of Wisconsin-Milwaukee,
and author of *The Waters Under the Earth* and *A Pentecost of Finches*

A powerful and moving book that will bring faith and inspiration to those fortunate enough to read it. This book serves as a testament that there is heart in Hollywood. I know firsthand that my amazing friend and colleague Lee Stanley puts his heart into everything he does.

Neal Moritz, producer of the motion picture *Gridiron Gang*

After reading *Faith in the Land of Make-Believe*, Jane and I had the same reaction as we did to the Desperate Passage docu-drama series, which we had the pleasure of financing. What an insightful, inspiring look behind the scenes of a life lived so meaningfully! We are very proud to partner with Lee and Linda Stanley.

Bert and Jane Boeckmann, owners of Galpin Motors, Inc.

What wondrous—and wild—things happen when a tough guy asks God to take over the reins of his life! Lee Stanley clearly was called to step out in faith and risk everything for a mission greater than anything he'd ever imagined— helping kids who'd messed up and inspiring the world. The multiple Emmy-winning filmmaker's journey is funny, shocking, poignant, and sweet. Lee and Linda's love story is a testimony to the power of a faithful, faith-filled marriage. I laughed a lot, gasped a few times, and, yes, was moved to tears as I read *Faith in the Land of Make-Believe*.

Stacy Jenel Smith, syndicated Hollywood columnist

Lee's story is that of an artist who keeps faith and finds beauty in the midst of desolation. In shipwrecking storms and blinding fog, he keeps his faith. Take this opportunity to hear from someone worth knowing, whose vision is made real through courage. Parents of all ages need to read this insightful autobiography.

Jahn Rokicki, director of Early Childhood Services,
Harbor Regional Center, Torrance, California

Powerful, transparent, and inspirational—a must-read for anyone considering working in the entertainment industry! Save yourself significant grief by learning from a master teacher trained by experience.

Dr. Rick Bee, senior director, alumni and friends development, Biola University

If ever there was a lion of God, it's Lee Stanley. Lots of people talk the talk, but this man walks every step of the walk. Stanley doesn't know how to quit. For him, closed doors and the word *no* are simply battle cries to begin the war. *Faith in the Land of Make-Believe* is an inspiring account of how one person can change the world—if he trusts his God and refuses to back down. You don't have to know or even like Hollywood to be encouraged that, whatever your sphere of influence may be, if you take God at his word and fight the fight, you will set the captives free.

Bill Myers, bestselling author of *The God Hater*

This book is a fabulous inside view of two completely different worlds that are never talked about in the same sentence. Read it and be challenged to be a difference maker in your generation.

David Loveless, lead pastor of Discovery Church, Orlando, Florida

This book is about more than the battles and triumphs in Lee's life. It is about the spirit of a man who is driven by his commitment, dedication, faith, and vision in a world far too driven by immediate gratification. Lee has had a positive impact on thousands of lives, including mine. Without his vision and conviction, the *Gridiron Gang* story never would have been told. I recommend this book to all in need of a little inspiration to stay the course without compromising their personal values.

Sean Porter (portrayed by Dwayne Johnson in the movie *Gridiron Gang*), senior probation director of the Los Angeles County Probation Department

Intimate, honest, and truly original. Lee's adventures, both at sea and on land, kept me turning pages until midnight.

Lin Pardey, sailor and author

Lee's book is an incredible journey of putting others first and making extreme sacrifices to see to it that no one gets left behind.

Bret Michaels, multi-platinum recording artist, reality television star, and winner of *Celebrity Apprentice*

Faith in the Land of Make-Believe is awesome and represents everything that needs to be talked about every day: GOD is everything—See ya in the ring.

Antonio Sabato Jr., actor, reality television star of *My Antonio*, winner of TV's *Celebrity Circus*, and sparring partner

FAITH
in the Land of
MAKE-BELIEVE

WHAT GOD CAN DO ... EVEN IN

HOLLYWOOD

LEE STANLEY
Award-winning Filmmaker and Producer of *Gridiron Gang*

Foreword by
DWAYNE JOHNSON

ZONDERVAN

ZONDERVAN.com/
AUTHORTRACKER
follow your favorite authors

ZONDERVAN

Faith in the Land of Make-Believe
Copyright © 2011 by Lee Stanley

This title is also available as a Zondervan ebook.
Visit www.zondervan.com/ebooks.

This title is also available in a Zondervan audio edition.
Visit www.zondervan.fm.

Requests for information should be addressed to:

Zondervan, *Grand Rapids, Michigan* 49530

Library of Congress Cataloging-in-Publication Data

Stanley, Lee.
    Faith in the land of make-believe: what God can do . . . even in Hollywood /
Lee Stanley.
        p.   cm.
    ISBN 978-0-310-32545-1 (hardcover, jacketed)
        1. Stanley, Lee, 1943- 2. Christian biography—United States. 3. Christian
converts—United States—Biography. 4. Motion picture producers and
directors—United States—Biography. 5. Church work with juvenile
delinquents—United States—Case studies. I. Title.
BR1725.L363A3 2010
277.3'082092—dc22   2010003540

Cover design: Curt Diepenhorst
Cover photography: Martin Barraud / Getty Images
Interior design: Michelle Espinoza

Printed in the United States of America

11 12 13 14 15 /DCI/ 22 21 20 19 18 17 16 15 14 13 12 11 10 9 8 7 6 5 4 3 2 1

To Linda,
forever my love

Let this be written for a future generation,
   that a people not yet created may praise the LORD.

Psalm 102:18

CONTENTS

FOREWORD

From the day I met Lee Stanley, I knew he was a unique and special man. I was so overwhelmingly moved by his documentary *Gridiron Gang* that I immediately agreed to make the film. I was eager to meet the man responsible for actually changing the lives of these young men. When we shook hands for the first time, he looked me straight in the eye and thanked me wholeheartedly for doing the movie. It was then that I could see Lee was comprised of pure truth, compassion, and conviction. Those are indicative adjectives when I describe Lee Stanley and certainly truthful words to describe this book, *Faith in the Land of Make-Believe*.

As for many of us, Lee's journey through life has been full of countless struggles and setbacks. Yet it was always Lee's unwavering conviction and compassion that allowed him to realize that those same countless struggles were, in fact, countless blessings. Over twenty years ago, Lee dedicated his life to helping at-risk youth. Incarcerated youth. He devoted his life to empowering them with self-esteem and, more important, self-respect. Lee's efforts to change these kids' lives have been tireless. The impact he has had on literally thousands of kids is priceless. I feel fortunate to know Lee and his amazing family. I am eternally grateful to him, and more than anything, I am proud to call him my friend. It is an honor to write the foreword for this book. Lee, as you know, "there is no success without struggle." Congratulations. You are a true blessing.

Your friend,
Dwayne Johnson

INTRODUCTION

Heart. This book is all about heart. It's about more than heart as in "guts" or gut feelings, but it includes them. It's about passion, determination, and a refusal to give up when there was every reason to do so — but even more, it's also ...

about having a heart for people, especially those society tends to give up on.

about having a heart for your marriage, especially when it's stressed by the pressures that break up a lot of them.

about having a heart for your kids, especially when everything you hoped for them seems to backfire.

And it's also about having a heart for God, especially about God in his *reality* — which means you encounter his *nonreligiousness.* (Contrary to what many suppose, the Real God doesn't even need to be religious.)

Anyway, Lee Stanley asked me to jot a quick note to you introducing his book. He said, "Pastor Jack, I'm asking you to do this, hoping you think I'm reflecting those values it's about." Since you're reading this, I obviously do.

I was in week-to-week touch with Lee and his dear wife, Linda, for the middle years of the story here. This centerpiece to it climaxes with the release of a movie — with the fulfillment of a dream. You'll like the way it reveals the *real world* of fulfilled dreams — and they don't come easy. More important, the greatest dreams are never self-centered. They may be yours, but they are focused on helping others—on making a difference. That's why the best dreams include God—because they could never be told without God's being invited in. (And when he is—I mean *really*, and with no pretense—he accepts the invitation.)

You'll love finding out how God does that—in this bluntly honest, totally up-front account of how God meets real people in the middle of real problems. You'll find yourself moved too, because, frankly, it's emotional to read the great things that happen when *tough love* begins to transform *tough kids*.

And by the way, if anyone familiar with me wonders why I would endorse a book that uses some language I don't, here are two reasons. First, this story can't be told credibly without taking us into its setting. Lee had to tell it *real*, and he has. Second, since the Bible tells us, "God displayed his love for us when all of us were distant and opposed to him—and Christ died for us" (my paraphrase of Romans 5:8), I conclude that a frank telling of a real story about the "before and after" of some tough guys doesn't offend God when the "before" is told as it is.

So read—and meet Lee Stanley, *a real man with a really great heart*. It's a story that is as wild as the kids involved, as exciting as life can get, and as wonderful as God really is.

Dr. Jack W. Hayford,
president, Four Square International;
founding pastor, The Church On The Way,
Van Nuys, California

A BROTHER'S "FOREWORD"

I am Lee's only brother. When Lee asked me to read his autobiography, I expected a somewhat dry, predictable tome. I was wrong "per usual" (inside joke). Lee's story is so pure and human in its telling that you find yourself right beside Lee at each turn, crying, cheering, wanting to jump into the fight to help him win.

I was there for some of it; for some of it I was not. I had no idea how serious and powerful his story is and how his story would impact me emotionally and, in parts, actually physically. Lee has a way of describing events that makes them so real that you can actually see them develop in an almost surreal manner.

Jump into Lee's life and you will see for yourself . . .

Oh, Lee asked me to make suggestions to improve it. For some reason, he has been deluded into thinking I am a writer on the same level as is he. He is wrong, but to try to maintain the illusion, I diligently went about the task. I found two spelling errors.

I should be so blessed as to have his talent.

Love, and God bless.

Unca Ricky

AUTHOR'S NOTE

Some of the names, locations, and dates have been changed so I don't get sued — or shot.

L.S.

PART 1

CHAPTER 1

THIS IS NO HONOR FARM

CAMP DAVID GONZALES —

LOS ANGELES COUNTY PROBATION DEPARTMENT

I'd driven past this small wooden sign in Malibu Canyon dozens of times on the way down to our sailboat in Marina del Rey. I thought it was an honor farm, a minimum-security detention facility, tucked beneath the rocky peaks of the Santa Monica Mountains in Malibu and surrounded by sprawling horse ranches and multimillion-dollar estates.

I turned my four-wheel-drive truck down the short, tree-lined lane and realized the massive compound before me was no "honor farm," but a maximum-security juvenile prison. Behind the two-story wall, an eighty-foot metal pole supported a small cluster of powerful floodlights.

I turned into the empty, unkempt visitor parking lot and looked around for some signs of life. A screeching red-tailed hawk circled in the distance. I rolled up my window, climbed out of my truck, and locked all the doors. Invisible surveillance cameras tracked my every move as I walked self-consciously along the narrow concrete path to the prison entrance. A small sign below a dime-sized electronic button told me to "ring bell." I looked up to see the red-tailed hawk, now circling directly overhead, when a loud buzzer startled me, releasing an invisible steel bolt. I pushed against the double-plated bulletproof glass door and entered the prison.

The year was 1981.

"I'm here to see Chaplain Fox," I told the male guard behind the counter.

Chaplain Fox had found my film company's name in the Yellow Pages earlier that morning and asked if I would splice a film that the camp projector had damaged the night before. Why not? I was "between projects," as filmmakers like to say. Besides, I was curious to see what Camp David Gonzales was really all about.

"What's your name?"

"Lee Stanley."

The guard checked the handwritten entries in the dog-eared ledger chained to the countertop.

"Wait right there," he ordered before disappearing down a bleak hallway.

The poorly lit, hospital-green front office smelled like a wet dog.

"You a cop?"

I turned to see a teen in baggy jeans and a crisp white T-shirt gripping a push broom, staring at me through half-closed eyes. He was medium height, with pockmarked, pasty skin. Tattoos marked his bare, muscular arms and thick neck, while his shaved head was a hockey rink of scars.

"Nope," I replied.

He kept his menacing eyes on me.

"You look like a cop—I hate cops!"

"Chaplain's on the phone," announced the guard as he returned to the front office. He eyeballed his one-man cleaning crew. "Mr. Rhodes, give Mr. Stanley a tour."

The teen prisoner, Mr. Rhodes, looking away from me, leaned the broom against the scuffed green wall and pushed open the heavy door that led to the camp's enclosed compound. I grabbed the door just before it slammed shut. Mr. Rhodes stayed a pace or two ahead, walking with a strange, limping gait.

The grassy "yard," which was about the size of an oval football field, was surrounded by a high wall. One-story cinder block buildings topped with rusty cyclone fencing and barbwire were integrated into the wall. We walked in uncomfortable silence past the shabby softball diamond and weight-lifting pit, then across a cracked and bumpy asphalt basketball court where chain nets hung from bent hoops. In front of us, a squad of twenty-five sullen juveniles, hands clasped behind their backs, moved toward a nearby building under the watchful eye of a powerfully built probation officer.

"How many kids are here?" I asked Mr. Rhodes.

"One-twenty," he said without turning, his voice flat and cold.

As the silent squad of prisoners neared, my tour guide's strange gait amplified, and he purposefully worked his baggy jeans lower and lower until his butt crack was in plain sight.

"You're saggin', Rhodes!"

A voice bellowed over the yard's loudspeaker. Rhodes pulled up his baggy jeans with one hand, slowly.

"And stop strollin'!"

My escort cursed under his breath and continued walking, minus the strange gait. He spat, not quite clearing his chin, and wiped it off with the back of his scarred fist.

Trying to ease the tension, I pointed to a building that was obviously a gym and asked, "What's that over there?"

"Gym!"

"Can I ask you something else?"

Mr. Rhodes slowed to a stop, his mad-dog stare trying to bore holes in my head.

"How old are you," I continued, "seventeen, eighteen?"

"I'll be eighteen in a minute," he claimed, puffing up his chest and sneaking an admiring glance at his muscled arms.

I thought I was about to get coldcocked, so I quickly continued. "I don't know why you're locked up, but to my understanding, they cut you loose when you're eighteen. You got a whole life ahead of you. What are you going to do with it?"

His eyes squinted as if he'd never considered a future.

"You can be anything you want to be—doctor, welder, probation officer, even a filmmaker." I watched as curiosity began to creep onto his face. "Juvenile records are confidential, right?" He nodded, almost childlike. "No one ever has to know that you messed up."

I felt like I was talking at myself.

■ ■ ■

At age nineteen, I hopped a twin-engine commercial "tail dragger" out to the West Coast via Chicago after "messing up." I arrived in Burbank, California, on a foggy May morning with fifty-five bucks in my pocket, a small tattered suitcase stuffed with a couple pairs of Levis, T-shirts, fins, mask, snorkel, and scuba regulator— and no plans. I'd left Connecticut after taking a smack in the face from my mother and being told to go to hell. I was trying to escape my reputation: *You're a damn bum, and everybody knows you're a damn bum!*

I'd already dropped out of college, and I had no plans. I realized that no one ever taught me how to be a man, a husband, or a father, and I was scared to death that somebody would find out.

"What you doing in California?"

An elderly black man, sucking on a well-worn pipe, was emptying trash cans at the Burbank Airport where I was waiting for a Greyhound bus. He had a peaceful way about him.

"Do some scuba diving, write articles for adventure magazines. Stuff like that."

The answer sounded good to my ears—in California I could pretend to be anybody I wanted to be. I could escape my past.

"Well, son," said the man, tapping his old pipe on his calloused hand. "If you can't make it in California, you can't make it anywhere."

■ ■ ■

"Mr. Stanley, return to the front office!" the camp loudspeaker echoed across the compound.

I extended my hand to inmate Rhodes. He looked at it and then took it limply.

"When you shake a man's hand," I said, "grab on to it." He quickly squeezed my hand. "And look me in the eye!" He did. "Thanks for the tour" — then I headed toward the front office.

"Mr. Stanley!" I turned back. "Will you — will you come back and visit me? Sir?"

I thought for a long moment. "I don't know."

I collected the tattered film reel from Chaplain Fox and left the facility. Once back on the outside of the brick wall, I took a deep breath. I felt numb, unsure where to put all that I had just experienced.

"Line up and shut up!" the camp loudspeaker bellowed from inside the prison. I turned and looked up at the shiny gray loudspeakers bolted to the tall light pole. "Hands behind your back! Move it out! On quiet!"

I wandered back to my truck, climbed in, and sat behind the wheel.

I don't know why, but I cried.

That first "up-front and personal" encounter with "killer kids" at Camp David Gonzales was an alarming wake-up call. Within moments, I sensed those hostile teen predators had me locked in their invisible crosshairs; they knew who I was (and I'm not talking about my name), what they thought of me and why.

Killer kids can read your eyes, your body language, your muscle tone, your gait, your hairstyle, your clothes, and the tone of your voice, even your choice of words. To them you represent an "opportunity," a walking billboard, a living testament of your net worth. They gauge your strengths and weaknesses. In the flick of a switchblade they know if they should play you, when they should play you, and how they should play you.

If you do get "the nod," please know that you have been hand-picked for one or all of the above reasons, and your chances of survival are slim to none.

I got the nod—and it changed every area of my life.

■ ■ ■

My custom-built cedar home was in the same Santa Monica Mountains as Camp Gonzales, but three miles farther west and overlooking picturesque Malibu Lake. I was a documentary film-maker obsessed with doing things "my way" and thus always scrambling for work to feed my blended family of five. I'd been married and divorced twice and had a five-year-old son, Shane, when I met Linda, my third wife. I also had a nine-year-old daughter whom I had never met from my first marriage. Linda brought two sons to the party, ages nine and twelve. We added Wiley the goat and Star the dog shortly thereafter. So far, we'd survived four bumpy years.

We couldn't see the lake from our home because of the thick stand of pines and leafy sycamores between us and the water. In our garage we maintained our off-road motorcycles, organized our sailing and camping gear, and worked out with our boxing equipment. My private studio was perched over the garage, its high ceiling and windows creating the perfect setting for filmmaking—and wrestling matches with my kids.

Another short flight of stairs led to the main house. While not large, it was romantic and always smelled of fresh air, pine trees, and Linda's home cooking. At nighttime, we could hear the coyotes and sometimes the screech of an owl. Our distant neighbors were quiet and friendly and always smiled and waved when we drove past or took out our trash barrels.

Nobody ever mentioned Camp David Gonzales.

"Chaplain Fox called while you were out," my wife announced as she entered the studio and placed a tray of iced lemonade and Fig Newtons on my cluttered desk.

"Any message?"

"She's very nice." Linda poured the lemonade. "I set up a screening of *Mountain Tops* for next Saturday at Sylmar Juvenile Hall."

"You did *what?*"

"Chaplain Fox asked if you had any films that would inspire the prison kids. When I told her about *Mountain Tops*, she got all excited." Linda leaned down and kissed me and then headed for the door. "I already talked to Rick. He and Esther will meet us there."

My friend Rick and his fiancée, Esther, were the subject of the documentary.

CHAPTER 2

FORTY-ACRE KID CAGE

Sylmar Juvenile Hall (now called Barry J. Nidorf Juvenile Hall) is located in the foothills of the smoggy San Fernando Valley. It houses a pimple-faced potpourri of more than 350 tough, angry, scared, confused, violent, abandoned, deranged, and sometimes innocent kids. Surrounded by a twenty-foot-high brick wall that is topped with razor wire, it is continuously monitored by surveillance cameras and blasted by dozens of massive mercury-vapor floodlights that illuminate every square inch of this forty-acre kid cage.

The boys and girls inside range from age nine to eighteen. Most look twice their age and have committed every crime you can imagine. The majority are expressionless, slovenly, pissed-off underachievers who were given up on by parents and society long ago.

The sad part is, most of these kids know it.

■ ■ ■

When a kid gets busted in Los Angeles, he or she first goes to the hall for sentencing, then waits for an available bed to open up at one of the county's fourteen juvenile camps. Some of the kids do their entire time in the hall.

Eighty-five percent of the kids have divorced parents or never knew their parents.

Every year, a handful of kids manage to escape the overpopulated and understaffed juvenile hall. Stupidly, they scoot back to their home turf, only to be scooped up in a day or two by the local cops and carted back to jail.

The juvenile system is peppered with euphemisms. The so-called *hall* is really a *jail*. *Program* means *sentence*; a child is not *sentenced* but rather *placed* in detention. *Prisons* are called *camps, guards* are *counselors*, and those incarcerated — oops, those *detained* — are not *prisoners* but *wards* who will be released when they *graduate* from the *program*.

Most noteworthy, a ward is never found guilty of a crime (only adults can be found "guilty" — unless the juvenile is tried as an adult); guilt is referred to as *a sustained petition.* Thus, a juvenile who may have participated in a similar crime as an adult can honestly say they have not been convicted. The court can seal a ward's records when he or she turns eighteen, and while wards are in the system, their names and identification cannot be made public. Identifiable photographs of juveniles are absolutely forbidden — no exceptions — without the court's written consent. Only licensed professionals, members of the probation department, law enforcement officials, legal defense folks (usually an overworked and inexperienced public defender), ministers, or court-approved family members may visit a ward while he or she is incarcerated.

Regardless of the system's efforts, every year, juvenile crime persists, with kids continuing to kill, sell drugs, rob people, stab people, turn tricks, steal cars, and get "jumped in" to violent street gangs. In its 120-plus-year history, nothing the juvenile justice system has ever created, established, developed, or implemented to "rehabilitate" wards of the court has ever worked to reduce juvenile crime. And yet year after year, billions of taxpayer dollars are poured into the same programs, institutions, frustrated social workers, and researchers under the guise of solving the problem.

About a couple of dozen years ago, and without admitting failure, the "shot callers" in our state capitals decided that we need to focus efforts (which means spend *your* money) on rehabilitating "at-risk" juveniles (those currently doing drugs, gangbanging, hooking, knocking up their thirteen-year-old girlfriends, and whacking people upside the head—yet who haven't been caught or have been placed on probation instead of doing time in our grossly overcrowded jails—I mean halls).

Programs were quickly created, funded, staffed, and carried out. The phrase *at-risk children* became a cause célèbre for those wanting a one-shot pat on the back for volunteering their time or ponying up a fistful of dollars to save these little boys and girls from a life of crime.

Regardless of the "focused efforts," an increasingly steady flow of fresh, new "at-risk kids" nationwide make their way into the bulging-at-the-seams system each year.

And how were those kids already in the system affected?

Existing programs were cut, and aftercare programs (after a ward would graduate) became nonexistent.

What's a mother to do?

■ ■ ■

Dozens of brooding wards shuffled into Sylmar Juvenile Hall's 350-seat chapel in single file, hands clasped behind their backs "on quiet" for the Saturday night screening of *Mountain Tops*. The half-hour documentary film features Rick Leavenworth, a twenty-three-year-old paraplegic, who sets out to climb a jagged mountain in the High Sierra. Rick is a mechanical draftsman and one of the most amazing and content human beings I have ever known.

I first discovered Rick on the cover of a Christian magazine. He had been photographed sitting in his wheelchair somewhere on a wooded trail, a backpack strapped to his flimsy legs and a big smile on his wide, happy face. I quickly called the editor of the small publication and announced that I was a filmmaker and was considering doing a film on his cover boy.

A week later, the editor called back.

"Rick said 'thank you very much,' but he's going to pass on the opportunity. He said he just wasn't worthy to have a film done on him."

A year later, I called again. This time, Rick called me back. "Hey, how you doing?" he asked in a cheerful voice. I could feel that smile coming right through the phone. "Why would you want to do a film about me?" he queried with the innocence of a schoolboy.

"You're an inspiration," I said from my heart. "And I can't stop thinking about that picture of you on the magazine cover. Have you ever climbed a mountain, Rick?"

"No! Have you?"

"Nope. I'm afraid of heights."

"Cool! Let's do it!"

■ ■ ■

The chapel at Sylmar filled quickly. Rick sat quietly in his wheelchair at the back, all smiles, with his lovely fiancée, Esther, by his side. Guards (aka "counselors") were strategically positioned throughout the small auditorium. Linda and I stood against the back wall, watching the tension build as the disgruntled teen girls and boys flopped into their seats, flashing an occasional "finger" or gang sign at rival groups. Others were busy checking out the opposite sex.

As the kids filed in, the hall's assistant director barked out unnecessary direction through his bullhorn, irritating the already edgy teens. The last of the wards entered, strutting their stuff and mad-doggin' everyone. These were the bad boys, the "vets" who had been in and out of the juvenile system for years. The lead tough, a good-looking Hispanic with gang tattoos and a thick scar running the length of his face, eyeballed my wife as if I weren't there and squeezed his crotch a couple of times.

"Welcome to the Hall!"

Chaplain Sonja Fox stood near the bullhorn-toting Gene Waterman. A plain woman with short, bobbed hair and horn-rimmed glasses, Chaplain Fox was as real as they came, without the phony God talk that makes unbelievers want to stay that way.

Assistant warden Waterman suddenly aimed the bullhorn in my direction.

"Shut up and sit down!" he shouted at the kids near me, causing a sudden painful ringing in both my ears. "I will not tolerate inappropriate behavior! Mr. Stanley has come here on his own time, and frankly I would not blame him if he decided not to show you his film!" Waterman scanned the inmates with his squinty eyes. "Any more disruptions, and you'll be on lockdown for the week—every one of you!"

He waited until there was absolute quiet and then turned to me. "Go up and say a few words about the movie."

I took a deep breath and, with ears still ringing, started the long walk to the front of the crowded chapel to face the motley mix of kids. Some slouched low in their chairs, strong arms folded defiantly across their chests. Others stared back with hooded eyes or exchanged jaded looks with their homeboys or homegirls.

"Hi, my name's Lee Stanley." The mic shrieked with feedback, causing all of us to wince. A probation officer scrambled to turn down the mic while I took a few steps back to regain my composure. "*Mountain Tops* is a documentary about a guy who attempts to climb Red Slate Mountain, a 13,163-foot peak up in the central part of California. We filmed it as it actually happened." I scanned the room, looking for some signs of life or interest. There were none.

"Hope you enjoy the film. Thank you." I put down the mic with a loud thud and returned to the back of the auditorium where I could scan the audience as they watched the movie.

Mountain Tops always screens well. I am very proud of Rick Leavenworth, especially after we nearly lost him during our initial attempt, when on the final morning of the climb we were hit by a violent storm at eleven thousand feet with sixty-knot winds packing a wind-chill factor of twenty below. Rick went into hypothermia, shivering uncontrollably, his breathing quick and shallow. I knew if we didn't get help fast, Rick would soon be dead.

I put out an emergency call on my two-way radio.

"Helicopter film crew, helicopter film crew, this is Red Slate Attack (our code name). Over!"

"Red Slate Attack, this is helicopter film crew, go ahead. Over!"

I yelled above the wind. "We're at eleven thousand feet and need an emergency evacuation. Rick has gone into hypothermia. Over!"

"We're on our way. Out!"

Rick stopped shivering, a sure sign that his body was shutting down. I climbed into his sleeping bag, hoping my body warmth would keep him alive.

Forty minutes later, and fighting hurricane-force winds, a helicopter miraculously plucked paraplegic mountaineer Rick Leavenworth off the side of the mountain and raced him back to civilization, where he spent five days in the local hospital.

"I want to go back to Red Slate and finish my climb," Rick told me once he was home. "Hey, maybe this time we'll see an eagle — my favorite bird."

Ten days later, Rick Leavenworth crawled up to the summit of Red Slate Mountain and looked out in every direction for hundreds of miles.

"Thank you, Lord," he said with a smile.

We both heard a loud screech. Two hundred feet overhead, a bald eagle circled majestically on outstretched wings. One of its feathers dislodged and floated lazily down through the crisp, clean air. The feather landed in Rick's open palm. Then the eagle disappeared — straight up!

■ ■ ■

I usually get emotional watching the final scene in *Mountain Tops* in which Rick crawls those last few yards on his elbows, dragging his body up to the summit of Red Slate Mountain.

Not this time.

Some of the kids were laughing as they watched Rick flop in and out of his wheelchair or struggle to drag his droopy legs up the steep mountain. As the lights came up, I walked to the front of the chapel to scattered applause.

"Thank you!" This time all eyes were on me. "I'd like to introduce you to a friend of mine." I pointed toward the back of the chapel. "Rick Leavenworth!"

The room went silent. The kids had no idea Rick was there. Rick beamed back a smile as I gestured to him to come forward. The kid sitting directly in front of Rick had been laughing throughout the film. He turned as Rick rolled past and looked him right in the eye. "Sorry, man," he mumbled.

Rick smiled back and grabbed the boy's hand. Some of the kids stood to get a better look at the broad-shouldered mountaineer scrunched down in his wheelchair. Others just stared in silent admiration.

"Anybody have any questions?" I asked as Rick rolled in next to me.

There was a long pause. Then, "What happened to your legs?"

When Rick agreed to make the movie, he had one condition: He would never have to explain to me or anyone else how he became paralyzed. He simply stated that there was an accident when he was four years old, and we were told to leave it at that.

Here, in front of 350 hardened kids, Rick looked out over the audience toward his fiancée, Esther, standing in the back of the room. He then took the microphone and allowed himself a thoughtful moment.

"When I was four years old," he began, "my mother drove me and my eight-year-old sister, Kathy, into the Mojave Desert. Mom parked about a half mile off the main road and then told us to get out of the car. 'We're going to play a game of blindman's bluff,' she said, and then she folded a scarf and wrapped it around Kathy's head. She took a second scarf and wrapped it tightly around my head so I couldn't see. I heard a clicking sound, then a sharp explosion that dropped me to the ground. My sister screamed and took off running. My mom walked over and shot me two more times with a 38-caliber handgun. Kathy flagged down an 18-wheeler and escaped.

"By God's miraculous grace I lived, but one of the three bullets that hit me severed my spine and paralyzed me from the waist down."

Rick breathed a deep sigh and looked at the now motionless audience. Someone in the back sobbed. It was Esther.

"Is your mother in prison?" asked a girl in the second row.

"My mom was very sick. She was put in a mental hospital where she could get help. We see each other often. I love her — she's my mom, and I forgive her."

Mr. Waterman walked over to us and tapped his wristwatch. "We're going to have to wrap it up," he warned.

"Do you mind if I conclude in prayer?" I asked.

He wasn't expecting that.

My prayer was short and sweet. All bowed their heads in quiet reverence.

When I finished, the kids stood on command as their dorm was called, and they exited in single file lines. As they walked past, they nodded respectfully, and some even shook our hands and thanked us for being there.

When the chapel was empty, Waterman pulled me aside.

"If you want to come back tomorrow," he offered, "I'll make arrangements."

CHAPTER 3

"I DIE, YOU GO TO PRISON"

The next day Rick and I returned to Sylmar Juvenile Hall.

"We're here to see Mr. Waterman," I told the woman behind the bulletproof glass at the hall's musty front entrance.

"He don't come in on Sundays," she replied indifferently, her nose in a cruise ship brochure.

"How about Chaplain Fox?"

"She's down at Central." Then the keeper of the gate looked up for the first time and saw Rick. "Praise God!" she trumpeted, tossing down her brochure and pushing open the metal door to smother Rick in a massive hug. "I told those kids you'd come back!"

She handed me a small envelope with my name printed on it. Inside was a heavy key attached to a leather cord tied at the ends.

"Don't lose it, honey," she said as she placed the leather strap around my neck.

"What's this?" I asked.

"Mr. Waterman's master key. You can go wherever you want. I'll call A-Dorm, first building on the right, and let them know you're coming."

Without escort, Rick and I "walked and rolled" along the concrete path leading to the various one-story buildings that were enclosed by the massive brick fortress. I sensed hundreds of oppressed eyes tracking us through windows that were painted over, leaving only the top six inches clear.

I gripped the large bronze key dangling from my leather neck-lace, leaned down, and inserted it into the oversized lock. I pushed open the heavy metal door to A-Dorm to find two dozen girls in their early teens, quietly seated at some stainless steel lunch tables, staring back at us. They were dressed in matching baby blue button-up shirts and khaki pants. Most looked old beyond their years, and expressions ranged from sullen to angry, vulnerable to shy, and vacant to sexy. The open room had a gray concrete floor with pink cinder block walls that were chipped and stained. A female counselor smiled a greeting just as the steel door slammed closed behind us.

"Ladies, if you have any questions for Mr. Stanley or Mr. Leav-enworth, raise your hand."

No one responded. Some turned apathetically back to their scratched and discolored plastic food trays. The silence stretched out.

"I'm sorry we interrupted your lunch," I said. "We'll stop back later," and turned for the door.

"Do you have any kids?" a young voice asked, stopping me.

A young teen with soft brown hair and liquid eyes was look-ing at me. What was she doing in jail? She belonged at the beach with her friends or at home painting her toenails and giggling on the phone with her boyfriend.

"Yes, I do."

I knew what was coming next.

"Any girls?" she asked.

"I have one daughter and three sons."

"How old is your daughter?" she asked, continuing her tender interrogation.

"She will be fourteen in March," I said, having to check myself on the date.

"Is she pretty?"

My heart was racing. A simple yes, and I was off the hot seat, on to B-Dorm, and away from this nosy, doe-eyed runaway.

"Is she?" the girl persisted, tilting her head just enough.

"I don't know," I said softly. "I've never seen my daughter."

■ ■ ■

In March 1967, I was awakened by an early morning phone call from my brother in Connecticut.

"Congratulations, bro!" Ricky said. "We just heard the great news!"

"What great news?" I said, now wide-awake.

My brother's wife had spoken to her best friend on the West Coast, who happened to be a close friend of my daughter's mother. My daughter, I learned, was born — two days earlier.

I quickly called the ex-mother-in-law, who informed me in guarded tones that baby and mother were at her home in Beverly Hills.

"The baby is weak and cannot see any outsiders for a while," she stated. "Doctor's orders."

"I am not an outsider," I bellowed. "I want to see my daughter!"

The phone went dead. I went ballistic and called back.

"If you call again or attempt to come over here," she warned, "I'll call the police!"

What was going on? I was feeling like Dustin Hoffman in *The Graduate* trying to get to Elaine, and she was Mrs. Robinson blocking the way. Granted, this was no ordinary mother-in-law — she was someone you didn't want to tangle horns with. Bess was fifty-two and still gorgeous, with the body of a woman half her age — and the heir to a substantial fortune left by her late estranged and famous composer husband. She had twin daughters, a son who was a twentysomething homosexual, and a nine-year-old daughter going on thirty. Bess lived in modest seclusion, having succumbed to Catholic guilt after divorcing her composer/voyeur husband when he boogied to New York City to buy a room with a view. Her twin daughters were real showstoppers — loud, filled with gaiety, and when one or both dyed their blonde hair dark, they became Elizabeth Taylor look-alikes, à la Cleopatra.

I first met one-half of the twins (whom I nicknamed "Kiki") at Catalina Island the summer of 1963. I was living on a twenty-three-foot speedboat in Avalon Harbor with my buddy Art. We would start each morning diving overboard and swimming the fifty yards to shore for breakfast. By the time we hit the main drag, the warm sun and cool sea breeze had dried our tanned bodies. As we passed a waterfront restaurant, I noticed two girls leaving their table — and a plate of food that had barely been touched. We quickly elbowed our way past the busboy and sat down to a breakfast of slightly poked-at pancakes and crisp bacon.

"You've got to be kidding!" I heard a female's laughing voice declare as she approached our table.

It was Kiki and her traveling companion — a foxy, thin blonde girl in an obviously padded bra — returning to the table to leave their tip.

We became fast friends. They stayed at the island an extra week, and Art and I took them out on the boat to sunbathe and watch us dive. Nothing more.

Back on the mainland we would ride our matching 250 Honda Scrambler motorcycles up from Newport Beach to join Kiki and friends at a local nightclub or dinner spot. We were a novelty item — beach bums on Hondas living on a boat, rubbing elbows with the rich and phobic. Sometimes it got too late or we got too drunk to ride back to Newport, so we would stay at Kiki's Beverly Hills house that she shared with mama Bess.

Everybody got to know each other real well. Kiki was entertaining and pretty and had lots of her daddy's money. Then over coffee and sweet rolls one morning, I announced my plans to jump a tramp freighter to Greece.

Awkward silence.

I took a bite of breakfast and smiled, sort of.

"You should work in films," Kiki announced.

Bess made a phone call to her close buddy Frank, and the next day Art and I were extras on the big-budget motion picture *Von Ryan's Express*, starring Frank — as in Sinatra.

The job lasted two weeks and paid well. I never did get to meet "Ole Blue Eyes," but one day on the set he pushed through the crowd of three hundred extras with actress Mia Farrow in tow. I was tempted to jump out and say, "Hey, Frank, it's me!" but better judgment prevailed. Besides, extras in the film business learn early that they are not supposed to have any meaningful exchange with stars, unless of course the extra is a gorgeous blonde.

I'm a brunette.

The next job followed the first and so on down the line. I ran with some stunt guys, took up racing motorcycles, and started doubling stars who couldn't tie their shoelaces without tipping over.

I had met a boatful of famous actor types over at Catalina and during our motorcycle runs up to Beverly Hills. Most tended to play out snippets of different characters performed in the past and were always "holding court." Once you got them alone, they were as nervous as puppies in traffic.

There was one actor, however, whom I always wanted to meet — Paul Newman. I studied him in *Sweet Bird of Youth*, in *Hud*, and (as Fast Eddie) in *The Hustler*. This guy was cool to the bone.

During a fight scene I was in for a *Mr. Novak* television episode, a small Jiminy Cricket–type man asked if I ever thought about acting.

"I can lie just as good as the next guy," I boasted.

Three weeks later, Jiminy Cricket, acting coach extraordinaire, invited me to be part of MGM's new talent program along with a handful of other young hopefuls.

My new profession did not go over well with Kiki. I was getting too much attention and having too much fun.

Finally, after a screen test at Warner Brothers, I came home super-late. Kiki turned peculiar and began screaming accusations at the top of her lungs so all of Beverly Hills could hear that I had bedded down my leading lady.

She was wrong — this time.

Out of customary guilt, I married Kiki but didn't change my habits. Shortly thereafter, Kiki came home from a night on the town with her gay friends. I was playing poker with a motorcycle buddy at our dining table. Without a word Kiki disappeared into the back bedroom and returned gripping my semiautomatic, hair-trigger, loaded hunting rifle and pushed the cold steel barrel right between my startled eyes.

"You bastard!" she seethed through clenched teeth.

One of Kiki's gay pals had seen me out on the town with the "padded bra" Catalina girlfriend.

My biker tablemate made a move toward the front door. Kiki swung the loaded rifle at him.

"Sit down!" she warned.

"Let him go!" I pleaded. "He hasn't done anything!"

She swung the rifle back toward me. My pal ran out of the house. Kiki began shaking, eyes filled with rage, foam forming in the corners of her quivering mouth.

"Kiki, put the gun down!" I pleaded.

"You bastard!" she screamed and aimed right at my face.

"Think it through, Kiki. I die, you go to prison!"

I suddenly flipped the heavy oak table over on her and scrambled out the back door.

That was the last time I saw Kiki — until March 1994, twenty-seven years later, and the day before our daughter's wedding. Linda and I spotted Kiki in a local restaurant. Kiki didn't see us, and though invited, she did not come to her daughter's wedding.

■ ■ ■

"Why haven't you ever seen your daughter?"

This little knock-off Penelope Cruz was pressing for the truth, perhaps to help understand why her own father abandoned her or to make me accountable for not being there for my daughter.

"Her mother hated me and did everything she could to keep us apart."

"Why?" she demanded.

I darted a look over to the female counselor. She stared back with a slight smirk.

"Because I was unfaithful."

Unfaithful and afraid. I had seen Kiki flip out. She was, at times, frightening — seemingly possessed. I was convinced she would cut our daughter, Quinn, in half before allowing me to see her.

Over the years, I wrote my daughter letters and sent her cards. Linda and I prayed for her daily. We learned that Quinn was attending Bel Air Prep in Hollywood. On her eighteenth birthday, we drove to the school. Linda walked in with a birthday card expressing our heartfelt desire for Quinn to become part of our family and gave it to the principal.

Two weeks later, I received a handwritten note from Quinn: *You're too late.*

I continued sending cards and letters. She never responded.

Nine years later, in 1994, my twenty-two-year-old son, Shane (from my second wife, Carol), pulled me aside.

"I just had lunch with your daughter," he beamed.

He told me how he miraculously found her and how they connected with each other the moment they met. Then he showed me her picture — beautiful! I know that's what every father says about his daughter, but Quinn is a knockout.

"She can't see you yet," Shane explained. "This is going to take time, Dad. Quinn has no idea who you are or what you are really like — only what her mother told her."

Two months later, Shane invited Linda and me to hear his rock band perform at a local club. The room was packed, and as my son rocked out onstage, the silhouette of a girl walked toward me— darting off at the last second like a scared deer. I couldn't see her face, but I turned to Linda.

"That's my daughter!"

A few minutes passed, then I felt a tug on my shirtsleeve. Without looking, I grabbed the person and held her tight.

"I love you, Quinn!" were my first words to my daughter.

"I love you too."

After a joyous celebration, and well wishes and tears from an audience of absolute strangers, we returned to our home. Quinn and I went into the living room and talked until dawn. Quinn asked me every question you can imagine—and a few I hadn't counted on.

I told her the truth.

CHAPTER 4

YOU BETTER BE WHO YOU CLAIM TO BE

In May 1976, I was standing outside a church in the San Fernando Valley watching the "Jesus freaks" greeting one another with holy hugs and praising "You Know Who" for such a beautiful day. All I knew from the time I was in pants was that church was boring, and I didn't appreciate being told by my Sunday school teachers that I was a sinner who was going straight to hell.

I've always felt uncomfortable around people who act religious — that's one reason why I steered clear of Christ for the first thirty-three years of my life.

As I watched the seemingly happy scene in front of me, I thought, "Get real, folks. It's hot, it's sticky, and the Valley smog sucks — I'm thirty-three, divorced twice, a single dad, and you better not try to hug me!"

I self-consciously scanned the large, bubbly group for the film producer who tricked me into joining him for Sunday morning service. Dave Adams first invited me to have brunch poolside at his Bel Air estate. He was writing the checks for my educational films, and his company, Pyramid Films, was distributing them, so of course I said yes.

Then he brought up the church part.

"I don't own a sport jacket," I complained.

"You won't need one," he replied.

"I don't even have a tie!"

"We'll meet you out front," Dave said.

The longer I stayed out front, the better things were looking. I scanned the crowd and zeroed in on some really gorgeous women. I caught one lovely's eye and managed my first smile of the day.

"Good morning, Lee!" Producer Dave was pushing through the crowd with his wife, Lynn, by his side. He grabbed my hand and shook it with heartfelt enthusiasm. "Isn't this a beautiful day?"

The double doors of The Church On The Way kicked open, spilling a wave of people down the steps and onto the sidewalk. They seemed strangely joyful, energized, and refreshed. Then I found myself moving with the " 'second service" crowd toward the main entrance and separated from Dave and Lynn. Dave waved me on with a smile.

As I pressed my way inside the small church, I sensed a Voice speaking to me—as if no one else were around. "Welcome home, Lee. We have a lot of things to do together."

Silent tears of release began to pour down my cheeks. Once the two-hour service was over, I couldn't wait to come back.

A week later, I returned to The Church On The Way and accepted Jesus Christ as my personal Lord and Savior—with the condition that if he were not *exactly* who he claimed to be, I would drop him like a bad habit.

One of my first prayers after the dust settled was, "Lord, if you have someone out there for me, you're going to have to bring her to me. I'm done chasing your lambs."

Ten days later, Linda and I met in a bookstore.

What a woman! She was tall and trim, with a beautiful, tanned body, auburn hair, a sensuous mouth, and a gorgeous smile. She recommended a book on tennis; I recommended we have coffee next door. Before Linda could say no, I gathered her parcels and escorted her around the corner. We sipped coffee and talked for an hour. We made the long walk back to her car in awkward silence. My heart was racing, and I was dreading the fact that she would soon be gone.

"I've been looking for you all my life," I said, then gently kissed her on the mouth.

Stunned, and with visibly shaking knees, Linda climbed into her pale yellow Buick Skylark and, without a word, drove off.

The next morning, I called Los Angeles Children's Hospital, where Linda told me she taught school. A cranky, officious nurse answered the phone.

"Dialysis Unit, this is Mrs. Talbert."

"May I speak with Linda, please?"

There were probably two dozen Lindas working at Children's Hospital, and I couldn't remember her last name.

"You mean 'the one and only Linda'?" asked the head nurse.

"That's the one."

She put me on hold for what seemed like forever.

"This is Linda," a soft, warm voice said on the other end of the line.

"This is Lee."

"I know."

That felt nice.

"May I take you to lunch today?"

Long pause.

"All right."

I packed a small picnic basket of cheese, bread, and wine, including cloth napkins, then drove the twenty-plus miles down to Los Angeles Children's Hospital, feeling like an overanxious, love-sick teenager.

Linda was waiting in the hospital lobby. We drove in silence to a nearby park and found a remote picnic table under a large shade tree. I uncorked the chilled wine, filled two plastic glasses, handed one to Linda, and asked her to be my wife.

Linda was raised in a middle-class Christian home under the covering of a father who loved God and family, went to church every Sunday, and played by the rules. When she was a senior in high school, thirty-eight-year-old John Petrie, Linda's adoring dad, was killed in a United Airlines midair collision with a military jet over Las Vegas, Nevada. Devastated beyond words, the family turned to their pastor for answers.

"I don't know why," confessed the family's Methodist minister. "Sometimes God just lets things happen."

Not very comforting for a beautiful young woman who loved her father.

Linda turned her back on God and his reps and spent the next eighteen years "uncovered," which means no one was overseeing and protecting her spiritually — at least, no one on the Lord's team.

Father's Day, June 1976, Linda and I walked into the church for our first "official" date. The congregation was singing and clapping and praising the Lord — with hands lifted up, mind you!

Linda turned to me with a startled look. "Lee, this is a Holy Roller church."

I had no idea if that was a good thing or a bad thing. After fifteen minutes of jubilation, Pastor Jack Hayford gave his sermon on the role and character of a father, both our earthly fathers and our heavenly Father. Pastor Jack is respected around the world. The first time I sat under his teaching, I felt like Jimmy Stewart was talking to me. I trusted him immediately — no manipulation, no grandstanding, just the truth.

He concluded the Father's Day sermon by asking everyone to bow their heads, inviting anyone who wanted to accept Christ to signal him with their hand and then to come down front to the prayer room. The service closed, and Linda started toward the altar.

"Linda," I said, gently steering her toward the back exit, "that's only for the people who signaled Pastor Jack."

"I know," she said with moist eyes. "I just accepted Jesus as my Lord and Savior."

CHAPTER 5

HOMESICK— BUT FOR WHAT?

A week after the *Mountain Tops* screening, I went back to Sylmar Juvenile Hall on my own. I noticed a miserable kid sitting on a bench all by himself, studying his county-issued black Converse sneakers.

I scooped up a nearby foam football and signaled him to go out for a pass. He fumbled my first throw but scooped it up and returned a sidearm wobbler that I had to chase after. We continued to play for about five minutes without any talking. Finally, I signaled him to go long and deep, and then I threw a bomb. My rookie wide receiver made a diving catch.

One of the nastiest reactions a human being can experience is one of disrespect. If you dis a street thug, he'll blast you. Dis your woman, she'll scratch your eyes out — or stick a loaded semiautomatic rifle between your terrified eyes.

The only thing worse is to believe that you are not worthy of respect. Very crippling. To survive, you join a gang, do uncaring things, wet the bed, take drugs, become a hermit, lie when it's cheaper to tell the truth, take a shot at the "enemy" before they get a shot off at you — or jump a twin-engine commercial "tail dragger" out to Southern California.

How I responded to that measure of inadequacy early on in my life was who I became — defensive, paranoid, intimidating, hot-headed, and extremely competitive. Weakness was a no-no, and I made damn sure that I never got myself into any situation where I would be embarrassed or beaten. Too often, those traits trampled potential relationships, opportunities, and gentle souls. But now those same traits worked to my benefit, allowing me tremendous insight and revelation into the "throwaway" kids who would consume fifteen years of my life.

"Touchdown!" I yelled, my words echoing off Sylmar's surrounding brick wall and across the yard. The boy scrambled to his feet, grinning from ear to ear.

"Would you like to become one of my volunteers?"

Chaplain Amalia Torres was making her way toward our imaginary end zone. I sensed a tone of admonishment in the woman's question and wondered why she felt the need to interrupt our game.

The chaplain was pushing forty, really leaning into it, with bleached blonde hair, a tight print dress, and enough makeup to make even me look pretty. Her jewelry was noisy, and she smelled good. "I oversee all Christian activities," she stated. "Would you come with me, please."

That was not a question.

I tossed the foam football to my jilted teammate and followed Chaplain Torres back to her office, speculating how she could walk on the grass in stiletto heels and wondering why I felt like I had been caught doing something wrong.

In her large office she handed me an official-looking form. "You need to fill out an application and mail it back to my office before you return here." I stared down at the form. "All religious programs must go through me," she added as if I should know better.

"I don't have a religious program. I just wanted to make myself available to kids who want to talk."

"You're the moviemaker, aren't you?"

I sensed a trap.

"You reference your Christian faith when speaking to the children and you pray. *If* you would like to come back on a regular basis, you can become one of my volunteer interns."

"What would that require?" I asked, feeling like a lamb being cut from the flock.

"Coming in one day a week, after you've been given clearance and training," she answered with a rather unholy look. "You are a member of a church, aren't you?"

"Yes. My wife and I are members of The Church On The Way."

"I know that church," said the good chaplain without conviction. She pranced around to my side of her oversized desk, her heels clicking on the smooth concrete floor. "I've always wanted a film done on our work with these children." She stopped directly in front of me and cocked her blonde head innocently to one side. "What do you think about that?"

"That would be interesting," I said, waiting for the next stiletto to drop.

"You'd have to photograph them without identifying them." Sensing victory, she excitedly opened a black leather book perched on the corner of her desk and flipped a few blank pages. "Tomorrow, 10:00 a.m.?"

She scribbled in the journal.

"What about my application and training?" I asked, hoping to sidestep.

"*I'll* train you!"

■ ■ ■

I was in jail once when I was twenty-eight years old. It was May 1971, a month before my son, Shane, was born. I was full of myself—producing and directing my first documentary film, *On the Line*, about "the men who risk it all in the perilous sport of desert motorcycle racing, and the women who wait," starring yours truly.

For those of you who have never thrown a leg over a Greeves 250 Challenger or a Husqvarna, desert racing is an American Motorcycle Association–sanctioned event where five hundred to a thousand riders (at least in my time) line up on their bikes with their engines off. All are aimed toward the ominous unknown horizon, accented by a billowing smoke bomb a mile or two away that signals the start of the hundred-mile race course consisting (usually) of two 50-mile loops of dangerous, uncharted desert terrain laid out in a figure eight. A huge banner drops, and hundreds of motorcycles explode to life, taking off in roaring, dust-spewing wheelies and charging flat-out toward the distant smoke bomb.

Those out in front escape the broiling thunderheads of dust that make seeing and breathing next to impossible and risk the danger of crashing and becoming helpless targets of the next tidal wave of high-speed heavy metal. The scaredy-cats wait for the dust to settle and then head for the bomb, where the wide-open chaos narrows down to animal trails, natural jumps, bumps, drop-offs, canyons, yucca trees, and dried-up riverbeds. Bikes were geared for about 95 mph, rocketing us over impossible terrain that, when you stayed "on it," would set your eyes vibrating in their sockets.

If you made it through the first grueling fifty miles, you'd loop back through the pit area for gas, water, clean goggles or whatever, then tear off on the second equally treacherous, death-defying loop.

The worst thing about desert racing was crashing miles away from the pit area or the half dozen checkpoints sprinkled along the course. It could take a long time for the mobile emergency medical team to get to you, and sometimes it was too late. There were no spectators, just family, friends, and lovers who drove the couple of hundred miles each Sunday to cheer you on or twist a wrench when you came flying into the pits. There was no glory. No prize money. Top riders were paid a couple hundred bucks to "show up." I wrestled a 20 percent discount from my sponsor for parts and labor.

In my very first Hare Scrambles, which is what they called them, I was running in the top ten out of five hundred riders. My accelerator cable snapped during the second fifty miles, but dueling it out with the best-of-the-best was the ultimate high and I suddenly realized that I was just as good as the next guy—even better—no matter what you or anybody else thought of me.

■ ■ ■

As the twenty-eight-year-old producer/director/star of the racing documentary *On the Line*, I was obsessed with my work and prepared to attack anyone who showed the slightest doubt of my genius or opposed my dreams.

Once, while filming a desert motorcycle race, my cameraman informed me that his Berkeley buddy had come along to watch him ply his craft and shoot some still photographs. I welcomed the bearded scholar around the campfire, which means I agreed to feed, tent, and water the lad for three days. The second morning of filming, we climbed a steep, rocky hill to catch riders charging through a narrow canyon—with the sun blasting right down on our camera lens. I asked the scholar if he would "shade the lens" (hold a small square of cardboard to block out the sun) while his buddy operated camera and I "pulled focus."

"No!" he responded, with a trace of scrambled egg that I had fed him earlier that day still clinging to his shaggy red beard. "That's not why I'm out here." He plopped down on a rock shelf overlooking the desert. "Also, I don't work for you!"

He unscrewed the black plastic top chained to his aluminum army canteen, took a swig of water—which was also provided by me—then looked out toward the distant tornado of dust from the first wave of fast-charging motorcycles.

"Here they come," he announced to no one in particular as he screwed the black plastic top back on the canteen and pushed the metal container into its padded canvas pouch.

"Get off the hill!" I ordered.

He looked in my direction for the first time.

"You don't own this desert," he stated, sending a shot of

adrenaline racing through my system and slamming my heart into overdrive.

He aimed his brand-new 35mm, single-lens reflex Nikon with the 300mm telephoto lens toward the approaching racers and started firing off motorized shots. I smacked the camera into thin air, grabbed a fistful of red beard, and dragged my ungrateful guest headfirst down the rocky slope, bouncing him off of sharp rocks and yucca trees shrieking and kicking the entire way.

My cameraman came stumbling down the hill after us, screeching at the top of his lungs. "Stop it, Lee. Stop it!"

He was wide-eyed and gasping for breath.

I yanked Berkeley Boy to his feet and booted him in the butt. "Get out of here!" I roared.

The red-haired scholar scrambled around on all fours, whimpering, scooping up bits and pieces of his shattered equipment. My cameraman quit on the spot, and his now bruised, blotch-bearded partner threatened a lawsuit.

I never did get the shot I wanted, wasted two days of time and money, and lost a damn good cinematographer.

That's when I decided to teach myself how to be a cameraman.

Early the next morning, I rented a fluid head tripod, 16mm Arri S camera with a zoom lens and excitedly headed for the Pacific Ocean in my VW station wagon to shoot my first roll of film. A motorcycle cop followed me into the beach parking lot and pulled me over.

"May I see your driver's license, please?" he asked, appearing ominous behind sunglasses and helmet.

"Yes, sir," I said, trying to hide my apprehension.

A few weeks earlier, I had outrun the police on Mulholland Highway, a winding single-lane road with twisting turns and deadly drop-offs topping the Santa Monica Mountains that separate San Fernando Valley from the rich and stuffy of Beverly Hills. A cop spotted me riding the parallel dirt fire roads on my Greeves Challenger motorcycle. That was a big $500 no-no.

With lights flashing and siren squealing, he swung his black-and-white in my direction. I took off like a startled kangaroo, then looked back once to see his rear wheels spraying dirt and the cruiser fishtailing all over the place—right into a ditch. I literally jumped onto Mulholland Highway and "wheelied" halfway home. It was no contest, but I wondered if the cop noted the AMA racing number on the front and sides of my motorcycle.

"What's the problem, Officer?" I asked with the respect and courtesy I had learned during three productive years at Vermont Academy Prep School.

"Faulty directional signal." He took my driver's license. "Stay in the car, please."

The officer returned to his motorcycle. I breathed a deep sigh of relief and promised myself never to ride the fire roads again and to obey all laws, so help me God.

"Step out of the vehicle!" The motorcycle cop had walked up next to me, balanced on the balls of his booted feet, with right hand poised over his holstered weapon. I felt my body go numb. My mouth turned to cotton. "Place your hands on the hood of the car, feet apart."

I reached for the hood and jumped back from the frying pan—hot metal. He slammed my hands down on the car and pulled out his revolver.

"Don't move!" he barked and radioed for backup.

Burning palms or not, this was pre–Rodney King, and I was not about to test this cop's field etiquette.

"Do you mind my asking what this is all about?" I said, voice quivering, hands one-eighth of an inch above the burning metal.

"There's a warrant out for your arrest!"

Those damn number plates on my Greeves Challenger. I should have removed them!

"What for?"

"I can't find the code violation in my book."

He was getting frustrated.

A backup cruiser rolled onto the scene, lights flashing. Hands cuffed, I was sequestered in the caged backseat of the sizzling-hot squad car. I peeked out the closed rear window and felt the condemnation from the neck-craning, drive-by lookie-loos.

"You got a dog?" the newly arrived cop asked as he looked at me through the steel cage.

"Yes, sir. A German shepherd."

I almost said "police dog" but checked myself.

"You never responded to a ticket for having a dog on the beach."

That was last summer. I had brought Porsche, my newly acquired seven-week-old shepherd, down to the beach in a picnic basket while I flew my custom-designed kite to new heights. A large, young crowd gathered to cheer me on, when a uniformed municipal officer came over to see what was going on. With dubious authority, he pointed his sausagelike finger at the puppy in the basket.

"Dogs are not allowed on the beach," the pudgy, self-conscious officer declared.

"She's not on the beach," I stated, playing to my young audience. "She's in a basket."

The suntanned crowd roared with laughter. The unarmed officer blushed, pulled out his dog-eared (pardon the pun) ticket book, and, to the jeers and boos of the crowd, wrote me up. I stuffed the ticket in my bathing suit, basked in the affection of my supporters, and never gave it a second thought.

"We've got to take you in," said the motorcycle cop.

The local police station was old, stuffy, and in need of everything. Out in the potholed parking lot I was searched — rather intimately, I might add — and brought inside for fingerprints, mug shot, and my one phone call.

"Carol," I said into the jail's pay phone to my future son's mother, "get someone to bring down thirty-six bucks to get me out of here!"

During that unfortunate "BC" chapter of my life, I didn't ask, I told, loved ones what to do.

The jailer escorted me back to the holding cells. He didn't smile or make eye contact and would have benefited greatly from a double shot of Listerine.

"You have any books or magazines?" I inquired.

"This ain't a damn liberry, ya know," he snapped as he unlocked my cell and ordered, "Inside!"

I can still hear the echoing sound of the heavy steel door slamming shut behind me. The cell was small, maybe six by eight, with a badly scuffed concrete floor and bars that had been painted dark green so many times they had increased in diameter. In one corner stood a filthy washbasin. Alongside it was a filthier toilet with an empty roll of toilet paper hanging off the flush handle. The air was thick and smelled like piss on a hot radiator. High up on the back wall a crack of a window, maybe a foot wide and six inches tall, let in a sliver of smog-filtered sunlight. I felt vulnerable, abandoned, frightened, and stripped of all rights and my individuality. It was not quite noon.

"What you doing in here?" asked a gravelly voice, not really needing an answer.

I looked up to see a bumlike man who was probably forty but looked old enough for AARP. He had not shaved in days, and the couple of teeth he had were crooked and stained yellow-brown. He was in the cell across from mine, scrunched up in a corner, indifferent to his bleak surroundings and empty life. I told him my circumstances, and he laughed out loud.

"Tell him what *you're* in for, Doc," he said, as he called over to the distinguished-looking hollow-eyed man in the cell next to mine.

"Doc," it turned out, was a well-known West Coast gynecologist awaiting sentencing for sexually assaulting his teenage clients.

Five o'clock rolled around, and a slovenly trustee brought me and my "cellies" each a metal tray of baked beans, lumpy mashed potatoes, some gray meat, and a small, smudged carton of room-temperature milk.

"No, thanks," I said, sounding a bit optimistic. "I've got someone coming down for me."

My bum-friend laughed out loud and farted as if he were alone in the woods.

I clung to the cold steel bars and stared longingly as the last ray of sunlight disappeared from view. Outside, the sounds of rush-hour traffic had faded, and people found their way home to awaiting families. My small window to the outside world turned black. Now a dim nicotine-stained bulb supplied the only light.

I found myself desperately homesick, but for what?

PART 2

CHAPTER 6

PIGEONHOLED INTO HOPELESSNESS

The role of a volunteer chaplain in the Los Angeles County Probation Department was to offer spiritual guidance to those wards who wanted it, intercede when they were broadsided by emotional crises, hold church services at the facility on Sunday mornings, and pray for all concerned.

After being trained, fingerprinted, background checked, licensed by the church, and blessed by the flamboyant Chaplain Torres, I began making my once-a-week eight-hour unrestricted rounds as assistant chaplain at Sylmar Juvenile Hall, along with a half dozen other volunteers. We worked alone and on separate days.

I was given a roster with the names of children requesting to see a chaplain. We would meet in their individual cells or the recreation/lunch room, or stroll around the enclosed compound — unless the kid was in ICU, the Intensive Care Unit, another Juvenile Justice euphemism.

My untainted opinion of each kid began the moment we met. I didn't want to be prejudiced by their juvenile records or psychiatric assessments. Besides, those records only reflect what they are arrested for, not what they managed to get away with — and too many psychs and social workers are street-dumb. They have all the terms and definitions down, but they can't touch a heart or impact a desperate child's life.

Am I being judgmental? Yes!

Too many children (one of my own included) are pigeonholed into hopelessness by the label of some scholarly "expert." I wanted to help every kid — if they wanted help.

My first official visit was in the boys' ICU, a stagnant container of confused, frightened, and unparented children. I used my newly assigned master key to unlock the heavy, painted steel door, my Bible tucked securely under my arm. Chaplains in probation always carry a Bible to mark their role.

The lights inside ICU were dim. There was no recreation/lunch area in this hospital-green building, only a centrally located glass control room from which the staff monitored the two dozen or so locked quarters, each with its own steel door and small opaque window. A clipboard hung by every cell with the name of the contained child and a space for the probation officer to sign after checking in on the child on the hour, every hour. The Intensive Care Unit was jarringly quiet and felt more like a hospice for the terminally ill than a juvenile rehabilitation center.

"Morning!" a deep voice echoed across the room.

Vince, a neatly dressed, athletic probation officer in his mid-forties, stepped out from behind the glass cage. A phone call from Chaplain Torres had alerted him to my pending arrival.

"You're the new chaplain," he stated with a welcoming smile.

Boy, did that ever feel uncomfortable! I pictured chaplains as dainty men with smooth hands and manicured fingernails. They had soft muscles and became short of breath after one flight of stairs — and I'd never met a chaplain who could throw a perfect spiral pass.

"*Assistant volunteer*," I clarified. "I'm a filmmaker, actually."

"I saw *Mountain Tops*," Vince declared. "When Rick started sprinting for the top, I lost it."

Vince handed over a short list of kids who wanted to see the chaplain.

"Would you mind seeing the boy in 16? His name isn't on there."

"What's the problem?"

Vince shrugged, searching for the appropriate answer. "He just won't talk — to anyone. He's never had a visit and he's never gotten any mail. I really feel bad for the kid."

"Why's he locked up?"

"Took a fire poker to his foster parent. Was on the lam for a couple of years when they finally caught up with him living on the streets in New Mexico."

"Did he kill the foster parent?"

Vince shook his head and gestured down the hall. "He's been in here for ten weeks. They're afraid he'll jackrabbit — go AWOL — so they won't put him in general population." Vince studied me a moment. "One other thing."

"What's that?"

"Boy's got a temper."

Kids had heard our voices, and their silhouettes were now pressed up against the small opaque windows of each cell door, desperate for human contact and needing to know they were not forgotten.

I took a deep breath and started down the dim concrete hallway. ICU was at full capacity. I stopped at door number 16. No silhouette. I checked the name on the dangling clipboard and, although I had a key, decided to knock lightly. After a few moments, I knocked again.

"Anybody home?" I asked.

The opaque window showed movement. I unlocked the door and leaned in. "Can I come in?"

The air was stale and reeked of body odor. A pasty-skinned boy with a flattened nose stood up from the bunk, seemingly confused that I had asked permission to enter. He positioned himself strategically against the back cinder block wall. His county-issued boxer shorts were wrinkled and freshly stained, his stenciled T-shirt at least two sizes too small. He stood about six feet tall and weighed nearly two hundred pounds. A vacant, institutionalized stare emanated from his fifteen-year-old eyes.

Must be on some kind of drug, I thought.

"I'm a volunteer chaplain. My name's Lee," I said, locking the cell door behind me. I wondered if I was the first person Ronnie ever shook hands with. An old *Cycle Guide* magazine was in a short stack of reading material next to his bed. His "bed" was nothing more than an elevated slab of concrete with a thin, discolored mattress covered by a knotted mess of sheets.

"Can I look at your magazine?"

Ronnie nodded.

I picked up the *Cycle Guide* and scanned the pages. It brought back happy memories, which I was now reliving through my son, Shane.

Shane got his first motorcycle when he was three years old. We loaded up the brand-new 50cc Indian and drove through the night to Soggy Dry Lake—California's answer to the Bonneville Salt Flats. We awoke with sun and frost on the windows of our rented motor home. That's when I realized I had forgotten to bring gloves. Shane spent the morning with my socks taped tightly around his little hands, riding that bike until it ran out of gas.

"Anything I can do for you?" I asked.

Ronnie looked at me without the slightest clue how to respond. He finally shook his head. I smiled and continued to page through the magazine.

"Do you ride?" he asked in a near whisper.

"Sometimes, with my son. How about you?"

Ronnie slowly shook his head and stared down at the floor. I studied Ronnie as he studied the floor.

"Ronnie, I need to ask you something." I closed the magazine. "What happened to your nose?"

He reached up and felt his mushy nose as if trying to remember. "Broke it," he murmured.

"How?" No response. "What happened?"

After a long moment, a tear spilled down Ronnie's cheek.

"It's OK, man," I said softly. More tears. I stepped closer and gently placed my hand on his shoulder. "It's OK."

Ronnie sobbed uncontrollably. He was loud and his breath was sour, born out of the pit of insufferable pain and terminal hopelessness. Ronnie's foster parent didn't like it when little Ronnie cried. To shut him up, he would grab Ronnie by the ankles and smash his head into the piss-filled toilet bowl. This went on for years until little Ronnie became big Ronnie and finally clobbered his abuser with a fire poker and took off running with just the clothes on his back—and no one to tape socks around his cold hands.

I drove home and hugged my son.

■ ■ ■

As I had promised, I returned the following morning. Ronnie was on his feet, wearing yesterday's shorts and T-shirt. He was holding a raggedy two-year-old copy of *Sports Illustrated* in his hands. We scanned the magazine together. One particular photo of a joyful family taken at a popular ski resort, their arms wrapped around each other, held his attention.

"What happened to your parents?" I asked.

"My father's dead—and my mom . . ." He paused as he rubbed "sleep" from the corner of one eye and flicked it indifferently from his finger. "I dunno what happened."

Later, Vince told me Ronnie's parents were drug dealers. We were standing outside ICU. He lit up his first smoke of the morning, took a deep, satisfying drag, and turned the freshly opened box of Marlboros toward me.

I waved it off.

"They had a full-blown meth lab going on in an abandoned

ranch out in Palmdale nine or ten years ago. Got raided by the cops. The mother's out in New Mexico, living with some loser," Vince told me. "That's how they found Ronnie. He showed up one day at his mom's and wouldn't leave. Her boyfriend called the cops." Vince sucked on the Marlboro, exhaled slowly, and shook his head. "And people wonder why these kids are messed up."

Across the compound, a lanky white boy was being escorted toward one of the dorms by an officious-looking probation officer. It was obvious the youngster had been crying hard and was visibly afraid. Vince tracked the odd couple.

"Do you know him?" I asked.

"New meat. Family probably thinks this will teach him a lesson."

"Will it?" I asked.

Vince snorted with disgust. "Kids in here will teach him how to be a criminal. Scratch in a tattoo someplace where his buddies can see it, and once he gets out he'll show them what he learned. He'll be the hometown hero."

Vince pinched the ash off his cigarette butt and flicked it away. "Never enough time. Soon as you think you're making a difference, the kid gets transferred or released back into the same old crap."

He pulled out another Marlboro. "Feel like I'm not doing my job, you know." He fired up the cigarette and automatically offered me one. I smiled back. "That wouldn't look too good," he said. "Cigarette in one hand, Bible in the other." He took a drag and gestured toward my Bible. "So you believe all that?"

"I bought the whole book, Vince. How 'bout you?"

This time he didn't take a drag.

"I see kids getting 'saved,' as you guys call it, every day — and six months later they're right back in here for the same damn thing, or worse." He thought for a moment and looked at my Bible. "If all that's true, they wouldn't be coming back here after they found God."

"You want my opinion?" I asked.

"No." Vince laughed nervously and blushed. "Nothing personal." He took another deep drag off his Marlboro and stared at it. "One of these days I'm gonna quit."

I liked and respected Vince. He cared deeply about the kids and made the volunteers feel welcome. More important, he made us feel needed. A few years later, Vince did stop smoking.

It was Christmas Eve in the commercial section of San Pedro Harbor, where he lived alone on a powerboat. The coroner estimated that time of death was approximately an hour before midnight. There were no signs of forced entry aboard Vince's well-maintained twenty-seven-foot cabin cruiser. No signs of a struggle. Vince bit down on the barrel of his .357 Magnum and blew off the back of his head.

He didn't leave a note.

And I never gave Vince my opinion about the Bible.

■ ■ ■

Before I left ICU, I asked Ronnie if I could pray with him. I gripped his cold damp hand. He bowed his head and squeezed his eyes shut.

"Will you come back tomorrow?" he murmured as I stood to leave.

"Yes."

"What time?" he asked.

"Same time. Same station. Will you be here?" I asked, trying to lighten the moment.

Ronnie stared back curiously, then smiled for the first time. "Yes, sir."

I walked over to the clean, quiet chapel and ate my bag lunch and thought about Dave and Lynn Adams, owners of Pyramid Films. They never acted stuffy or religious; they didn't have posters on the wall or little Scriptures tacked up in the lunchroom or

Jesus fish stuck on the back of the Rolls or Ferrari. They just lived their lives properly.

When I first started working with Pyramid Films, I would check out the secretaries as they walked out of the room. Dave didn't clear his throat and recite Matthew 5:28. That wasn't important, for now. He did have a short fuse and stood his ground on certain issues, but I never heard him curse. Me, I was good at it. I'm sure I used the Lord's name my way as often as Dave used it his way. But he never scolded me. He never told me I was in violation of the Ten Commandments. Dave had bigger fish to fry. He wanted *my life* to change, not just my conduct.

I was just finishing my lunch when an alarm went off outside.

All hell was breaking loose in ICU. I ran across the compound, catching up with three other staffers before we charged into the building. Two burly probation officers and Vince were looking into the rubber room at the end of the hall. The kid inside was scream-ing violently, cursing them with every disgusting word imaginable.

After fair warning, Vince slammed the door, locked it, and started back toward me. He was huffing and puffing and had a fresh cut under his left eye. His dress shirt was torn from collar to waist. I grabbed a white towel from a clean stack and gave it to him. Vince wiped his face and reacted to the amount of blood on the towel.

"Coldcocked me," he said, then pushed past.

The others walked back, barking stern warnings to kids with their silhouettes pressed against their small opaque windows. I looked but couldn't see if anyone was in room 16.

"Get off the door — now!" the officers bellowed as they banged a fist against each cell door.

One grabbed a handful of ice from the nearby refrigerator, plopped it in a Ziploc bag, and pressed it against Vince's bloody and swollen face. The others gathered close to check out the damage.

I couldn't help but listen to the rubber room screams that now were louder than ever.

"You want him?" One of the probation officers looked at me and gestured toward the rubber room.

I walked slowly down the hall toward the animal-like screaming. None of the silhouettes were watching, and the rubber room door was solid steel with no window. I stood before it, wondering if it was Ronnie inside. I unlocked the steel door and entered the rubber room. Every surface was padded. There were no windows. A Hispanic youth was sprawled out on the floor, hogtied and screaming louder than anyone I had ever heard. His thin, muscular arms were handcuffed behind his arched back and chain-locked to his ankles. His county underpants were soaking wet, his T-shirt torn loose at the neck.

I locked the heavy door behind me and walked around where I could see the boy lying facedown in a large puddle of his own urine. I knelt beside him, rested his head on my knee, and wiped his face with my sleeve. His screaming turned into gut-wrenching sobs as he began to settle down.

I stayed in the rubber room for about an hour.

■ ■ ■

I read all I could get my hands on about violent juvenile offenders — reports, manuscripts, textbooks, even a plethora of Christian titles from *The Cross and the Switchblade* to *Where Flies Don't Land*.

Most Christian books were blandly predictable. By the second act, the bad and the blind got born again and lived to sin no more.

Secular books were steeped with arm's-length observations from articulate scholars who had never experienced an unmonitored day in the life of a troubled kid. True, there were those rare exceptions, but usually that lone compassionate voice crying in the wilderness was muted by the verbose and well funded. And not one secular manuscript that I read quoted the one and only true experts — the kids themselves.

All case studies were conducted by heady experts asking leading questions to troubled kids with damaged hearts who knew the answers long before the sessions began. Reports were filed, and treatment was recommended. There were three earthly choices: professional therapy, prescribed medication, or both — all at a hefty price. No guarantees, and if you checked out the success rate, you'd understand why.

I did discover one consistent element in reading Christian biographies and testimonies. The lives featured were changed because some nice folks, usually nonprofessionals, invested their personal time and hearts into the troubled soul, not because it was their job, but because they cared. They wanted to share God's love. They knew from personal experience that God was in the business of changing lives — without pills and free of charge.

■ ■ ■

The request list to see the chaplain at Sylmar Juvenile Hall grew longer with every visit. I began showing up three or four times a week — and nearly every weekend.

"Mr. Stanley, we need your help." It was an official from the Hall.

I had just returned from a full day at the facility and was about to tear into the clogged carburetor of my son Shane's YZ80 minibike.

"What's the problem?" I asked into the cordless phone in our garage. My ten-year-old son was standing anxiously nearby with his toolbox open, ready to go to work.

"One of the ward's fathers was murdered," the AD explained. "He doesn't know yet."

"Why don't *you* tell him?" I suggested.

"It's a little more complicated than that."

"Give me an hour," I said and hung up.

Family interruptions were becoming a regular occurrence.

I turned to my son. "Shane, I'm sorry," I said, really meaning it. "I've got to go back to Sylmar."

"I understand, Dad." Shane checked his emotions, as he would a thousand times to come.

Volunteering can become a full-time job if you let it, with lots of overtime and no pay. Was this a door God was opening — was this where he was going to use me?

I had to find out.

I walked into the assistant director's office. He was pretending to talk to someone on the telephone. I waited impatiently for about fifteen seconds and then turned to leave. He quickly hung up the phone.

"Sorry. Thank you for coming in," he said, keeping his eyes on the open file on his cluttered desk. "The ward's name is Leon Brewer."

"Don't know him."

"Yes, I realize that," the AD confessed, "but due to the circumstances, we felt it would be better if you told him."

I walked across the compound alone. It was quarter to nine and eerily quiet. Inside K-Dorm, the sixteen- to eighteen-year-old boys were showering their scarred and tattooed bodies and brushing their teeth. All eyes focused on me as I walked through the metal door. The night shift team came over and, in hushed tones, pointed out one of the toothbrushers as Leon Brewer.

"Brewer!" a counselor called out. "Get dressed! The chaplain wants to talk to you."

Leon was as confused as he was hulking. He methodically climbed into a pair of county-issued jeans, wedged his huge flat feet into blue corduroy slippers, pulled on a wrinkled white T-shirt, and followed me outside.

He remained an arm's length away as we walked in uncomfortable silence toward a picnic bench in the corner of the compound. We sat down across from each other. No one else was around.

"Leon, I got a tough one for you." My voice sounded strange, as if exploring new territory. "Last night your father was murdered."

He looked away without emotion. This guy was used to bad news.

"Who killed him?" he asked.

"Your mother," I said as gently as I could.

Leon stared at his corduroy slippers for a long time without a word. I could see his mind sifting through the pain, his life, not knowing where to put any of it.

"What am I supposed to do?" he mumbled.

Fair question. Leon had been locked up for seven months and was scheduled to go home in two days. But with father dead and mother locked up in county jail looking at twenty-five to life for blasting Pops over the last few drops of Rémy Martin, Leon Brewer would have to remain in Sylmar Juvenile Hall until the courts found suitable placement for this homely, fat, seventeen-year-old black loner.

Good luck, Leon.

CHAPTER 7

"NO ONE RESPONDED TO MY VISION FROM GOD"

"Thar she blows!"

A California gray whale breached a quarter mile off the port bow of our thirty-six-foot Cheoy Lee Clipper ketch during the sail back from Catalina Island. It was a beautiful, breezy Sunday afternoon, and I had successfully managed to stay away from Sylmar Juvenile Hall for three whole days.

Shane and Brett, Linda's youngest, who was fourteen at the time and three and a half years older than Shane, were standing barefoot on the foredeck, pointing in the direction of the forty-foot-long mammal. Sixteen-year-old Christopher, Linda's firstborn, was not on board. After four rebellious years he had opted to leave our nest and live with his father in nearby San Fernando Valley.

"Get closer, Dad!" Shane yelled.

The whale sounded. I quickly changed course and headed south, following the whale's annual migration run to Baja, Mexico.

The shiny black-hulled ketch was our second sailboat. Linda and I bought our first boat a year after we were married and before we purchased our first home.

It was a foggy, irresponsible morning and our weekend without the kids. We were standing alone on the end of Paradise Cove

Pier, just north of Malibu. First light revealed a small sailing ketch at anchor less than a hundred yards off. The skipper came topside holding a steaming cup of hot coffee. He scanned the horizon, and after enjoying a few sips, he quietly went forward to raise the mainsail.

An attractive woman with long dark hair wearing a man's shirt appeared from below and sat at the helm. She was tanned and smiling. The early-morning breeze gently pushed the boat slowly into the silver-gray fog when I noticed an insignia on the mainsail: H28.

That boat was the exact replica of the sailboat pictured over my desk at Vermont Academy Prep School.

"For Sale — H28. Excellent condition. $24,000. Firm!"

I read the ad out loud to Linda that same morning. By noon we were in Redondo Beach Harbor standing aboard *Princess*, the twenty-eight-foot wooden Herreshoff ketch advertised in the *Los Angeles Times*.

She was as the ad promised. Everywhere we looked was pleasing to the eye. Linda ran her fingers over the galley's small two-burner alcohol stove and smiled. "I'll cook us wonderful meals under way!" She looked around pensively, fore and aft. "Honey, where's everybody going to sleep?"

I slid my arm around Linda's trim waist. "We'll manage."

I kissed my wife. This was one of the happiest days of my life.

The seller rejected my offer of $20,000.

I went ballistic — yelling and stomping around our rented home like some revolutionary on the loose, calling that good-for-nothing seller every degrading term that popped into my raging head. Linda watched in amazement. She had not witnessed her sailor's rejection button.

After the dust settled, my calm and beautiful wife made a suggestion. "Why don't you make another offer?"

A week later, *Princess* was christened *Linda~Lee*.

Nine months later, we sold the ketch after finding a bigger boat lying in Seattle, Washington. I called the "for sale by owner" phone number and asked the price: $42,000. The classic-looking thirty-six-foot Cheoy Lee was way out of our price range, which realistically was about $10, but we decided to drive up and see it anyway.

I bought a used camper shell for our mini Datsun pickup; loaded up our sleeping bags, Coleman lantern, and clean clothes; and headed north. We stayed at beachfront campgrounds and cooked over open fires, watching the sunset each evening. If the stars were out, we'd sleep on the sand. It was like a second honeymoon.

"What are you going to do if we like the boat?" Linda asked with reasonable concern.

"It's priced below market. Probably needs a lot of TLC and stuff," I assured her.

We turned off the highway just south of Seattle and followed a narrow winding road through tall pines down to where the boat was moored. We parked in the gravel parking lot. The sun was shining, the sky was blue, and there was a light late-morning breeze.

"Kind of nice, huh?" Linda said with an excited smile.

The clipper ketch was moored at the end of the two-hundred-foot-long main dock. I locked up the truck, took Linda's hand, and headed for the boat. The closer we got, the better she looked.

Once we were alongside, Linda squeezed my hand. "Kind of nice, huh?"

A pleasant-looking man in his early seventies poked his head through the perfectly varnished forward hatch. He had permanent crow's-feet accenting his smiling blue eyes.

"Hi! You must be the Stanleys. I'm Hal Thorston."

And as if on cue, his lovely, equally smiling wife popped her head up. "Come on aboard!" she said cheerfully. "I'm Rita."

We stepped aboard the perfectly maintained ketch. I couldn't help but notice the near-new teak decks.

"Hope you like fried chicken," Rita said.

After a delicious lunch of chicken, salad, corn on the cob,

freshly squeezed lemonade, and homemade chocolate chip cook-
ies, we went for a sail on Puget Sound. Hal showed me how to work
the boat. Rita was busy down below teaching Linda how the galley
operated. The wind was out of the northwest at twelve knots, with
two- to three-foot seas. About a mile out, Hal turned the helm over
to me.

I looked up at the pristine white sails and cranked in two full
turns on the jib sheet winch with one hand, while my other gripped
the shiny wooden spoke of the helm.

"Why are you selling her?" I asked, keeping an eye on the main
telltales.

"It's time," he said with a touch of sadness in his eyes.

Back at the dock, the men washed and wiped the boat down in
silence. The women were below cleaning up.

"Would you like to buy her?" Hal asked once we were done.

I looked back to find Linda and Rita standing in the cockpit.
They had obviously bonded.

"We'd like you and Linda to have her," Rita said with a smile.

"Mr. Thorston, I can't afford your boat right now." The Thor-
stons just kept smiling. "Will you take $40,000, and a $100 deposit
to hold her?" I asked, embarrassed by my own insanity.

"That would be fine," Hal said. "We can carry paper for you
if you'd like."

That was in October 1979. Mr. and Mrs. Thorston carried
paper at 8 percent with $100 dollars down. My monthly payments
began eight months later in May 1980, after Hal and his friends
delivered the boat at no charge to Los Angeles.

Whenever Shane and Brett were on board, they would keep
one eye on the horizon, hoping to spot a whale, a shark, or some
other form of marine life. Whoever spotted a whale got "a pound
o' tobacco," which meant a Snickers bar. If it was a false alarm,
the other would be awarded the candy. Sometimes they would get

fooled by the splash of a diving pelican and in midsentence change their cry to "thar she—pecks!"

Whoosh!

The California gray whale breached fifty feet away. The wind blew the mist from her spout across our bow and into the cockpit.

"Pee-you!"

Brett grabbed his nose and fanned the air. Shane laughed out loud.

"Those jail kids would love this," I said to Linda. She looked back with a dubious smile, while I grinned.

■ ■ ■

Shortly after Chaplain Fox called me down to Camp Gonzales, I was working alone in my studio when the Lord gave me a vision. I grabbed a clean sheet of paper and started writing it down as fast as I could. The first part was more of a command:

> You will take kids out of jail and go to sea aboard a sail-boat and you will film the adventure in detail and the kids will return to camp. The completed project will impact the nation as nothing ever before.

I raced upstairs clutching the paper and read it aloud to Linda. She looked at me as if I had slipped over the edge.

"Linda, I *know* this is from the Lord!"

Nice try. Too often, believers had crossed our path emphatically declaring that the Lord had given them a vision for a film project or the Lord had told them we were to work together. It took a few seasons, but I learned to agree only when the Lord spoke to me directly.

I was now reaping what I had sown.

I called my agent, Ben Conway, and told him the premise of the project—leaving out the God part.

"Fantastic!" was Ben's excited response. "I can sell it in a heart-beat as a *Movie of the Week* with you attached as the writer."

"No script, Ben," I said. "I want to do a documentary."

"You mean like *Scared Straight?*"

I could feel Ben's enthusiasm free-fall. The popular *Scared Straight* featured problem kids who agreed to the experiment of visiting a prison for the day and getting screamed at by the inmates, then returning home to their disgruntled parents.

"Nothing like *Scared Straight.* There will be no theatrics or screaming, unless the kids start screaming at me." I laughed, trying to win back his enthusiasm.

"OK!" He was starting to get pumped again. "Real kids temporarily released from a real prison go out to sea on a sailboat. Lee, can you pull that off?"

"Yes!"

I had no idea *how* to make it happen or even *if* I could make it happen, but I was trying to be convincing.

Ben continued, "We'll get some TV star to go with you, like Tom Selleck or Jim Arness. Arness is a sailor — has a boat, *Sea Smoke* I think he calls it. Could probably work out a deal with him." Ben was riding high again. "The networks will love it. That I can sell!"

I interrupted him. "No! The kids will act different if a star is on board. They won't be themselves. I want the real thing, Ben."

The "real thing" brought Ben back to earth again. Regardless, good friend that he was, Ben pitched the concept all over town.

No one responded to my vision from God.

CHAPTER 8

"WAKE UP, FOLKS! THERE IS A BATTLE FOR YOUR KID'S SOUL"

The swamp coolers did a lousy job chilling down the hot-tempered teens and overworked staff at Sylmar. It was the summer of 1982, and the Hall was at 120 percent capacity, with juveniles sleeping in the halls, literally, on thin mattresses and dirty floors.

Sylmar was an hour's drive through the hot San Fernando Valley from our Malibu Lake home, and, as luck would have it, the air conditioner in the Land Cruiser decided to quit. Usually, we'd get something like that fixed on the spot. But a month earlier, our film company's two biggest clients, McDonald's and Encyclopedia Britannica, each closed down the divisions where we produced films.

Money was getting tight.

I still had high hopes for a big project we'd been developing for months about an American doctor in Africa who had dedicated his professional life to helping lepers. The project was to be funded by the same group that funded *Mountain Tops*. Close friend Dan Matthews, executive director of Faith For Today, was very pleased with the success of *Mountain Tops* and wanted the African project to be next, but it kept getting pushed back for one reason or another.

"Come on, Lord!" I bellowed. "I've been doing good for a lot of seasons. What's up?"

I was referencing the Scripture that the Lord gave Linda and me after we returned from our five-day honeymoon in Rosarito Beach, Mexico. I wrote the promise in white grease pencil on the full-length mirror in our bedroom.

It was Galatians 6:9:

Let us not become weary in doing good, for at the proper time we will reap a harvest if we do not give up.

"We need to think about selling the boat," Linda suggested with great trepidation.

"No way!" I countered.

That beautiful black-hulled classic was one of the most admired yachts in the biggest small boat harbor in the world. It affirmed every adjective I equated with Lee Stanley — successful, adventurous, a free-spirited stud with a gorgeous first mate who was a "10" in any bikini. I was living my childhood dream. I loved sailing!

But what upset me most and became my deepest concern was how I could, without this boat, fulfill my vision from God.

"I'm going to take kids out of jail and go to sea and make a film," I told Linda.

"All right," she answered matter-of-factly.

"All right?!" I snapped. "Is that all you can say — 'all right'? I believe in that project, and I believe it's from the Lord!"

"Then it will happen," she said, leaving the room.

I tailgated her into the kitchen.

"Those kids need help, and I'm going to help them!" I felt close to tears. "I *have* to!"

Linda turned and faced me. "I know," she said deep from within her soul. "You helped Brett. You did it for one; you can do it for a thousand."

Linda's younger son, Brett, had (we were told) undisclosed learning problems (notice I didn't say "disabilities"). I sensed it during our first family time together. He was one of the cutest kids

I had ever seen. He wasn't frail or fragile, and his hair was never slicked down like some parents do to their kids for church. He was naturally gorgeous, with twinkling blue eyes and near-white blond hair. He was trim and bouncy and a joyful little gentleman who instantly stole the show whenever he was introduced to adults.

I vividly remember the day we met up at Linda's house. She had told her nine- and twelve-year-old sons I was coming over. Before I could get out of the car, they appeared in cowboy boots and jeans. Christopher, the older of the two, dove quickly into the shadow of Brett as they clip-clopped around the corner. Brett was smiling inside and out and shook my hand. When he smiled, his whole face joined in. But when he wasn't smiling, he appeared to be in a mental tug-of-war as if no one else were around.

After our first year of marriage and after Brett completed his first semester in a new school, Linda and I received a disturbing telephone call.

"Mr. Stanley, we would like you and Mrs. Stanley to come in for a conference."

It was the head honcho calling from Lupin Hill Elementary School. Brett's grades were consistently poor, and his behavior irrational. One of the reasons we moved out to Calabasas, some twenty miles northwest of Los Angeles, was because the school district was rated as one of the finest in the nation.

The conference was set for the following day.

Lupin Hill was an ideal setting for learning, sitting on a dozen acres of green grass overlooking the distant Santa Monica Mountains. The school was a new, sprawling, one-story building with lots of room and happy middle-class children running around inside and outside.

The counselor stood as we entered her well-organized and comfortably sized office. She was in her late thirties — attractive and well groomed. We exchanged pleasantries and sat down. Brett's files were spread out neatly on her desk. Off to the side were photographs of her preteen children, two girls and a boy. They were professional photographs taken at Sears or J. C. Penny, featuring photographic backdrops of autumn leaves. The two oldest children had big toothy smiles, but their eyes were not involved. The youngest was about three and hadn't been trained to respond when the photographer said "cheese" or "whisky" or whatever other word made a child look happy.

There were no pictures of the children's father. I was told they were divorced. How strange, I thought. This woman was the district's senior counselor, an accomplished professional, yet her family had fallen apart.

"Thank you for coming," she said with a pleasant smile.

"Sure. What's up?" I asked a tad defensively.

The counselor clicked into gear and spoke carefully and concisely, explaining that she and Brett's teacher had gone over his files extensively — which included the transcripts from his previous school. She used professional terms and lost me after the first one. They were deeply concerned with their findings and were placing Linda's now eleven-year-old son in the district's "special" classes, effective immediately.

Then she hit us with the real kicker.

"Our primary goal is to prepare Brett in such a way that when he is an adult, he will not have to live with his parents."

"What do you mean?" I asked, feeling like I had just been kicked in the stomach.

"We are hoping that as a young man your son will be able to care for himself."

Linda turned white-faced. She gripped my hand so hard that it hurt.

"What do you suggest we do?" I asked.

"You need to have your son examined thoroughly by a medical doctor and by a child psychologist. Once we've had a chance to review their reports, we will then assign Brett to the special classes that would benefit him the most."

Linda and I spent the weekend walking around like zombies, as if a cobra had struck us in the heart. Oh, we prayed, but our voices sounded flat and lacking in faith. I had never seen Linda depressed. Fortunately, the boys were with their other parents.

"We're going to get the best doctors in the world, and we're going to beat this thing," I told Linda with ungrounded conviction.

It was well past midnight. We were in bed, with the moon shining through the open window. Linda looked up at me and smiled, with her lips pressed tightly together and tears in her eyes.

Why is it that when credentialed professionals make a conclusive pronouncement, we mere mortals accept it as gospel?

The following Monday afternoon, I booked an appointment with our associate pastor to get his recommendation for the best doctors in Southern California. It was a bright, beautiful spring day without a cloud in the sky, and I was feeling like hell. I started the drive, anxiously talking to God as if he were unaware of our dilemma.

One of the draws of Christianity was "that they may have life, and have it to the full."

OK, God, I'm going to take you at your word, and if it ain't true, I'm dropping you like a bad habit, remember?

About a quarter mile into the drive, I got sick of hearing my voice, so I shut up. My mind started racing. I began to speculate on the future with a problem child/adult. Linda's heart would always ache, though she would not complain. But the dark cloud would always be there, reminding us of Brett's condition, his circumstances, his needs — day after day, night after night, in our thoughts, in our conversations, in our prayers, in our bedroom.

I started speeding, with both hands tightly gripping the wheel, recklessly cutting in and out of the heavy morning traffic.

"If you commit to parent Brett on my terms, I promise you total victory in every area of his life!"

I swerved hard right across the freeway, seemingly on two wheels, to make the exit, jumped back on the 101 North, and headed for home.

Linda was at the sink, head down, washing dishes. I came through the door like the White Tornado and took her in my arms.

"Brett's going to be fine!" I declared with tears in my eyes. I shared the word that the Lord had given me as I was driving to town. "Honey, I commit to do whatever it takes to fulfill that promise for Brett."

We hugged for a long time.

I had no idea where to begin.

I greeted Brett when he came home from school. I knew I had my work cut out, not only because of the promise, but because Christopher and Brett had been with their father for the last three days. Today was Monday. It usually took until Wednesday to get them back on our track. Nobody told us about *that* part during premarital counseling or in the many books we read about "blended families."

They didn't tell us a lot of things. We found out the hard way, and years later, we produced a two-hour television special titled *A Step Apart*, hosted by Marlo Thomas. The show stayed clear of the psychobabble and let the members of blended families tell their personal stories of pain, fear, trials, victory, and joy — and that ongoing struggle to "blend." The show was a national hit and a gift that Linda and I give to friends who are starting over.

I sat my eleven-year-old son (we don't use the word *step*son) down at the worktable in his room. He was tired and drifting away. It was three thirty in the afternoon. As soon as I began to talk, his eyes would default to that mental tug-of-war.

"Brett, look at me! We are going to change your life, beginning right now."

From that moment on, I addressed everything Brett did or said that supported whatever it was that wanted his soul. No matter what the situation, whenever he said he couldn't do something, I would ask him a simple question: *Why?* And when he answered, I would challenge that with another *Why?*

What we would eventually get down to was the root of the problem.

"Why didn't you do your assignment?"

"Because I didn't understand it," Brett would murmur.

"Why?"

"I don't know!"

"Why don't you know?" I persisted.

He would clam up, eyes swollen. Tug-of-war time.

"Brett, look at me!" He would. "Did you pay attention to the teacher?"

"Maybe. I don't know."

"Yes, you do know. Why didn't you pay attention in class?"

He stared back, his mind sifting through a thousand answers. Then he smiled that full-face smile.

"Because I didn't *want* to!"

Bingo! But we've only just begun, as the song says.

"Why didn't you want to?"

The smile was gone. Brett started searching for answers. Eventually, I would get the real answer. They were never "heavy-heavy," introspective chin strokers. They were simple decisions — choices, if you will — to take the path that felt the best or some other path that was trying to pull him away.

This revelation didn't happen overnight, or even during the first year. It took hundreds of intense hours and four long, thorny years before Brett stepped into the promised land.

Did Brett want to change?

No!

I mean, think about it. Can you imagine any pint-size handful strolling up to his or her beleaguered parent(s) and declaring, "You know, Mommy and Daddy, I've been thinking. I want to change my behavior for the good, and I'm going to start right now!" Kiss, kiss, kiss.

Music up.

Fade out.

The end.

For years I have watched professionals deal with delinquent kids (meaning murderers, robbers, rapists, sourpusses, and the like) who continually sucked the joy, hope, purpose, and peace out of the day and out of their loved ones.

"Tell me how you feel about this. Tell me what you're feeling now. And why do you think you feel like that, Johnny?" said the good doctors, not needing to take notes because Johnny had previously been pigeonholed — I mean "evaluated" — by their colleagues.

Hey, Doc, what about a little accountability here? What about consequences for bad and disruptive behavior? And please, folks, I am not talking about those precious young lives who have been beaten, either verbally or physically, or tormented or provoked and have lost heart, abandoned to their own devices. I am talking about the little tykes who have decided — for no *earthly* (key word here) reason — to be problem children.

My approach to redemption was (and still is) a tad different, quite unacceptable in today's marketplace and nowhere near as lucrative.

I refused to give a place (or a foothold, if you get my spiritual drift) to whatever or whoever it was that wanted Brett's soul. It was a never-ending battle. Sometimes Brett would come down to breakfast with a beleaguered scowl and sour attitude. I'd send him back to his room, inviting him to return only if and when he changed his demeanor. If the 'tude resurfaced after bacon and eggs, I would point to his room.

Did these demands and conditions upset our home, our marriage, and Linda?

What do you think, Mom?

Whenever he'd slip into the fog or cop an attitude, I would ID the problem and tell him how to correct his behavior, conduct, or whatever you want to call it. I didn't blame God or quote Scripture to justify my stance. That's one sure way to drive any soul from heaven. All Brett knew was that his life was going to change. As a matter of fact, he never knew about the guru of Lupin Hill's little kicker, nor God's promise of victory, until he was thirty years old.

Brett didn't have learning disabilities. Brett had *undetected correctable problems* (my term), as most of us do. And remember—you cannot solve a problem until you discover what that problem is.

If a child of any age says he can't do something, that doesn't mean he has learning disabilities or ADD (attention deficit disorder, as if we all didn't know) or ADHD (H for hyperactivity). He doesn't need pills; he doesn't need therapy. He needs someone who will invest the hundreds of one-on-one, nonpaying hours it will take to pull him out of the quicksand and onto solid ground (aka "parenting").

Of course there are exceptions, but we have lost millions of kids to prescription pills and expensive therapy—and we continue to do so because some bearded wizard with a PhD diagnosed him or her with ADHD, or whatever other terms they come up with to describe a child's imperfect behavior.

Brett was accused of being disruptive, not paying attention in class, having poor retentive skills, not being able to focus on the task at hand, and a host of other clinical catchphrases that would cause any parent's head to spin right off his or her shoulders.

Hey, don't change the kid; that would take a personal investment of unconditional love and time. Change his circumstances, his surroundings and conditions. Put him in special classes, give him therapy, and, if there is no acceptable progress, toss the lad a pill.

Once again times a million, we have given our children over to experts who most likely can't make their own lives work or keep their own families intact.

Wake up, folks! There is a battle for your kid's soul long before the first cry escapes the lips. Roll up your sleeves and be a parent. You may not have time to watch TV, play golf on the weekends, or go sailing, unless you do it with your kid—on God's terms. And if you don't know what those terms are, learn them!

Am I the perfect parent? So far from it that if you knew the total, unbridled truth, you'd chuck this tome in the trash can and write me off as a hypocrite.

When Shane was born, I collected him in my loving, protective arms and promised him—out loud in front of God (whom I didn't know)—that he would not go through the things that I went through as a child.

Nice try, Daddy.

Brett is another story. I was on his case 24/7. No grace. I was right—and don't get in my way! After the first year I ordered the school to take him out of the special ed classes.

"I wash my hands of this and will not take any responsibility for what will become of your child," warned the Pontius Pilate of the Las Virgenes Unified School District.

Linda and others fought my decision. It wasn't open for discussion.

Was it ego?

Hell, no! I believed deep in my soul that Brett was someday going to walk in the promise of "total victory."

Our biggest battle was with Satan himself (don't you just hate it when believers talk like that?). I will spare you the assorted and ongoing attacks, but one biggie is worth noting.

Brett was bedridden and had not eaten in three days. He didn't have a fever, no flu signs, just weak beyond description. At the end of the third day, his skin was pearl white. I put my ear close to his dry open mouth. I could barely feel his breath. I took his pulse. It was forty-plus beats per minute. I ran down the stairs to alert Linda to call for medical help and then ran back upstairs.

I was stopped as I entered the room.

"In my name you will cast out demons. Praise my name!"

I took Brett's lifeless hands in mine and began softly praising the Lord. I continued for minutes, when I felt Brett's hand move. I continued to praise the Lord, louder and louder. I wasn't being fanatic; I was being obedient. I wasn't risking Brett's life; I was watching it slowly return to him.

After a few minutes, he sat up in bed.

"I'm hungry," he whispered and then smiled.

It was finished, as they say. We got our son back, but at a price.

My constant monitoring and correcting of Brett's conduct wore on my and Linda's relationship. The time I allotted Shane was not the quality time we had known together in our past. To help offset my guilt, I was lax in disciplining my own son and got on Linda's case whenever she did. Christopher was running his own life and didn't want me in it.

Did God fulfill his promise for Brett?

To the max!

Today, at forty-two, Brett is a very successful businessman, and he and his two sons are committed to the Lord. He is a fine athlete in skiing, golf, mountain climbing, and swimming — and a pillar in the church. He could retire tomorrow and live like a king. Instead, he continues to work hard in commercial real estate (flies around in a private jet) and plays hard — with his beautiful and healthy family.

Brett couldn't be happier, and neither could Linda and I.

Years later, we visited the guru of Lupin Hill Elementary School and told the woman our story.

She listened with keen interest and smiled. "In all my years as a counselor, I have only heard of such a transformation in a young person's life one other time." She checked her emotions and continued. "Like you, they were Christians."

If I had to do it all over again, would I do it differently?

Absolutely!

My flesh got in the way more often than I would seek God's way. I was impatient with Brett, irritated by his ways and the attention and time his circumstances demanded. Linda's and my weekly battles were always — *always* — about the kids. Why didn't I treat her kids like I treated Shane? Why didn't I treat Shane like I treated her kids?

During one season of total frustration, I cornered producer Dave Adams, who had become like a father to both Linda and me.

"Those kids of hers are a constant drain, Dave," I pronounced. "They are not mine, and she expects me to raise them as if they were. I'm really sick of it!"

"Those children are a gift from God!" Dave began shaking with emotion. "He entrusted them to you." His face turned bright red, and his eyes welled up with tears. Dave wasn't yelling; he was hurting. "You raise those boys as if they were your own!"

CHAPTER 9

A GREAT WAY TO TURN KILLER KIDS ON TO LIFE

While making my rounds at Sylmar Juvenile Hall, I encountered the assistant director, Mr. Waterman.

"Gene, can I talk with you for a moment?" Waterman waited for me to speak, as if expecting bad news. "I want permission to take some kids sailing."

"Sailing?" he asked incredulously.

"Great way to turn a kid on to life, Gene! Have you ever been?"

"No!"

"Well, then," I said with a smile, "you better come along too."

"That's out of the question!"

"Why?" I asked.

"Mr. Stanley, the minors here are not Sea Scouts."

I never could figure out why Gene continued to call me Mr. Stanley. I'd been coming to Sylmar for well over a year.

"We'd teach them the basics," I replied. "How to sail, navigate, cook, scrub the decks. They'd become a team and learn to depend on each other."

"It's also against the rules."

He started to walk away.

I went with him.

"Change the rules—just for a day."

No response.

"Most of these kids have probably never been to the ocean."

He turned to look at me. "We don't change rules around here, Mr. Stanley. Not even for you!"

He continued walking to his office, alone.

■ ■ ■

I had become so confident that I would be taking jail kids out to sea and filming the adventure that I had stopped developing new film projects. The African deal was put on hold. Cameras and Moviolas were gathering dust, and the Stanleys were running out of money.

As I drove home from Sylmar, my headlights picked up the silhouettes of Linda and Star, our black Lab mutt, walking the narrow Malibu Lake road. I slowed the Land Cruiser as I approached.

"Nice-looking dog," I said flirtatiously.

Star was happy to see me, but Linda cut across a moonlit field and kept walking. I got out of the car and followed after her.

"What are you doing?" I asked.

Linda's arms were folded tightly against her chest. She had been crying.

"I'm walking. I'm angry, and I'm scared!"

"Linda, I have to help those kids."

"Cure the kids so you can cure yourself!"

Ouch! That hurt.

She picked up her pace. "Ever since those camp kids came along, you've abandoned the business and our sons."

"I haven't abandoned anybody. You're just used to having me around all the time."

"I called Dave and Lynn. They offered me a job at Pyramid Films, and I'm taking it!"

"Linda, you should have asked me first!"

"I'm a USC graduate. Look what's happened to my life!" She

stopped and turned to me. "We can't make the house payment, Lee, and we're two months behind on the boat."

My pride didn't want to hear it.

■ ■ ■

I grew up in a home with constant money problems. My father was a famous artist who watched it all slip away through bad planning, unchecked spending, and changing times. Correction: He didn't "watch"—he looked the other way, and my mother was forced to get a job.

He was fifty years old when I was brought home from the maternity ward to The White House—the biggest and nicest home in Essex Junction, Vermont, outside of Burlington. My mother had just turned thirty. Dad was broad-shouldered, loved people, had a twinkle in his eye, and never cursed. While in the army, he had taught enlisted men how to box, and years later he taught me too. I took him on when I was sixteen years old and he was sixty-six. I never knew what hit me. He helped me up off the kitchen floor and sat me down in a chair.

"Keep that left up, son," was all he said.

I never challenged him again.

His original oil paintings graced the covers of *Saturday Evening Post, Liberty* magazine, and dozens more. As kids driving through New England, my brother, Ricky, and I yelled, "There's one!" every time we saw a billboard displaying one of Dad's commercial illustrations. In the course of a hundred-mile trip, we would count dozens of Dad's billboards promoting Mobil Oil, Coca-Cola, Buick, Sinclair Paint, Budweiser beer, and more.

Dad was the greatest listener in the world. Only problem was, he wasn't home very often to listen. He was either in his studio in Burlington or in New York.

The last time I saw Dad was in a Florida hospital. I was twenty-four and hadn't seen my parents in over three years. The twinkle in his eye was still there, and his handshake was firm. He acted like it was the happiest day of his seventy-four years and asked questions about my life and about California.

It felt good to be with him.

The next morning, he told us it was too beautiful a day to be in a hospital.

"Go to the beach, sons." He smiled. "I'm fine."

Four hours later, the Florida State Police called our names over their squad car's loudspeaker.

Ricky and I rushed to the hospital to find nurses, doctors, and orderlies working feverishly over Dad. He yanked off the large oxygen mask that was being held over his nose and mouth.

"Go back outside, son!" he gasped.

I did what he asked.

A few minutes later, he died.

The funeral was held in a small chapel in North Miami, where my parents had moved five years earlier. I was surprised by the large turnout and the number of old friends who made the long trip south from New England.

After the service, brother Ricky and I stood alone before Dad's closed coffin. An American flag was properly folded and placed on top. I was doing just fine until Ricky reached out and touched the shiny gray coffin. I bolted for the door and ran off into an overgrown vacant field after nearly being hit by a car.

I cried harder than I had ever cried before.

I never took the time to really get to know my dad. I was too busy with Little League baseball, trapping muskrat, and playing my drums. I never hugged him or told him I loved him.

"So long, Dad. I love you."

■ ■ ■

The African project was canceled. Our friend called to tell us that the American doctor had become too ill to continue his work helping lepers. "I'm sorry, Lee," Dan said. "I know you would have done an outstanding job. Let's have a word of prayer."

Dan, the wonderful man of God that he is, prayed for the good doctor in Africa, the doctor's family, and the poor lepers who would no longer benefit from his work. Then he prayed for me and Linda, not knowing that the financial rug had just been yanked out from under us.

Linda and I walked around the lake at Malibu. The African romance was over. As a filmmaker, I felt empty, knowing I would never see that project—in which I had already invested much creativity and energy—come to fruition. I wasn't feeling sorry for myself; I simply felt abandoned.

To make matters more confusing, Chaplain Torres had offered me my own probation camps to oversee—nearby Camp Miller and Camp Kilpatrick.

"What do you want to do?" Linda asked. "You can't be a filmmaker and a full-time chaplain."

"It looks like the decision is being made for me," I said meekly.

"Remember the Scripture Mickey gave you?"

In 1981, a week before I made the fateful trip to Camp Gonzales to fix the camp's film, a woman in our church, Mickey Moore, pulled me aside.

"I have a Scripture for you," she said in a confident, levelheaded tone. "Isaiah 42:6–9." She smiled, then gave me a hug and left.

I recited the first part to Linda.

"I, the LORD, have called you in righteousness; I will take hold of your hand."

"And the rest?"

"I will keep you and make you to be a covenant for the people and a light for the Gentiles," I continued softly, *"to open eyes that are blind, to free captives from prison and to release from the dungeon those who sit in darkness. I am the LORD; that is my name! I will not give my glory to another or my praise to idols. See, the former things*

have taken place, and new things I declare; before they spring into being I announce them to you."

We kept walking in the darkness, together.

■ ■ ■

That evening, we gathered our two sons, Shane and Brett, for a family powwow in the living room. The full moon was already illuminating Sugarloaf Mountain across the way. Star curled up at Linda's feet. Outside, Wiley Goat, our two-year-old Nubian, was standing unfettered on the wooden balcony, staring at us through the glass slider and chewing his cud.

"I've been asked to be the chaplain at two nearby juvenile camps."

"Does it pay a lot?" Brett asked.

At fifteen he had become very practical.

"It doesn't pay anything," I said.

Brett darted a quick look at his mother.

"Mom and I have also talked about forming a foundation to help kids and to provide us with an income. What do you think?"

"Go for it!" Brett said with a smile.

"Just like that, huh?"

"You always told me," Brett continued, "that if I believe in something and it's right, then that's what I should do!"

■ ■ ■

Our lifestyle changed quickly and dramatically. We put our home and boat on the market.

"Dad, how are you going to take those kids sailing and make a film without our boat?" Shane asked.

"I'll charter one," I said with a confident smile.

Inside I was smarting. Our yacht was meant to become the flagship of our foundation. Chartering a stranger's boat to fulfill the vision was not supposed to be part of the deal.

I met with Chaplain Torres in her office at Sylmar Juvenile Hall to explain our plan for the foundation and to gain her support.

"The purpose of the foundation," I began, "is to teach boys how to become men, husbands, and fathers and to teach girls how to be ladies, wives, and mothers — all on God's terms! We will train volunteers to effectively minister to kids while in detention, when they are the most vulnerable and susceptible to change." I was excited. This was the first time I had pitched our concept to anyone.

"We would call the volunteers *caretakers*. Once the child is released, he or she would have the option to contact the caretaker. The caretaker would then commit to seeing the kid at least one day a week, sort of like a Big Brother, and help him or her get back into school, into church, get a job, or go to college — whatever it takes to become a productive, law-abiding, God-fearing citizen."

Chaplain Torres had not changed her expression since I started talking, but I plowed ahead. "And we would set up sailing expeditions for the caretakers and kids so they could experience adventures at sea together without having to watch their backs."

"You'll have to excuse me," she interrupted. "I've got a meeting downtown." She smiled as if waiting for her picture to be taken. "I'll give it some thought."

That's it? I said to myself. *You'll give it some thought? You should be leaping out of your oversized chair, twirling around with upraised arms, and chanting, "Go, Jesus, go!"*

Instead, Chaplain Torres collected her patent leather purse and stood next to her open door, waiting for me to exit.

"God bless you!" I uttered out of habit.

■ ■ ■

I poured myself into establishing the foundation. Linda came up with the name one morning after working out.

"Wings!" she said as she hustled up the stairs with a big smile.

"What?" I asked curiously.

"That's the name of our foundation."

I agreed.

Later we read these verses from Isaiah 40:

Even youths grow tired and weary,
and young men stumble and fall;
but those who hope in the LORD
will renew their strength.
They will soar on wings like eagles;
they will run and not grow weary,
they will walk and not be faint.

Film work dried up like an autumn leaf. No new projects and no returned phone calls. We were definitely in this foundation thing for the long haul. "Hello! Is anybody up there?" I yelled from the mountaintops, reminding God of his promise.

It felt like someone pulled the financial plug and I was spinning out of control down into a deep, dark abyss.

I have since learned that when God wants my attention or is about to make a major shift in my life, he puts me in ICU, opaque window and all. The phones stop ringing, the projects dry up, the money gets scarce — and I get mad at God.

I hated it then, and I hate it now. But I'm not the one in charge.

Linda put in long hours at Dave and Lynn's Pyramid Films. My mother, without being asked, sent $10,000 to keep our house from going into foreclosure. My brother was there for us as well.

"We're going skiing!" he announced over the phone.

I love to ski, but such a trip was out of the question. "Thanks, bro, but we're just trying to make it till Sunday, if you get my drift."

"Got you covered," he said. Ricky had already rented a five-bedroom house for one week in Taos, New Mexico. My brother believes that "if you got it, you share it." He wouldn't allow us to spend a dime, not even on ski rentals or junk food. "Thanks, Uncle Ricky!" was the constant refrain of us West Coast Stanleys.

After our ski holiday, I did what I thought I was supposed to do — I turned my collar around, so to speak, and headed for the hills.

■ ■ ■

My assignments, Camp Fred Miller and Camp Vernon Kilpatrick, were nestled discreetly in the Santa Monica Mountains less than seven miles from Malibu Lake. Their buildings were one story, and the two camps shared a common wall and full-service kitchen that was run by camp wards and overseen by a professional cook. Camp Miller was an open camp without fences, housing boys between the ages of fourteen and seventeen. Camp Kilpatrick was maximum security, surrounded by cyclone fencing and razor wire.

A kid's length of stay at either camp was between three and nine months, depending on his behavior. If the boy went along with the program, he would "graduate" early. The boys in Kilpatrick were fifteen- to eighteen-year-olds, mostly violent, hard-core juvenile offenders or repeat offenders. The majority of the kids in Camp Miller were first-timers who had not committed violent crimes — or at least hadn't been *caught* committing violent crimes.

I learned this from the first camp graduate Linda and I took into our home — seventeen-year-old Dee Middleton. Dee was black, trim, and handsome, with a smile that resonated from deep within. He was better at making friends than I was at winning souls.

Dee got busted for stealing a silk shirt from a men's store in downtown LA. The fleet-footed proprietor chased after him. Deladea pulled out a switchblade, looked back to threaten his pursuer, and slammed right into a light pole.

During his tenure at Miller, Mr. Dee, as he was called, became "camp governor," a title reserved for the number one, all-around best guy in the camp.

"Was that the first crime you ever committed?" I asked Dee over a home-cooked breakfast of bacon and eggs.

"Oh, Lee, no," he confessed with an embarrassed laugh. "I was doing it like vitamins, a crime a day — just like most everybody else in camp. You lie in bed and think, OK, what crime am I going to commit today? Then you plan it, and you just do it!"

"What kind of crimes?"

"Everything. Just before I got busted, I was stealing some guy's car. He reached in to grab the keys out of the ignition, and I shot him."

"Did you kill him?"

Dee shook his head. "Don't know. I mean, you don't wait for the body-drop, know what I'm saying? Just *bam*, and go! I don't watch the news or read the paper, so I don't know if the guy made it or not."

Dee's admissions showed us the depth of the problem we were facing. The majority of kids doing time get "saved" and find Christ. Outsiders (and judges) call it "jailhouse religion." I believe the kids really mean it at the time, but once they "graduate," they go right back to the same ol' same ol'. Before the first free sunset, they get high, get crazy, and get laid.

And that feels better than God.

We believed that the Wings Foundation would help probated youth keep their commitment to God on "the outs" and stay straight. It would be a hard job, but there was nothing more necessary. We just had to figure out how it was all going to work.

"Getting financial support is going to be tough."

I was meeting with Max Lyle, director of finances at The Church On The Way. Max, an ex-Marine, shared our vision and eventually became one of our board members. He was a man of few words and talked straight without diffusing his comments with sappy God talk. "Count the cost, Lee," he warned. That was pure Scripture. "Most churches won't get behind prison ministries."

"Why?" I asked.

"They don't want ex-cons in the church. Many ex-cons intimidate people. They dress differently, have prison tattoos, con people in the church, and give very little financially, if anything at all."

"Is that Pastor Jack's stance?" I asked.

"Jack Hayford cares about being obedient to God. He's not caught up in a popularity contest."

Linda and I witnessed that truth our first season at The Church On The Way. Jack and his wife, Anna, had returned from vacation. After a joyful reunion of praise and worship, Jack asked everyone to be seated.

"I understand church attendance dropped off 50 percent while we were away," he said. Some in the congregation felt they had to affirm that truth and applauded enthusiastically. Jack waited for the room to settle. "If you're coming here to see Jack Hayford, please don't come back." You could have heard an angel's wing flap. "We gather at The Church On The Way in the Lord's name—not mine."

"People who give expect results," Max continued. "How many of your Wings kids will walk the walk once they get out—or even stay out?"

CHAPTER 10

"EVERYTHING I WANT TO DO IS AGAINST THE LAW"

Dave and Lynn Adams put up the necessary funds to legally form the foundation. Dave also became our first official board member. Miraculously, our home sold the day before it was foreclosed. Unfortunately, it was already "on the books" at the bank, and Linda wrestled for the next seven years trying to repair our damaged credit.

We moved into an eight-hundred-square-foot converted chicken coop out in the rural section of Agoura Hills, just a couple of miles from Malibu Lake. The two bedrooms were so tiny that I had to build bunk beds for Shane and Brett, and I cut our king-size waterbed down to queen-size. We crammed two school-type desks in the laundry room and hauled the washer and dryer outdoors, running hoses through the window and dodging the occasional rattlesnake.

To get to the house, we turned off on a dirt lane that dipped sharply through a dried-up riverbed, then climbed straight up a hill for about a quarter of a mile. We parked our vehicles on the main road whenever rain was forecast because the dried-up riverbed turned into "Raging Waters." To get to the cars or back to our rented house, we walked a quarter mile through the woods to a footbridge.

Once, during a sudden downpour, Linda, Shane, and Brett

were alone in the chicken coop with one car and two mini pickup trucks parked outside.

"I'll drive Dad's pickup!" said thirteen-year-old Shane excitedly to Linda, scrambling out the door with Star running after him. At the time, Shane was five feet tall. He jumped behind the wheel, stuffed a couch pillow under his rear, fired up the engine, and sped down the quarter-mile driveway, with Star running like a wild deer after him. Sixteen-year-old Brett followed in his pickup, laughing hysterically.

By the time they got to the bottom of the hill, it was pouring rain, and the now-swollen river was sweeping up over the banks. Shane jammed the mini pickup into gear and shot full speed ahead, right into the raging river! The truck splash-landed and was swept sideways downstream. Just before tumbling over a small waterfall, the pickup's spinning rear tires touched the shallows, and Shane "wheelied" safely out of the river up onto the other side.

Our chicken coop, besides being the perfect escape from suburban apartment dwelling, was out in the remote, hilly countryside on four private acres, surrounded by dusty horse ranches and a secreted mobile home or two. It would make a perfect out-of-the-way, low-profile gathering place for Wings Foundation.

Our Cheoy Lee Clipper ketch sold. I paid off our debt to Hal Thorston and thanked him for his patience and understanding. He mailed back a check for $100, made out to Wings Foundation.

Linda worked hard as director of publicity for Pyramid Films, and I continued volunteering full-time as chaplain at Camps Miller and Kilpatrick. The first couple of months, we sent out Wings mailers to our immediate "circle of influence." The meager donations mailed back barely covered our time and materials.

Linda and I also worked at a friend's mobile pet clinic part-time, driving a three-quarter-ton pickup towing a thirty-foot mobile home to predetermined strip malls and shopping centers. People stood in the hot sun with their animals for hours at a time to get discounted rabies, parvo, and 3-in-1 puppy vaccines. It was more like a three-ring circus with dogfights, runaway cats, fender benders, and hot tempers. My job was to break up fights and clean up dog poop.

During one clinic, Wayne, the elderly, arthritic veterinarian, knocked over a quart of rubbing alcohol inside the trailer. The kitchen stove caused a flash fire. I was outside working the "pooper scooper" when I saw black smoke pouring out of the open side door. I yelled for someone to call the fire department, and Linda screamed that Wayne was still inside the trailer. I busted out the rear window and climbed in. I couldn't see through the billowing smoke and called out his name without a response. I found Doctor Wayne crouched on the floor of the closet, wide-eyed and frozen with fear. I lifted the panic-stricken veterinarian out the broken window to waiting hands and jumped out after him.

The trailer burned to the ground and I was out of a job.

■ ■ ■

We needed the Los Angeles County Probation Department's blessing to get Wings Foundation up and running inside the county juvenile detention centers. Outside of God's promise, I was totally unqualified. I did not go to college. I did not work for the Los Angeles County Probation Department, and I already had the reputation of being "aggressive" (another county euphemism).

"Mr. Stanley, what's on your mind?" asked the assistant to the chief probation officer.

Linda and I were seated at a long mahogany table in the Los Angeles County Probation Department headquarters' conference room. Seven executives stared at us without a single smile. At the head of the table was chief probation officer Kenneth E. Kirkpatrick, an elderly, pale-faced man seemingly void of emotion and on the brink of retirement. A black woman in her fifties by the name of Teena Lambert sat across from the chief. I introduced my wife and my plan to save the world.

"Thank you for setting the time aside for us."

I was as nervous as a first-grader in a school play. In football, I was always nervous before the first explosive tackle; in baseball, until my first defensive play at shortstop; racing motorcycles, I would get the dry heaves on the line, waiting for the starting banner to drop. Here at the Los Angeles County Probation Department, I had no idea what I was waiting for or why I was feeling so edgy.

I was distracted as one of the tall wooden doors of the conference room pushed open and in walked Chaplain Torres. She sat down in a vacant chair without acknowledging my wife or me.

The "starting banner" had dropped. I was no longer nervous.

"In my two years as a volunteer," I began, "I have witnessed the overcrowded and understaffed facilities, Proposition 13's stripping of in-camp programs and activities, and the termination of all after-care programs, along with the 20 percent increase in juvenile crime. It is clear to me that the problem of juvenile crime and the escalating rate of recidivism have become bigger than the county's resources."

I walked around the heavy rectangular table distributing the printed documents I had prepared. "The purpose of Wings Foundation is to help solve that problem." I ended up back at my chair and remained standing. Those present silently skimmed through my nine-page proposal. Not wanting to cause a meltdown, I had left out the sailing part. "What we are asking for is your permission to begin a pilot program with our Wings volunteers at Camp Miller, where I am currently the chaplain."

"Is this a religious program?" asked the director of public relations.

"Not exactly," I said. "We have two choices — we can teach either godly or ungodly principles to those kids. They're already living proof that the ungodly approach doesn't work."

"You have a very convincing way about you, Mr. Stanley," said Teena Lambert, director of community affairs, with a smile.

"Unqualified personnel are not permitted exclusive meetings with juvenile wards of the court." All eyes turned to Chaplain Torres. She continued. "It would violate their confidentiality."

I took a slow, deep breath.

"Chaplain, our volunteers would not be there to discuss the kids' criminal records," I explained, "but rather to teach them how to become productive members of their community."

"I understand," she said, smiling back. "However, only licensed chaplains, family members, and credentialed professionals are allowed one-on-one visits inside a juvenile facility." Chaplain Torres batted her baby browns innocently toward the members of probation. "That is the law — isn't it?"

All eyes shifted to the chief.

"Yes," the chief confirmed.

"That law was made to protect the identity of juveniles." I raised my voice. Linda shot me a warning look. "It was not meant to isolate them from capable, qualified volunteers who care about kids!"

"We'll get back to you, Mr. Stanley." The chief probation officer stood and sidestepped toward the open door. Everyone else rose in compliance.

"These kids need help — now!" I snapped, stalling the herd's migration. Linda handed me my leather briefcase, trying to keep me calm. "If you don't allow caring people to get to those throwaway kids, sir" — I pointed an accusatory finger at the chief probation officer — "then you are forcing them to go right back to the only thing they know, which is crime and gangs!"

There was an awkward silence, and the herd followed the leader out of the conference room. Tight-lipped, I grabbed my things and made a beeline for the parking lot, ahead of Linda.

"I'm beginning to know exactly how they feel," I snapped as Linda and I climbed into the Mazda.

"Who?" she asked.

"The kids. Everything I want to do is against the law!" I pulled out into the heavy afternoon traffic. "Those self-serving bureaucrats don't want anything to change." I was venting, as they say down at the clinic. "All they care about is hanging on to their fat paychecks and pension plans!" I leaned on the horn at the slow-moving car in front of me. "They're afraid of change!"

"They're afraid of you," Linda said as she picked up a little steam. "You come barging into their camps with no education, no experience, no game plan — and you win the heart of every kid you see."

"Because I care!" I shouted.

"*Then* you muscle your way into the Los Angeles County Probation Department — one of the biggest probation departments in the world, I might add — and tell them how you're going to make things better!"

"Whose side are you on, anyway?" I said, now driving too fast.

"Honey, they're not the enemy."

Wrong, lady! I thought to myself. *If they're against me, then they're the enemy.*

I don't know when I started believing that, but I can't remember life any other way. When I raced motorcycles, if someone blocked me, I'd yell and scream at him over the roaring engines. If that didn't work, I'd ram him or kick his bike until he moved out of the way or crashed. Anybody who opposed me was "the enemy" — both on and off the track. I learned long ago that thoughts and feelings were to be shared only with those who I sensed would support or agree with my plans, position, or dreams. "Us against them" was my mantra.

I think the furry-faced doctors with the horn-rimmed glasses call that *paranoia*.

When I fell in love with Linda (which took about fifteen minutes), my biggest fear was that she would discover I wasn't the hotshot lad that I alleged to be. Now, at the ripe old age of forty, I was president of a film company that wasn't making films, living in a converted chicken coop, raising other people's jailed kids for free, and buying Shane and Brett "knockoff" clothing and shoe brands because I couldn't afford the real thing.

The thing I feared the most had come to pass. Events were making things pretty clear: I wasn't the hotshot I pretended to be.

I couldn't even afford new tires for my used mini pickup truck.

■ ■ ■

"What's this?" I asked Brett as we dropped him off at his father's apartment one Sunday morning after church.

He handed me a wrinkled aluminum-foil envelope.

"Don't open it until you get home, OK?" he said with a happy smile, then kissed his mother and bailed out of the car.

I got halfway to the freeway on-ramp and started to pull open the foil.

Linda checked me. "Wait until you get home," she said.

"It's probably some project they had him do in church." I looked over to Linda. "A bomb, perhaps."

I ripped open the envelope. Four $50 bills tumbled out, along with a handwritten note. I pulled off to the side of the road and read it:

Dear Lee,
New tires for the pickup.
Love, Brett.

"I can't accept this," I said, half to myself, as I stared at the money.

Linda's eyes filled with tears. "He loves you," she said, as if I didn't know it.

I wanted to jump out of the car and run back to Brett, but he was already swallowed up in the other household.

I was tougher on him than anybody. He accepted my God, my rules, my methods, my lack of grace, my dreams — my everything — without complaint.

We'd always been told we needed to care for Brett.

Look who was caring for whom.

■ ■ ■

The phone rang. It was my ally from the Los Angeles County Probation Department, Teena Lambert.

"Mr. Stanley, may I speak candidly with you?" she asked.

Her voice was soft, caring, and concerned.

"Yes, ma'am," I said, already preparing my defense.

"I am also a Christian, and I believe in your project. Perhaps if you could be a little more patient with probation, and I know that's asking a lot," she laughed, "I think you can get their support."

To this day, I have no idea what that angel did, but a week later Wings Foundation was welcomed into Camp Miller and Camp Kilpatrick, where I served as chaplain.

I chose our initial volunteers carefully — guys like Hollywood stuntman Doc Duhame, retired Continental Airlines pilot Roy Houston, computer sage Freddie Kurtz, investment broker Tom Taylor, and ex-thug-turned-property-manager Andy Cotte, a man comfortable with presidents and kings, winos and Wings kids.

Andy was born in Puerto Rico, and when he was eight years old, he immigrated to New York City. He woke up one cold and rainy morning to find his mother lying next to him, dead. To survive, Andy hit the streets, joined a gang, ran drugs, and collected money. He quickly became an expert with zip guns, knives, chains, and tire irons — whatever it took to do the job effectively. For his unquestioned loyalty, the ringleaders gave their little Puerto Rican "runner" his own cache of drugs, turning Andy into a hard-core heroin addict. When he wasn't in jail, he was out terrorizing the neighborhood, stealing, robbing, shooting, shooting up, and eliminating anybody who got in his way.

Once, during a violent street fight, an opposing gang member nailed Andy with a brick thrown from a tenement rooftop. Andy lived, but the brick caved in the front part of his skull. One desperate, lonely New York City night a month later, Andy Cotte met his match when a street preacher looked past Andy's bruised and dented skull and drug-induced, glassy-eyed stupor and took the grungy little thug in for a hot meal, clean clothes, and prayer.

"I accepted Christ when I was whacked-out on heroin, Lee," Andy confessed with a smile. "My mind cleared — no withdrawals, no cold turkey. It was like I had never used drugs ever before!"

That was thirty-six years ago.

Andy is one of the main reasons I never lose hope for troubled kids — or anyone else still breathing.

CHAPTER 11

"IF YOU WANT HELP, RAISE YOUR HAND"

"Shut up and sit down!" a Camp Kilpatrick staffer yelled through an electric bullhorn at the slow-moving assembly of one-hundred-plus surly, troubled teens.

It was Sylmar Juvenile Hall all over again, only this time in a cold, concrete-floor gymnasium with cinder block walls painted puke yellow and lousy caged lighting overhead. Tonight's gathering was mandatory. Camp kids don't like mandatory anything, especially on Wednesday nights — Wednesday night was movie night.

Dressed in county-issue blue jeans, white T-shirts, and unbuttoned tan jackets, the brooding wards sidestepped their way along the narrow rows of metal folding chairs, darting veiled glances at the only three females in the gym. As they came to the last available seat, each ward flopped down in place.

The dozen Wings volunteers stood against the scuffed and scraped sidewall, along with the camp director, a trim man in his late fifties who had a wrinkled face void of emotion. He was a man of very few words who learned long ago that what he said, or what anyone else on the front lines said, really didn't matter much.

The bullhorn-toting probation officer walked to the front of the assembly, scanning the room with obvious displeasure. He seemed to relish yelling. "We got guests here tonight to present a special program!" Most of the kids craned their necks around and zeroed in on volunteer Doc Duhame's perky young wife. "The way some of you are behaving, I can't imagine why they'd want to get involved with you!"

"I can imagine why I'd want to get involved with her!" someone shouted.

The room exploded in laughter. A husky probation officer yanked the rude Romeo out of his metal chair and hauled him away.

Our perturbed host engaged his tin trumpet. "Another outburst, and you'll all be on lockdown for the rest of the week!"

He kept the bullhorn an inch from his angry mouth and scanned the now silent auditorium. He slowly lowered the tin trumpet and gave me a nod.

I walked to the front of the auditorium, footsteps echoing off the concrete floor and cinder block walls. I dismissed the bullhorn with a smile, and the host probation officer stepped off to the side, remaining in full view of his caged customers.

"Some of you know me as Chaplain Lee."

One of my "clients," a sixteen-year-old white wannabe sitting in the second row, signaled with a subtle nod and wave.

I took a few steps toward center stage. "The main reason I am here tonight is because I care about you."

Sarcastic moans and jeers erupted from the audience. Someone in the back of the auditorium called out a disgruntled, 'Yeah, right!' The host PO darted a concerned look toward the camp director. The assembly grew unruly. Two beefy probation officers moved quickly forward.

I was totally calm.

I looked at my audience, feeling strangely at peace, like a snake charmer must feel sitting before an angry cobra that's ready to strike. I didn't have a flute, but I had empathy — for every kid in the room. Deep inside I knew they were hurting and scared to death, and they had no idea how to undo the mess their lives had become. They didn't know how to do anything except cover up their true feelings.

I waited until there was silence. "And I want to help you." A handful uttered groans of doubt. "If you want help, raise your hand."

The gymnasium grew strangely quiet.

I surveyed my juvenile audience. A tough-looking Hispanic with muscles on top of muscles looked around, then slid up his hand. Then another ward, then two more—a dozen, a large group off to the side—until over half the prison population had their hands in the air.

The vipers decided not to strike. Instead, they looked back expectantly, waiting for direction.

"Good," I said. "You can put your hands down. Wings Foundation has been established for you and supported by people who are committed to making a godly impact in your lives. Our volunteers will come to camp one night a week." I quickly added, "Not on Wednesday nights." The group laughed appreciatively.

"The purpose of our gatherings is for you to get to know us and for us to get to know you, one-on-one. If you want to continue seeing one of our volunteers once you are on the outs, you can call the Wings office, and we'll hook you up."

A good-looking thug seated near Doc Duhame's wife, Cynthia, raised his hand with a cocky smile.

I pointed at him and cut him off before he could speak.

"No, we will not hook you up with any of our female volunteers."

The room burst out in laughter.

"How much this gonna cost?" a young black asked.

"Just your pride," I said. Others in the audience nodded knowingly.

"Let me introduce the Wings volunteers who are here tonight."

I introduced each one of our guests by name. I then asked the volunteers to explain their professions and why they wanted to help kids. It was a powerful, emotional time. Producer Dave Adams couldn't get halfway through his first sentence without tearing up.

"I just want to tell you what a privilege it is," he told the kids, "for me and my wife, Lynn, to" — he pressed his lips tightly together, arm wrestling with emotion, the kids waiting patiently for him to continue — "what a privilege it is to be here with you tonight!"

Dave waved and stepped back against the wall. The kids applauded his sincerity.

We ended the evening in prayer and stood on both sides of the door, shaking hands with the boys as they quietly filed out of the gymnasium and headed back to their dorms.

Outside the night air felt nippy. As we walked across Camp Kilpatrick's compound toward the front office, our shoes left a dark trail in the cold, silvery, wet grass. The overhead mercury vapor floodlights turned our breath into sulfurlike puffs of smoke. We passed B-Dorm and saw the silhouettes of two dozen boys through the windows as they silently undressed and lined up for head calls. Three young prisoners tracked our exit through cupped hands pressed against fog-smeared windows. One of the boys waved. I waved back. Producer Dave put his hand on my shoulder.

"Lee, if you get permission to take those kids sailing," he said, "I will give you $25,000 dollars toward your film."

■ ■ ■

The ninety-minute weekly Wings meeting drew from fifteen to twenty-five wards on a regular basis. As kids graduated from camp, they hooked up with our volunteer caretakers. We had monthly Wings gatherings at the chicken coop, our little eight-hundred-square-foot home in the remote hills of Agoura. Wings demanded all of my time and most of Linda's time.

Brett and Shane got used to having Wings kids around on weekends and sharing their dinner table and cramped quarters with teen Wings kids who didn't want to go home or whose parents didn't want them at home.

Not only did I expect Shane and Brett to behave perfectly around these imperfect children, but I also expected them to embrace Wings kids as if they were family.

Years later, I would learn that my blood son never did get used to sharing his father with every deprived teen soul who came through our open door or called collect in the wee hours of the morning. Shane's gracious behavior during those intense Wings years never gave me a clue about how he really felt, except that he didn't want to disappoint his dad.

The work of Wings grew quickly. We were successful in the camps and on the streets. The Church On The Way committed $500 a month toward our foundation, and Pastor Jack graciously allowed me to speak to the congregation.

It was a Wednesday night, and the main auditorium was filled with about fifteen hundred people. I poured out my heart and soul and watched dozens in the audience pour out their tears, nodding in agreement and praising God for our work. I told true stories about real kids who had "bent the knee" and cried out for help.

"By the time a kid gets locked up," I concluded, "everybody has given up. The kid's parents have given up, the social worker has given up, the probation officer has given up, and the judge has given up." I waited a thoughtful beat. "Well, God has not given up!" The audience applauded and cheered. "What these kids are discovering is that the God they were indifferent to is the One who reached down, gave them a new heart, breathed new hope into their lives, and got them excited about being alive" — I pointed to the audience — "because they were experiencing the love of God through people like you!"

After the service, dozens of compassionate believers filled out Wings volunteer cards. Before collecting the cards, I gave clear instruction to my volunteers.

"Be sure to tell the people Wings will not be calling them. They are to call Wings if they want to get involved."

"Lee," Doc Duhame interrupted, "Wings asked for the information. Wings should make the first contact."

"Tonight most of these people are responding to their emotions," I said. "I want the ones who will respond to the need."

Out of the 178 volunteer cards collected that Wednesday evening at The Church On The Way, seven people contacted Wings to offer their time and resources.

A writer known in local church circles jumped at the chance to volunteer. This middle-aged and handsome biblical scholar arrived at the detention camp early and geared up to save lost souls.

I opened the Wings gathering with a simple prayer and then did a twenty-minute teaching. After the teaching, our dozen volunteers paired up with the twenty or so wards in attendance. I watched as the writer made a beeline to a heavily tattooed Hispanic gang member in the back of the room who had slipped into our meeting late, "testing the waters," as so many do.

The writer boldly praised Jesus for the thug's attendance and told him what a wonderful God we served. He talked nonstop — and I mean *non*stop! At one point I asked him to lower his voice. He was all atwitter because God had just given him a word for the gangbanger, Chico.

Sensing his moment, the writer spoke it aloud, without being asked, in tongues, with one hand gripping Chico's arm. He quickly translated for the confused convicts. "You will set a standard for the boys in this camp, for they will realize that it takes a strong man to lay down his pride, and they will follow your lead and come to Wings and find the Lord." He raised his other hand to the heavens. "Hallelujah, thank you, Jesus; praise you, Jesus!"

Embarrassed, Chico asked to return to his dorm, which I allowed.

My spirit groaned. I turned to our writer volunteer. "I think you're a little ahead of the Lord," I said in my gentlest manner.

"I came here because God told me to come," the writer advised later in the camp's parking lot, "to help you and the Wings Foundation. I did not come here to be embarrassed or made a fool." I opened my mouth to respond but was cut off. "How long have you known the Lord?"

I had to do a little math. "About eight years!"

He pointed a finger at his chest and poked it with every syllable. "Twenty-*five* years," he declared. "And I have written a book!"

"You were out of order," I said with a gentle smile.

"You don't allow room for the Holy Spirit," he countered. "You control everybody." For the first time in my life I didn't strike back. "I won't be coming back!"

The writer stomped off, leaving me standing alone in the parking lot. The moon was just peeking out from behind a retreating storm cloud.

"Hit a few, miss a few," I said out loud.

That was pretty tame for me.

■ ■ ■

Chico never came back. I learned the following day that he had just been told before coming to Wings that his little brother had been gunned down in a drive-by shooting. Perhaps he had come to Wings to get some answers or pour out his pain, but instead he got a lecture.

He "graduated" from Camp Kilpatrick, and, as his probation officer reported, Chico tracked down his little brother's killer and stabbed him in the face. He then climbed into his gray Camaro and, before speeding off, ran over the killer—twice.

This was all accomplished before the sun went down on Chico's first day of freedom.

As of this writing, Chico has successfully completed nineteen years of a "twenty-five to life" sentence. He started out at ancient San Quentin Prison and was later transferred to the modern and more secure facility, Pelican Bay.

My writer friend wrote another book. It was pretty good.

Am I blaming him for Chico's "payback" stunt? No. But there are ways to work with troubled kids that exhibit more wisdom than other ways.

I looked into Chico's record before he came to Camp Kilpatrick, and I don't mean his criminal record. I spent some time with his homeboys, his pregnant girlfriend, and another homegirl, Maria, who was the proud mother of Chico's first heir apparent.

"Chico is loco," this fifteen-year-old mother told me.

The girl looked like the actress playing the role of Elvira, with sprayed black hair teased to the ceiling, tweezed eyebrows, and long, dark fingernails with matching dark lipstick. Scratched on her smooth shoulder was the jagged, blue-inked tattoo, *LOCO*. On the other was an equally jagged tattoo that spelled out the name of a Hispanic street gang.

Chico's precious five-month-old son was crawling around on the floor in front of us. His skinny grandmother, who couldn't have been a day over thirty, was curled up on a nearby couch, rolling a joint and watching a Spanish soap.

Maria took a drag on a Sherman, exhaled thick, white smoke out her flared nostrils, and turned her shoulder around for me to see.

"That's his street name — Loco."

Grandma took a hit off her joint and joined in the conversation.

"Whatever you need done, Chico's the man," she boasted through half-closed glassy eyes.

I guessed she was on her second or third joint. It was a few minutes past noon.

"You tell him to shoot somebody," Maria continued, "he'll shoot 'em. You tell him to stab somebody, he'll stab 'em. I guess that's why they call him Loco."

She snapped at her mother in Spanish.

Grandma waved the dope smoke away from the baby and

walked outside, letting the rusted metal screen door slam behind her.

"You know what 'Loco' means?" Maria asked, and before I could show off my Spanish, she blurted out, "Crazy!" She took another drag on her brown cigarette and exhaled reflectively. "He is one crazy dude."

"You just don't want to cross him," Grandma called from the porch.

Maria shrugged and gave me a smile. "You want a beer or Coke or something?" she asked.

CHAPTER 12

"YOUR REQUEST IS DENIED"

"Mr. Nidorf, members of Probation, I would like your permission to take kids from camp out sailing."

I was back at the Los Angeles County Probation Department. At the head of the table was the chief probation officer, Barry Nidorf, a tall, middle-aged man with broad shoulders who was the new kingpin of the Probation Department. He already had the look of an old-timer working unending hours without praise or progress. On his left sat the assistant to the chief, Steve Canon.

My advocate, Teena Lambert, sat quietly across from the chief.

I handed out my proposal titled "Hard-Core Cruise." On the cover was a penciled sketch of a wayward teen gripping the spoked helm of a sailboat.

"Today, thousands of hard-core juvenile criminals are locked up around the country," I read out loud from my presentation. "Statistics say that nearly three-quarters of them will move into adult crime and end up in the already overcrowded penitentiaries of our nation. "Hard-Core Cruise" is designed to change those statistics."

I darted a look at my audience to see if they were reading along. "In this innovative, life-changing project, I am going to take seven juvenile offenders out to sea for ten days aboard a sailboat. We will teach them how to sail, navigate, fish, and scrub the decks, and, in the process, we will allow them to make some exciting discoveries about themselves and their shipmates. We will film the cruise in detail and make it available for a one-hour television special."

I concluded by reading our basic cruise plan and daily activity plan aboard the yacht. I also included a chart of the cruise area, my biography, and personal references.

"That is a very ambitious project, Mr. Stanley, but identifiable photographs of wards are not allowed," Chief Nidorf said. He leaned way back in his chair. "Why don't you take kids who are out on probation. Then you won't need the department's permission."

"Kids out on probation are running on their own, with attitude," I said. "Viewers see them on the news every night, and they won't care about them. Kids in camp are vulnerable and transparent, and that's what will make our project unique and successful."

"I cannot allow you to photograph juvenile wards of the court." Nidorf looked around the table. "I'm sorry, Mr. Stanley," he said. "Your request is denied."

■ ■ ■

You will take kids out of jail and go to sea aboard a sailboat and you will film the adventure in detail and the kids will return to camp. The completed project will impact the nation as nothing ever before.

It was the end of a long and hollow day. I was standing on top of a ridge overlooking Camp Kilpatrick and Camp Miller, staring at the notes I had scribbled down on a legal tablet months earlier as the Lord unfolded his vision for the film. I was exhausted for no apparent reason.

I heard a loud voice echo off the surrounding hillside and saw a line of kids, hands clasped behind their backs, march glumly out of Kilpatrick's dining hall toward B-Dorm under the command of a probation officer. Off in the distance, the Pacific Ocean swallowed the sun.

Wings' most recent mailing reaped less than $100, and once again, unpaid bills were piling up. The Stanleys were broke, and Linda and I were arguing more than ever. Correction: I was taking out my frustrations on my wife.

"Is this for real, or what!" I snarled, shaking my legal tablet toward heaven.

What kind of person abandons a career because he thinks he heard a word from the Lord — a promise, a vision for his life? What about all the people who did not "hear the word" — like spouses, sons, brothers, mothers, and bill collectors? What about going from a life of tangible promise, tangible assets, and tangible income to a life of tangible poverty?

What have I done with my life? What have I done to my family?

I drove the winding, steep, and dangerous Kanan Road through the mountains toward home. We had prayed the length of Kanan Road just last month after witnessing a horrendous crash from our front yard. A pink Volkswagen Bug packed with teen girls skidded out of control and off the road, plummeting two hundred feet down an embankment into the ravine below. Our home (the chicken coop) was directly across from Kanan Road, perched on the side of Lady Face Mountain about a quarter mile away. I called 911 and prayed to God that lives were spared.

It was dark and began to rain. I flipped on the Mazda's windshield wipers. Suddenly a car appeared, fishtailing into my lane. I slammed on the brakes and swerved to the side of the road, barely avoiding a head-on collision. The driver miraculously regained control and, after scaring us both half to death, continued on.

Prayer works, I thought.

As I drove along in the rain, I could see the lights in our small home on the side of the hill. I knew Linda, Shane, and Brett were there waiting for me. The house would be filled with the aroma of my wife's incredible cooking. Brett would be at his desk quietly doing homework. Shane and the dog would be out in our freestanding, dirt floor garage, working on his Kawasaki KX80 motorcycle. When I came up the driveway, Shane and Star would come outside to greet me, rain or shine.

I couldn't go home.

You're a damn bum, and everybody knows you're a damn bum! The old label was back to haunt me.

I continued on into Agoura to the post office. I was on the verge of throwing in the towel. Faith is one thing, but not providing for your family is a bridge too far.

I parked in front of the outdoor mailboxes and unlocked the Wings Foundation post office box. The rain stopped. Inside the mailbox was one envelope. I opened it to find five crumpled-up $1 bills and thirty cents in change, along with a handwritten note:

Go for it, Dad!
Love from your son,
Shane

PART 3

CHAPTER 13

"SO YOU'RE THE ONE WHO'S TWEAKING PROBATION'S NOSE"

"Who has the ultimate authority over kids in camp?"

I was talking on the telephone to Teena Lambert from the Probation Department. Teena always fielded my calls, even when I was huffing and puffing and wanting to blow her department down.

"The presiding judge of the juvenile judicial system, H. Randolph Moore Jr."

"How do I get to him?" Teena gave me the judge's phone number. "Anything you can tell me about him?"

"I guess you could say he's feisty—kind of reminds me of you, Lee." Teena laughed. "His father is an Episcopal minister."

Two weeks later, I made the long drive from Agoura Hills to the Criminal Courts building in downtown Los Angeles to meet with the Honorable H. Randolph Moore Jr.

"Hey! Where do you think you're going, pal?"

I stopped abruptly and looked in the Mazda's rearview mirror to see a fat, uniformed Hispanic man leaning back on a bent metal chair next to the little hut by the entrance to the Criminal Courts building parking lot.

I rolled down my window and stuck my head out. "Name's not pal, *pal!*" I snapped. (This declaration came, of course, after I had spent the morning in stop-and-go traffic, praying and singing praises to the Lord.)

The keeper of the gate waddled up to my rolled-down window. His bulging belly was staring me right in the face. "Who you here to see?" he asked.

"Randolph Moore, presiding judge of the juvenile courts," I announced, as if putting the guy on notice.

"Park right there." He gestured toward a nearby empty space. "You know Randy?"

"No."

"He's the man! But hey — this area's for county employees only, OK?"

"I didn't know," I said, feeling bad about snapping at the guard.

"Randy's up on the twelfth floor." He extended his beefy hand. "You have a good day, sir."

I wandered off, feeling shamefully hypocritical.

I waited for the elevator with a dozen busy-looking folks clutching briefcases with the *Wall Street Journal* tucked under an arm, and with teen delinquents whose body language was announcing their disdain for a nearby parent.

How does a parent/child relationship get so infected? I thought to myself.

The elevator doors opened, and the crowd shuffled in as if we were one. I watched a mother out of the corner of my eye staring with contempt at her lanky young daughter less than a foot away. Mom was dressed in a gray sweatshirt, Levis, and rubber shower thongs. Her toenails were long, the silver metallic polish chipped. A light-blue scarf knotted under her double chin failed to cover a tight rack of pink hair rollers. I was curious about what other event the woman could possibly be prepping for. A worn imitation-leather purse dangled off her penguinlike shoulder. The clasp was broken, allowing anyone who cared to take a peek at her bent Virginia Slims. She coughed heavily, dislodging the morning's phlegm, and, thankfully, covered her mouth. The woman was not wearing a wedding ring and smelled like stale cigarette smoke.

The daughter was probably thirteen or fourteen, unkempt and defeated looking. Her eyes were more sad than frightened, and her skin was pale.

"Stand up straight, for God's sake!" Mom snapped and then looked over to me, shaking her tightly bound head with disgust as if we were comrades, and coughed again.

The door chimed open, and the bad seed was hauled out of the elevator. Mother and daughter stood there not knowing which way to turn. I watched them until the door closed.

■ ■ ■

"Lee, come on in!" a voice bellowed.

As I entered his chambers, Judge Moore bounded from behind a large mahogany desk with his right hand extended.

"Randy Moore!"

He shook my hand firmly.

The judge was a bundle of energy and charm, immaculately dressed and well groomed, with a neatly trimmed gray mustache and salt-and-pepper hair. His custom-tailored dress shirt accented his trim waist and strong shoulders. A silk tie was knotted perfectly at his neck.

We moved over to a comfortable leather seating area beneath a gallery wall of framed law degrees, civic awards, a photograph of a black minister — who I later learned was his father — and a photograph of the beautiful Mrs. Randy Moore. The most prominent display was a large black-and-white photo of a teenage Randy Moore in a boxing ring, slugging it out with another fighter.

"Golden Gloves?" I asked.

"My last fight," he said, darting a quick look up at the picture. "Got my butt kicked! Have a seat."

I sat down on the deep leather couch. Judge Moore sat in a matching leather armchair to my left.

"So you're the one who's tweaking probation's nose," he said, getting right to the point.

"Your Honor, I want permission to take a group of kids from Camp Kilpatrick and Camp Miller sailing on an overnight trip to Catalina Island."

"What happens after they get off the boat?"

"I have a nonprofit foundation that will hook them up with groups and churches in their communities to offer help and direction once the kids are released."

"How many kids?" the judge asked.

"Eight." I set my typed proposal on the glass coffee table in front of us. "This is a detailed outline of my plan, sailing credentials, insurance coverage, in-camp training program, and detailed procedures covering any situation; from man overboard to a full-blown mutiny."

"Mutiny?" Judge Moore smiled warmly. "You'll never get rid of them!" He walked over to the window and stared out at the city. "Did you know that a similar effort was tried about fifteen years ago?"

"No, sir."

"A dozen minors went out on a commercial fishing boat. They got caught in a freak storm. All twelve were lost at sea, along with the crew." The judge turned from the window and looked directly at me. "What else?"

"No police, no counselors, no probation officers. And I want a press conference at dockside — with no restrictions."

"Can't!" He walked back toward me and remained standing. "You're talking about juvenile wards of the court. Identifiable photographs and names are not allowed."

"Your Honor, I have read dozens of books and articles about today's troubled youth, and a lot of case studies too. I couldn't find one quote from a kid."

"What's your point?"

"My point, sir, is that no one has ever heard from *them*. The press conference will allow viewers to look into their eyes, to see if there's a kid left inside the criminal."

Judge Moore appeared to give this last thought consideration. "I'll get back to you."

■ ■ ■

"I hate it when decision makers tell you they'll get back to you!"

Linda had just walked through the door of the chicken coop after a very long day down at Pyramid Films in Santa Monica. I was pacing and giving her the rundown on my meeting with Judge Moore. She went into the teeny-tiny living room, with our black Lab mutt on her heels. Like everyone else in the family, Star was excited to have her home.

"Dave and Lynn gave me a raise today."

"Honey, I'm so proud of you."

I joined her on the couch.

"They know we're broke," Linda said with a smile.

I suddenly felt deflated, snapped back to reality. Broke! I stepped into my small study off the living room. Small is an under-statement — it was four feet by eight feet, with a window looking out toward Kanan Road.

"I'm calling the judge tomorrow morning!" I barked and wrote down a reminder — as if I needed one.

"Lee?" I looked over at my wife. "He said he would get back to you."

"I'm going to call him!"

Linda stared back at me with the most peaceful expression on her beautiful face, and then she left the room.

I didn't call the judge.

Instead, I started planning the sail to Catalina Island.

Wings volunteer Roy Houston committed $3,000 to cover a yacht charter and provisions. Roy was the retired Continental

Airlines pilot who cared about kids, especially Wings kids. He had bright blue eyes, silver-white hair, a George Hamilton tan, and pearly white teeth, and he rode a Honda Gold Wing motorcycle. He was also grumpy, stubborn, and opinionated, and he never said no to any request. That's probably what made Roy so grumpy. He was sixty-one going on sixteen.

Roy and I combed the docks from Santa Barbara to San Diego, talking with skippers and boat owners alike. We wanted a bareboat charter, which means all the yacht owner had to do was deliver a vessel that was seaworthy and passed Coast Guard inspection (that was my requirement). We would provide captain and crew.

Once they learned of our "cargo," they all rejected our proposal.

A week passed, and I still hadn't heard from Judge H. Randolph Moore Jr. To stay away from the phone, I stayed busy at Miller and Kilpatrick and started a mental list of juveniles to crew the boat. One kid caught my attention. He was fourteen but looked like he was ten, and he weighed less than one hundred pounds. "Little Corey" was doing time in Miller, the open camp, but he was currently in Camp Kilpatrick's A-Dorm, ICU, for disciplinary reasons.

"Kid's really amped," warned the counselor on duty.

"Why's he locked up?" I asked.

"Broke into a store and stole a bike. He's down at the end in 16."

I walked toward the last cell across from the intake area, nodding to the expressionless faces pressed against the small windows of each cell door. A small dark blur popped up in one window, disappeared, and popped up again. Cell 16.

Little Corey was all over me as soon as I entered.

"How much that Bible cost?" He rubbed his small brown fingers up and down the gilt-edged pages of my leather Bible, studied the embossed name on the cover, and furrowed his brow. "Lee Stanley!" He looked up at me. "That you?" he asked, not waiting for the answer to his first question.

"That's me," I said with a smile.

"You like Jonah?" He pulled me over toward the bed. "Will you read it to me?" We sat on the edge of his bunk. Corey started completing the verses with me about the time Jonah was thrown overboard. "That was a whale that ate Jonah!" he said with certainty. "Whales are the biggest fish in the ocean. My daddy's seen 'em!"

"Really?"

"Yup," he nodded. "I love whales!"

Corey had never seen a whale, never been on a boat. But he had seen the ocean, once. Little Corey's bus driver dad used to walk him down to the local bicycle store after hours so father and son could gaze at the brand-new purple and chrome bicycle in the storefront window. That was going to be Daddy's birthday gift to Corey, and he was saving up to make it happen. One night, a drug-crazed street thug stepped between father and son and stuck a double-barreled sawed-off shotgun in Daddy's ear. *Bam! Bam!* Corey was sprayed with red as his daddy fell to the ground, lifeless. The drug thug smacked the kid and took off running with a fistful of savings.

Once Daddy was buried, Corey returned to the bicycle shop after hours and hurled a thick chunk of concrete through the storefront window. The cops scooped up Little Corey about sunrise the next morning down at the end of Santa Monica Pier. He was straddling that brand-new purple and chrome bicycle, the sales ticket dangling in the breeze.

He was looking for whales.

"Medication time!"

A redheaded nurse leaned into her pill cart and banged it through Corey's open cell door.

"I don't want any," said Corey with a touch of wrath.

The nurse ignored my presence and extended a small pill cup and paper cup of water. Corey turned his face away. She put down the water and grabbed for Corey. He doubled over, head down between his knees, locking his little boy arms tightly beneath his skinny legs. The nurse jammed her chubby pink hand under his locked jaw and tried to jack up his head.

"Maybe he can take them later?" I suggested.

"Maybe you'd like to stop interfering and step outside!" snapped the nurse like an angry pit bull.

Little Corey got written up for refusing to take his medication, and a full week was added to his three-month "program." Two days later, he was returned to Camp Miller, and the following morning before breakfast he went AWOL.

I never did get to take Little Corey out to see the whales.

It was near dark by the time I got to the Agoura Hills Post Office. Storm clouds were forming off to the north. I pulled the lone piece of mail out of the Wings PO box, turned on the Mazda's dome light, and read the letter.

"You bitch!" I yelled out.

I jammed the car into gear and took off for home, setting a new speed record through the twists and turns of Kanan Road.

Shane was in the open garage working on his Kawasaki. As always, he came out to greet me as I drove down the dirt driveway. I skidded to a stop, bailed out of the car, and half-hugged my son.

"What happened, Dad?" he asked with obvious concern.

Linda appeared in the front doorway.

"What is it?" Linda asked as I strode into the house.

I handed her the letter.

She read it out loud, carefully.

... the goals and concepts of your Wings Foundation are most admirable. However, your new involvement with minors creates a conflict of interest, and therefore we must ask you to resign your post as chaplain of Camp Miller and Camp Kilpatrick, effective immediately.

In his service,
Chaplain Torres

Linda rescanned the letter and shrugged. "You don't need to be a chaplain to help those kids."

"If I'm not the chaplain, I can't get in to see the kids, Linda!" I grabbed the letter out of her hand. "Don't you understand? She shut me down!" I crumpled up the letter and hurled it across the room. "Same ol' same ol'. Nothing's changed since I started helping those kids, nothing — except the way we live!"

"What matters to me and to Shane and to Brett is that you believe in something and you want to make a difference!"

"True! When we started this — this walk of faith — that was true! But have you noticed that since we moved into this remodeled barn, they don't invite their friends over here. Neither do we, Linda, unless it's after dark. We're all too embarrassed!"

I stomped over to the window and saw Shane standing by the car with the dog at his side, listening. I leaned heavily on the kitchen counter and stared into the empty sink.

"You want to give up?" Linda asked. "That letter's your perfect exit. Just let me know what you want to do, and we'll do it!"

"Linda, don't start with me. This is not the time!"

"Nobody forced you into helping kids, Lee. That was your idea."

"My idea was to turn them on to life, not take on the system!"

"You wanted both, right from the beginning. I saw it. And that's what it will take to make a difference!"

Linda walked out of the room.

It rained hard that night. I got up around two in the morning and positioned three cooking pots on the living room floor. The water dripping into the empty aluminum pots was loud, so I put towels in each one. Our antique Seth Thomas clock chimed out the hour as I built a fire in the fireplace. Eventually, I went into Shane and Brett's bedroom. I covered Brett on the bottom bunk and stood up to cover Shane on the top bunk. He was awake.

"Hi," he whispered.

"You OK?" I whispered back as I tucked in his blanket.

"Yeah."

I gave him a hug.

I went back into the living room and sat quietly watching the fire and thinking about the day's events. I felt uncomfortable because I had called Chaplain Torres a bitch. Maybe I hadn't changed. I wondered if Pastor Jack swore when he got mad — what about Billy Graham or the pope? Will I ever gain perfect control over my flesh?

I got down on my knees and asked God to forgive my outburst.

The rain stopped, and the continual dripping of water into the pots slowed with every passing minute. I was no longer feeling uncomfortable. God had done a work in me. I thought back to what I was like before that fateful day in May 1976 at The Church On The Way. The rage was gone — temper tantrums, yes; rage, no. I was far from perfect but vastly "new and improved." I wanted to please God more than myself, and (the big *and*) I was delivered from that ever-present demon called "lust."

Now, this is an uncomfortable subject, especially when you are at the center of it, but one of the main reasons I believe God is exactly who he claims to be is that when I got saved, I got delivered — instantly! That does not mean I got "neutered" or became impotent. It means I was able to make choices that would please God — and not hurt, harm, mislead, or take advantage of others in my path.

One of my first prayers to him was "Lord, teach me how to love."

That was because I knew deep in my heart that I had never really loved anyone except my son, Shane.

Prayer answered — I fell in love with the Lord.

I then asked the Lord to bring his choice of a helpmate (wife) into my life. Ten days later, I met Linda in the bookstore. As a matter of fact, as I was sitting across the table from her in the coffee shop looking at her beautiful hands, I felt the Lord say, *There she is!*

That's when I fell in love with Linda.

That was more than thirty-three years ago, and she has far exceeded my hopes and dreams and expectations. And because of God, our love has grown deeper with every passing season and, yes, more passionate (that can only happen with God). True, we've had our screaming matches, thrown our clogs at each other, and broken a couple of windows, and I've spent my share of nights on the couch. But we have never shared ourselves with anyone else.

I went into our bedroom at dawn and whispered in Linda's ear. "I love you."

She smiled without opening her eyes. "Go to sleep," she said.

I couldn't. I was too excited about the days ahead.

■ ■ ■

Against my wife's better judgment, I called the presiding judge of the juvenile justice system, the Honorable H. Randolph Moore Jr. He agreed to a second meeting.

"What can I do for you?" the judge asked as we sat down on his leather couch.

I smiled back at him. "I want a court order to take camp kids sailing."

The judge studied me. He wasn't smiling. "You got it."

"Excuse me?" I asked, leaning forward.

"I'll give you the court order."

I wanted to grab "His Honor" in a bear hug.

"Thank you," I said, maintaining my cool and continuing. "With no guards, no counselors, and no cops, and I want to select the crew."

"As long as they are not in isolation."

"Agreed."

"What else?" asked Judge Moore.

My heart started thumping under my sport jacket.

"I want a press conference at dockside with no restrictions."

"No identifiable photographs. I already explained that to you, Lee."

"Your Honor, the purpose of the press conference is to introduce the community to the heart cry of these kids. Viewers won't respond unless they see their faces."

The judge stood and went behind his desk. I looked over at the photograph of H. Randolph Moore Sr., adorned in his Episcopal minister's wardrobe. For one split second, I thought about playing the "God gave me a vision" card.

"Judge Moore, when a kid comes before your bench, what influences you most in determining his fate?"

The judge spoke carefully and with deep reflection. "I look deep into his eyes for a glimpse of his soul. OK. We'll do it. But you will have to get signed releases from their parents and from each boy you take out on your boat trip."

"Thank you."

"Is that it?"

"One more thing," I said. "If this is a success, I want your permission to take the Wings program into every juvenile camp and detention facility in Los Angeles County."

"You don't want much, do you?" The judge was smiling. "What's next?"

"I find a sailboat!"

CHAPTER 14

"THOSE KIDS WILL KILL YOU IN A MINUTE"

I started combing the local boatyards, looking for owners of large sailing vessels who were doing their own work — a sure sign of limited funds. But nobody wanted prisoners aboard their yacht.

At the end of my third day of scouting, I was gnawing on a pretzel in Redondo Beach when I noticed a man working on a large sailboat in the very back corner of the congested boatyard I had just canvassed. I walked over to the chain-link security fence.

"She's pretty," I said to the middle-aged man scraping the bottom of the forty-seven-foot ketch.

"Thanks," he said, straightening his sore back as he stepped out from under the hull. He was a large man with a shaggy goatee. Sweat poured off his puffy, bright-red face. "She's for sale, you know."

He gestured to the yacht broker's sign attached to the bow pulpit.

"Would you be interested in chartering her out for a couple of days?" I asked, talking through the fence.

"Nope. But I'll sell her to you, direct. One seventy-five. No middleman. Stinkin' brokers get 10 percent, for what? The guy hasn't done squat to sell her." He pitched the metal scraper to the ground and wiped his dirty hands on his work overalls. "You got cash, I'll take one fifty. You can't find one of these anywhere for less than two hundred thousand. Come on in; I'll show her to you."

I had to go through the yard's main office to get back to the boat. I followed the skipper up the steep wooden ladder that was leaning against the hull. Everywhere I looked, I saw "deferred maintenance." But the sailboat was basically sound and just needed varnish and a good scrubbing. Below decks was dark but well laid out, with accommodations for ten, including two heads (bathrooms), a full galley with dirty dishes in the sink, and a well-equipped navigation station. A wrinkled sleeping bag was spread out on the owner's bunk, and clothes were scattered around on the floor.

"Why are you selling her?" I asked.

"Divorce."

"Sorry," I said.

His eyes reddened, and he turned away. "You want a beer?"

He bent down and pulled a cold one out of the ship's well-stocked booze locker.

"No thanks."

He popped the top, took a gulp, and stared at a framed picture of himself and an attractive blonde woman on the forward bulkhead. He took another swig of beer. I didn't say anything. He crushed the empty can in his strong hands and tossed it at a nearly full trash can. It bounced off of other crushed beer cans and fell to the teak floor.

"What's your name?" he asked.

I told him.

He extended his hand. "Darren Cooper. When do you want to charter?"

"First of the month. I want to take some kids from a detention camp out to sea for a few days."

"How long?"

"Four days during the week. We've budgeted three thousand to include everything — bareboat charter, provisions, the works."

"I'll do it for five hundred a day, two thousand in all, and that includes me as the skipper."

"That's very fair, but we were counting on a bareboat charter."

"I won't get in the way," he said. "I'd just like to be part of it." He gestured around the cluttered galley. "I'll get rid of all the booze and lock up the knives — make her look nice."

We stood below in silence for a moment.

"Why do you want to be part of it?" I asked.

"I was a camp kid."

■ ■ ■

Most of the Wings volunteers wanted to go on our maiden voyage. None were sailors. Some reminded me how long they had supported the program, how much they had donated, both in time and dollars, and — the real clincher — that they had "taken the matter to prayer."

Well, I had prayed long and hard about this voyage too — for years — and it was clear to me who went to sea and who stayed on the dock. I was to take only one Wings volunteer, Mr. Roy Houston. Roy had picked up the tab, but, more important, the kids liked Roy Houston. He treated everybody the same. He was grumpy, whether he was talking to camp kids or talking to God.

Two of my closest friends are atheists — one a sailor and one a writer.

Jac Flanders, the Emmy Award–winning writer, is one of the most gifted and creative people I have ever known, and one of the main reasons my *Desperate Passage* series won so many national and international awards, including a fistful of Emmys.

Jahn Rokicki, the sailor, is mellow, never raises his voice, and, by God's almighty grace, is still with us. At age twenty, he and a friend bought an old wooden boat in South Hampton, England, and set sail for California. While crossing the stormy Atlantic, they were knocked down three times, which means the wind and seas slammed their boat on its beam-ends, and, like Jonah, Jahn was thrown into the raging ocean. He was able to scramble back aboard on his own (so he thinks).

Jahn taught sailing to help pay his way through college. In January of 1977, I took his basic sailing course. Jahn would share his sailing knowledge, and I would share my newfound faith. He was a great instructor and a courteous listener who knew the Bible but not the Lord and wanted to keep it that way.

I chose Jahn as the other member of my support crew.

■ ■ ■

The Probation Department's major concern was that violent juvenile offenders were being released into my custody without law enforcement as backup. William Fredericks, a seasoned probation officer at Camp Kilpatrick, took me aside to express his concern.

"Lee, some of those kids are dangerous," he explained. "They are real smooth talkers. They are easy to get along with, but those kids will kill you in a minute!"

One Wings volunteer offered me his semiautomatic handgun, but those camp kids have stared down more gun barrels than I have, and I knew that if I drew, I'd better be prepared to shoot.

I passed on the pistol, but I did have a game plan. If a kid got out of hand, I would push him overboard—literally—followed by tossing out a life ring and pulling him back on board only after he had cooled off. I knew that when camp kids click into their attack mode, it takes something drastic to snap them out of it. My plan was cold—intentionally so!

The directors of both Camp Miller and Camp Kilpatrick called individual assemblies so I could explain the project to the kids. I told the boys there was only room for eight and that the crew would be representative of the camp's population and not a popularity contest.

I selected kids who were active members of my Wings Foundation in-camp program — two blacks, two whites, one Asian, two Hispanics, and one mutt, all between the ages of fourteen and seventeen. Their recorded crimes ranged from strong-armed robbery to grand theft auto.

My immediate goal was to gain the trust and confidence of the Los Angeles County Probation Department, the presiding judge, and law enforcement officials, so I selected crew members who were "manageable" — not convicted murderers or violent man-children or opposing gang members committed to killing one another on the street.

That would all come later.

For the most part, the parents of my camp crew were thrilled with the project and signed release forms. Others didn't respond, lost the paperwork, or didn't care. We tracked them down — often drunk or high on drugs — introduced them to a new word called *parenting*, and got them to sign their shaky signatures.

I taught basic sailing to our selected crew three nights a week, while Roy Houston ran around town buying sleeping bags, deck shoes, watch caps, sailing gloves, and toiletries. We bought each kid his own seabag and put his name on it.

Our last evening at camp, I explained to my crew that since the press was involved, they would be representing not only the kids in Camp Miller and Camp Kilpatrick but every kid in lockup across America.

"Be yourself and do what you know is right." I looked at each kid as I spoke. "Any questions?" No response.

"See you in the morning."

■ ■ ■

Roy Houston and I arrived at Camp Kilpatrick at 7:00 a.m. All eight kids were waiting in the front office dressed in Levis, gray sweatshirts, brown camp coats, and new boat shoes provided by Wings. They were silent and self-conscious. Each boy signed his name in the logbook, and together we walked through two sets of metal doors to a secure intake area where a white county van with barred windows waited, engine running. The kids and Roy climbed into the back rows of seats, and I sat up front.

The driver signaled a nearby guard. I heard a loud metallic thud, and the heavy electronic gates of Camp Kilpatrick swung open slowly with a deep humming sound.

We were on our way.

My crew stared silently through the steel-barred windows at the passing countryside. As we turned south on Kanan Road, the Pacific Ocean appeared in the distance. The water was sparkling blue, supporting Catalina Island on the horizon.

"That's where we're headed, guys." I pointed at Catalina.

"Will we see any whales?" asked Danny, a white boy with blond hair and acne.

"Hope so."

I turned back to look at my crew.

They all seemed anxious, except the youngest, Devon. This kid looked like a surly Mike Tyson. Devon, at fourteen, was locked up for sexually assaulting a neighborhood housewife.

"How you doing, Devon?" I asked. He gave me a look and then gazed out the window. "Devon?"

"All right," he murmured.

As we neared Marina del Rey, I noticed a sheriff helicopter circling overhead. We turned into the Harbor Patrol's parking area to see a sizable group of anxious reporters, TV crews, media trucks with satellite dishes extended overhead, and a crowd of three or four hundred friends, family members, volunteers, and curious onlookers.

Some of the kids began to mutter and exclaim.

Dee, the "governor" from Camp Miller, leaned forward. "Lee, what if they ask why we're locked up?"

"You don't have to answer any question you don't want to."

"I ain't doing this!" Devon was upset.

I turned and looked at my now very nervous crew.

"Everything's going to be all right," I said. "Stay close."

The van stopped. I got out and slid open the side door for my crew and Roy Houston. The huge gathering grew curiously quiet. Cameras were silently rolling, and flashes were popping like a Fourth of July grand finale. I scanned the crowd and saw Linda, Shane, and Brett smiling proudly. Judge Moore stepped forward. We shook hands, and I introduced him to the crew as an attractive female reporter approached with microphone in hand.

"Mr. Stanley, how did you get permission for this experiment?" Her cameraman moved in for my response.

"I presented my plan to Judge Moore, and he approved it."

"Are you a therapist or a clinical psychologist?" she asked.

"No."

More camera crews and reporters gathered in close.

A male reporter butted in. "Have you received any special training in dealing with violent juvenile offenders?" His tone was cold and arrogant.

"No."

"For this experiment, why did you choose hard-core prisoners—the worst of the worst, if you will?" he asked, as if the kids were not present.

"I thought reporters were the worst of the worst," I said, which caused slight laughter from the surrounding group.

A muscular male on roller skates called out from the crowd, "Hey, I got a question for you!" Cameras and microphones swung toward the skater as his burly buddy rolled up next to him. "What are you doing bringing that scum down here?"

The kids grew tense.

The disgruntled skater yelled out another degrading comment and rolled on with his partner.

A television reporter signaled the presiding judge. "Judge Moore, aren't you going out on a limb allowing this program?"

"It sounded like a good program, something that could give these kids some turnaround incentive," Judge Moore said. "I find that if somebody takes the time to pay attention and to let them know that they care, then you start to see a change in what they do and the directions that they take. Lee has supplied that."

"Mr. Stanley, may I ask the young man a question?"

It was the classy female reporter, and she was gesturing toward Dee.

"Dee! My name is Dee!" he said with an anxious grin.

"Dee, you are a member of Wings Foundation?"

"Oh, yes, ma'am!" Dee replied with a smile. "My life has changed by being a member of Wings."

"How has it changed?"

"If you've been in jail, it's like a name on you. People look at you different, and Wings looks at you in a more positive way."

The reporter turned to Victor, a Hispanic crewman. "Why is this program important—or is it important?"

"I've been locked up a lot," Victor said. "Mr. Stanley is making a lot of kids come out and show their real selves, ya know, instead of acting like hoodlums and getting in trouble and stuff like that. He's like, ya know, the shot caller."

"Shot caller?" asked the reporter.

"A leader."

Dee smiled. The other kids nodded their agreement.

On that note, I ushered my delinquent crew toward the waiting yacht. The crowd of reporters and others followed us toward the dock. My sailing buddy and friend Jahn Rokicki was waiting at the boarding steps alongside what appeared to be a different sailboat from the one I had found in the boatyard three weeks earlier. Her engine was running smoothly. The hull had been washed and waxed, the peeling varnish stripped, and new varnish applied. Even the ship's running lines had been washed clean and were coiled neatly in place.

Owner Darren Cooper appeared on cue from below decks. His goatee was neatly trimmed, and he was wearing pressed jeans, a black turtleneck, a yellow windbreaker, and brand-new deck shoes. Darren saluted with a proud smile. We shook hands.

"She looks great, Darren!" I turned to the kids waiting on the dock. "Come on aboard. This is your home for the next four days!"

The kids moved about slowly, strangers in a strange land. None of the boys had ever been aboard a sailboat or out on the ocean. Victor placed his hand on the wooden helm and moved the big wheel back and forth.

"Steers just like a Chevy, huh?" he said. "Except it ain't got no foot pedals."

Shane and Brett stepped down onto the dock while the rest of the crowd remained behind the fenced walkway.

I nodded to my sons. "Cast off all lines!"

Brett and Shane freed the lines and tossed them aboard. The big diesel engine accelerated, and the ship pulled away from the dock.

"Whoa!" Billy, one of our eight crew members, grabbed my arm. "We're moving."

My young crew seemed excited and happy. I looked back once, hoping to see Linda. There she was, pressed against the walkway fence with the rest of the crowd. She smiled and waved.

"Victor, take the helm," I ordered.

"Me?" he asked with a look of terror in his eyes.

"Yes, you! Steer course 1–6–8," I called out after giving him a quick lesson on steering a forty-seven-foot sailboat.

"Aye, aye, cap-pee-tan!"

Victor couldn't stop smiling.

The sun was warm, and the mid-October wind was coming out of the northwest at about ten knots. Jahn took three crew members forward and began raising sail. A few pleasure boats tracked our departure for a mile or two. The sheriff helicopter veered off and left us alone. About an hour out, the breeze freshened to fifteen knots, and the seas became choppy with a four-foot swell.

"I don't feel so good."

Billy was standing before me, his face a new shade of yellowish green. I helped him to the leeward side of the boat.

"Hold on, Billy, and keep your eye on the horizon. That should make you feel better."

Billy barfed.

"Hey, Billy's feeding the fish!" laughed one of the kids out loud.

Billy barfed again. Devon leaned over the weather rail and "did a Billy," as the kids later called it, into the wind. It blew back on my startled helmsman.

Victor cursed, yanked off his freshly soiled camp jacket, and threw it to the deck. I steered Devon to leeward. He got about halfway and vomited again. Skipper Darren Cooper hosed off the decks, and Wings volunteer Roy Houston held Devon's forehead while he puked over the side.

"Governor" Dee started moaning. "Lee, I think I'm gonna be sick."

My juvenile crew was dropping like flies, and we still had another four bumpy hours ahead of us until we reached the protected waters of Avalon Harbor at Catalina.

We were right on course.

CHAPTER 15

"WELCOME TO CATALINA!"

The winds had dropped, forcing us to motor through calm seas the last leg of our voyage. We kept the mainsail up to help dampen the yacht's yawing motion.

It was six thirty in the evening when we arrived outside of Avalon Harbor. The weather was pleasant, and the sun had already disappeared behind the island. Jahn was forward, helping Darren secure the yacht's running lines. Roy was admiring the extraordinary setting, having never been to Catalina. My juvenile crew was down below, sleeping, just like my sons when our family sailed to the island. I was at the helm.

Catalina is still one of my favorite places in the world. When I was nineteen, I lived there aboard a twenty-three-foot Chris-Craft Cavalier speedboat in Avalon Harbor. My wardrobe consisted of a black nylon bathing suit, a T-shirt or two, and my U.S. Divers swim fins. I wore a watch only when diving—the bell tower overlooking the harbor, or the comings and goings of the SS *Catalina*, told me the time of day, in case it mattered.

I awoke at sunrise and never missed a sunset. I ate when hungry, drank when I was thirsty, and slept when I was tired. I dove overboard and swam ashore each day for my morning coffee or some stolen pancakes. I was a dreamer living a dream without debt or regret. I didn't know God, but I felt his presence, his protection, his love. I wore a Saint Christopher medal given to me by a young girl with a dark tan and long, straight black hair.

"Saint Christopher will protect you in your travels," she promised as she placed the silver chain with the dangling saint around my neck. The chain never turned green, and the Saint Christopher medal made me feel "spiritual."

I liked being alone on board our Chris-Craft, and I liked having a girlfriend on board. I liked the freedom of saying good-bye without having to promise, "I'll call tomorrow." I didn't do drugs, and I wasn't a boozer. My greatest high was free diving with my speargun at the ready, tracking that evening's elusive dinner.

I seldom swore, if ever. I didn't like noisy parties, crowded bars, or watching television. I still don't. I was in perfect health, exercised "naturally" every day, and loved using my body because I was not fat and never got tired. Life was simple, good, and full of promise.

Sometimes I wish I were still nineteen and tanned, with sunbleached hair.

■ ■ ■

"Welcome to Avalon!"

A red launch with the words *Harbor Patrol* painted boldly in white on the sides motored out to greet us. The gray-haired uniformed officer at the helm handled the twenty-five-foot vessel as if he had skippered it most of his fifty-plus years.

"Thank you!" I said. I had not notified anyone on the island of our court-ordered cargo. "Can we get a mooring for a couple of nights?"

It was midweek—and a month after the island's peak season. There were very few boats in the harbor and little activity ashore.

"What's your length?" the officer asked.

I told him and then followed the red patrol boat through the breakwater inside the harbor.

"Where are we?" Billy asked.

My juvenile crew began to appear from below decks, stretching and rubbing their tired eyes. They seemed mesmerized by the small waterfront city set before them in the surrounding hillside. A handful of private yachts and fishing boats nodded quietly in the pristine, crystal-clear water. West of the harbor's entrance was the seven-story-tall casino, a large rotund structure housing the island's museum and movie theater.

Not much had changed since my first summer here at the island.

"What does he want?" Devon griped. He was watching the patrol boat.

"He's escorting us to our mooring."

Devon scowled and turned away.

We secured the ship and launched our fourteen-foot yacht tender and shuttled the crew to shore. It was dark, and one of the kids sat up in the bow holding a flashlight. Before leaving the yacht, I used the ship's two-way radio and made a reservation for twelve at Avalon's local pizza joint, half a block up from the waterfront. It was popular with the islanders—funky with good food, wooden captain's chairs, heavy oak tables, and sawdust on the floor. I hadn't been there in years.

The restaurant was crowded, and the owner intercepted us at the door, juggling a tray full of empty glasses. He asked us to wait outside and hurried back to his small kitchen.

"Why won't they let us inside?" whined Billy.

My dinner guests were hungry and irritable.

"They're afraid we'll steal something," Victor murmured.

"They're afraid *you'll* steal something," laughed Dee.

Victor's eyes turned angry-cold.

"We can't all fit inside," I said. "They have no idea what we're about, so relax!"

Half a dozen locals exited past us without a glance.

"OK!" The owner reappeared, wiping his wet hands on his food-stained apron. "Right this way, please."

The owner quickly shoved two large tables together while

a young waitress in a sauce-stained uniform gathered chairs. I instructed my crew to be seated.

"What would you like to drink, fellas?" The waitress smiled, and I saw she was missing a front tooth.

"How 'bout a pitcher of 7 Up and a pitcher of cola — that work for you guys?" I asked.

They nodded quietly and then watched the various families eating together and enjoying one another's company. I learned later that only one of my crew had ever been out to dinner with his family — with *any* family.

"Where you fellas from?" asked our waitress.

All the boys looked over at me.

"Los Angeles area," I said. "We just sailed over."

"What are you — Sea Scouts?" she asked, holding a curious smile.

"Something like that," I said, and ordered six large pizzas.

"How come there's so many forks?" Victor asked.

"That's in case you have a salad. The outside fork is smaller, and that would be your salad fork. The larger fork is for the main course."

"Why can't you use the same fork?" asked Billy.

"Good question," I replied, smiling.

Jahn and Darren poured soda for everyone at our two tables.

"How 'bout a toast?" Jahn asked, holding his glass up. "Here's to a great crew — and thanks for letting me be part of this."

We banged glasses.

"That like a prayer or something?" asked Victor.

"It's an old custom to make each person of the group feel welcome," I explained.

The waitress brought out six pizzas with the owner's help. They placed them on six metal stands lined up down the center of both tables. It looked like a party.

"I need to say a blessing!" announced Roy Houston. "Take the hand of the fellow next to you," Roy instructed, and then he began to pray. "Heavenly Father, we thank you for this time together and pray that—"

We all heard my name spoken aloud at the same time. I looked up to see both television sets featuring the female reporter broadcasting the evening news. "Lee was able to get a first-time-ever court order allowing eight juvenile offenders from two Los Angeles County detention camps released into his custody for a sailboat ride to Catalina Island."

The broadcast continued with highlights from our individual interviews and shots of the sailboat casting off for Catalina.

"Interesting story," declared the reporter's television cohost.

"Yes, a positive story, David. Teaching troubled kids how to sail."

No one moved. Every eye in the packed restaurant was on us.

"Enjoy your pizza, guys," I said softly with a smile.

Almost immediately, a large man with a beer belly and huge, swollen hands pushed back his chair and stood up. He looked like a professional wrestler. He walked over to me.

"Hey!" he said. I looked into his steel-gray eyes as he put his calloused hand on my shoulder.

"Welcome to Catalina!" He turned to my young crew. "We live on the *Hustler*—that large workboat anchored outside. Let us know if we can do anything for you boys while you're here!"

"Thank you," I said, surprised and grateful.

"I mean it!"

He walked out with his family.

Next the owner came over with a woman from the kitchen.

"Mr. Stanley?" We shook hands. "Tonight, you and the boys are our guests—OK?"

OK!

It was well after ten when we made it back to the boat. The boys went to bed. Jahn curled up with a book, while Roy and

Darren played chess in the main salon. I went topside and gazed at the heavens. It was a gin-clear night with no moon. I could faintly hear a young couple giggling aboard their small sloop two boats over. A dog barked somewhere onshore.

I counted eight shooting stars, and then I went to bed.

■ ■ ■

The warm morning sun reflected off the colorful buildings that are built into the lush hillsides overlooking Avalon Harbor. The ocean was calm and deep blue, and the water in the harbor was crystal clear and inviting. The waterfront was just waking up, and a handful of seagulls were exploring the wooden docks.

I found Jahn alone topside, sucking on a cigarette and nursing his first cup of hot coffee. For a split second, I thought about diving overboard and swimming ashore — but that was a long time ago.

"Thanks for not smoking in front of the crew," I said.

"Sure." Jahn watched a school of opaleye perch nibble on the yellow mooring line. "The kids up?"

"I'm letting them sleep in."

A yacht tender motored toward us with three adults onboard. It was the large, expensive sort, with a sturdy console and the name of the mother ship — *Destiny* — painted in gold leaf with a drop shadow on its port quarter. Two sets of leather golf bags were positioned amidships. A handsome, young uniformed captain was at the helm.

"Where are the boys?" the tanned and trim middle-aged woman near the bow called out.

She was dressed in a dark blue sweater and neatly pressed white slacks.

"Down below sleeping," I responded in a hushed voice.

"We saw you on television last night," added the smiling rich woman, standing up as if preparing to come alongside.

"Sit down, Marianne!" said the owner, forcing a smile at me.

I knew he was the owner because he was chewing on a large dark cigar, and he signaled the uniformed captain to continue on without even looking at him.

Another yacht tender — the economical type — angled over toward us with a father and small son and a dog on board. They stared in our direction, and as they passed, the father said something to his son. The boy spun around quickly for another look.

We were becoming quite the tourist attraction.

Billy came topside in his prison clothes and handed me a piece of paper with a crude drawing on it.

"I designed it myself," he boasted. I turned the paper and tried to figure out what I was looking at. "It's a tattoo." He traced the pencil drawing with his finger. "That's my area code there, and BNH is my neighborhood. These are the initials of my dead homeboys, kinda like a chain, ya know? And then that there's a cloud and RIP across the bottom." Billy pointed at his chest. "I'm gonna put it right here — as soon as I get out." He took the paper back. "Pretty cool, huh?"

"Pretty cool," I said.

The United States Coast Guard agreed to rendezvous with us at Moonstone Bay, five miles west of Avalon, at eleven o'clock. We freed our mooring at ten and motored out of the harbor with the mainsail set.

My juvenile crew stared at the luxury yacht *Destiny* anchored outside. Two uniformed crew members on board were busy polishing things.

"How much that boat cost?" asked Billy.

"Probably around three million," I guessed.

"How big is it?"

"Ninety to one hundred feet."

"That ain't no boat; that's a yacht!" Victor concluded.

By now, everyone had their sea legs, and we spent the hour-long run teaching the crew basic sailing: raising the sails, trimming the sails, and standing watch. Once we cleared Long Point, we could see the steel-white eighty-two-foot Coast Guard cutter *Point Camden* waiting a quarter mile offshore. We secured our sails and dropped anchor close to shore.

Before the hook was set, a *Los Angeles Times* newspaper reporter and still photographer motored up in a rented outboard and asked permission to cover the day and take photographs.

"We'll stay out of your way," the clean-cut reporter said.

He was dressed like he belonged on the island. The still photographer had on the typical shooter's vest, with bulging pockets and three well-worn 35mm Nikons draped over his neck. Both men displayed press credentials.

"No last names," I clarified.

We were piped aboard the cutter *Point Camden* and given a personal tour by the uniformed teenage seamen. Both sides were on their best behavior, and the young captain made all of us feel welcome — so much so that half my delinquent crew said they wanted to join the Coast Guard someday. We did learn that one of the seamen was an ex-gangbanger from Nickerson Gardens, a tough government-funded housing project in Los Angeles.

"I'd be dead if I stayed on the street," said the young seaman.

He had the battle scars and the tattoos of a hard-core gangbanger.

"That's where I'm from," boasted Devon.

"Where I'm from" in street talk means "in what part of the 'claimed' community I reside." "Where I stay" means "where I put my head at night." Devon "stayed" with his Auntie Pearl in the projects, so that made him "from" Nickerson Gardens. No one knew where Devon's mother stayed, and his father was missing.

I had to twist feisty Auntie Pearl's needle-pocked arm to get her to sign a release for Devon to go on the sailing trip, though I doubt she could recall the moment. Some spaced-out boy junkie greeted me at the door of her first-floor cave. Auntie Pearl's hunched-over silhouette could be seen at the kitchen table doing the pipe, and I don't mean Prince Albert. Her Prince Albert was passed out on the bathroom floor, door wide open, pants half down. For a split second I thought the man was dead, until he passed wind, startling himself.

"Hey!" I snapped at Devon. "No gang signs!" He was subtly making a gang sign with his left hand while being photographed for the *LA Times*. "This isn't about where you're *from*, Devon. It's about where you're *going*—where you can go if you want to turn your life around."

Devon seethed with half-closed eyes. He did not appreciate being called out in front of his peers.

I know of no school or handbook on how to confront teen murderers and criminals. To live to tell the tale requires a sixth sense. Come on too strong, and that suppressed teen rage will explode or be shrewdly postponed until a more convenient time to exact revenge. But act too soft, and their street sense will smell the coward and treat you accordingly.

To survive, I stand my ground. I stay in their faces with a strong, unwavering attitude of concern for their well-being. Concern, when played well, can cover up fear—even save your life.

The day before our sailing expedition, Devon's counselor cornered me. "Devon's a Crip. He'll kill anyone who disses his set. Don't take him out on that boat!"

I was not afraid of Devon. He just wasn't taking my "concern" bait. This fourteen-year-old little seagoing Mike Tyson had witnessed too much, was numb to life and death, and wasn't about to change for Captain Whitebread here. And the little thug wouldn't take the time or waste the energy to con me into believing anything different.

After an hour on board the Coast Guard cutter, we returned to our ketch. Left to ourselves, the boys began looking for something to do.

"Can we fish?" asked Billy.

"Who wants to learn how to dive?" I asked with unchecked enthusiasm.

My crew stared back at me as if I had asked them to go to Kuwait.

"Why can't we *fish?*" asked Victor with a touch of sour disappointment.

"You can fish," I sighed, giving Jahn the nod to drag out the fishing gear.

I don't have the patience to fish. Linda loves fishing, and all three of our sons love fishing and would fish all day long if given the chance.

I love diving. I strapped on my first fins, mask, and snorkel with the Ping-Pong ball in the little plastic cage to keep the water out when I was eleven years old.

By age fourteen, I had read every book I could find on scuba diving, including the *U.S. Navy Diving Manual.* The first magazine I subscribed to was *Skin Diver.* My first written article was published by *Skin Diver* magazine.

As a skinny fifteen-year-old, I watched a man "up close" set a New England record by staying underwater for nineteen hours and twenty-three minutes in a five-thousand-gallon tank. It was a promotional gimmick for the International Diving Center, a struggling dive shop housed in a four-hundred-square-foot storefront next to my barbershop in hometown Norwalk. When my "hero" diver emerged from the endurance tank, I tried to shake his hand, but he pushed me aside to get his picture taken by a Norwalk *The Hour* newspaper reporter.

I promised right then and there that someday, somehow, I would break his record.

Months later, I asked ex-Navy frogman and owner of the International Diving Center Don Lasky if I could help out around the shop. He said yes.

He never offered to pay me, and I never asked for money

because somewhere deep inside I believed that I had no right to be paid for doing something I really wanted to do — and I figured if I asked for money, he might fire me.

"We're going to Lake Candlewood Sunday to certify the class. Wanna go?"

Don had never asked me to go anywhere unless it was to make a dry-land delivery or to pick up lunch.

"Sure," I said, trying not to sound too excited.

Sunday morning, we drove the ninety miles north to Lake Candlewood and launched Don Lasky's Mercury outboard–powered twenty-four-foot pontoon boat. Eight wetsuit-clad adults, male and female alike, stood anxiously waiting for their first open-water dive. Don waved everyone on board, and we motored out two hundred yards and dropped anchor in the cold, murky water.

"Lee, check the depth!" ordered the frogman.

He grabbed a dive tank and guided my arms into the shoulder straps that would secure the steel fifty-pound compressed air cylinder onto my back. He draped the two-hose regulator over my head and turned on my air supply.

"Go down the anchor line and mark off each atmosphere." (An "atmosphere" is thirty-three feet in depth.)

I had never used dive tanks or scuba gear or any other kind of breathing apparatus, except a snorkel. I always free dived (held my breath). I never confessed this to the frogman for fear I would be fired for lack of experience.

Fear, even at fifteen, is very debilitating.

I took a few short breaths on my regulator. The dry air hissed in and expelled behind me through the round chrome-steel regulator secured to the tank valve. Lasky strapped a depth gauge around my wrist and clapped me on the back.

Over the side I went. I sank down around eight feet and grabbed the anchor line. Visibility was less than ten feet, and the water was chilly. I breathed through my self-contained underwater breathing apparatus for about thirty seconds until I felt relaxed and confident. I swam slowly down the rope line. At thirty-three feet I marked the anchor line with a heavy piece of twine. I continued deeper and deeper, and the water got colder and colder. I couldn't stop smiling. I settled on the bottom of Lake Candlewood and on top of our homemade thirty-pound concrete block anchor. Silt mushroomed up around me. I checked my depth gauge — seventy-five feet. I let out a war cry through an explosion of bubbles.

That was my first time using scuba gear, and I personally qualified all eight divers that day for their open-water certificate. One month later, I climbed into the International Diving Center's five-thousand-gallon tank and came out twenty-two hours and fifteen minutes later, establishing a New England record for living underwater. Shortly thereafter, I became a nationally certified YMCA scuba diving instructor.

I have a tremendous respect for the water. A lot of people accuse me of being overly cautious or too careful.

Too bad.

Twice I have personally experienced the grim consequences of carelessness on the water.

The first time I was seventeen years old and had gone ice diving with dive partner Bobby in an old abandoned quarry during Christmas vacation. We packed in through a hundred yards of Connecticut woods and two feet of deep snow to our secreted Rose Bowl–size limestone quarry.

I brushed back the snow and swung a heavy axe to cut a hole through the quarry's foot-thick ice. We had dived the quarry dozens of times over the summer, so I decided we didn't need to use a burdensome tether line to lead us back to our man-made hole in the ice.

One by one we slipped through the jagged round hole into the freezing water. We dived down sixty-five feet beneath the ice to explore ominous railcars, heavy tools, and twisted iron tracks scattered along the bottom. Our fins kicked up silt and restricted visibility. A hundred yards later, we were at the opposite end of the quarry, with half our air supply depleted.

I signaled my partner, and we started to double back. I looked up and discovered our exhaled air bubbles had been trapped beneath the ice. Each air pocket looked exactly like the exit hole I had chopped through the ice. We swam toward the surface. I unsheathed my diver's knife and tried jabbing away at the foot-thick ceiling overhead. Each effort pushed me back toward the bottom. I checked pressure gauges. I had 500 psi of air in my tank; Bobby had less than 400.

Under normal conditions, that was ten minutes' worth of air, but the water was cold and we were working hard and starting to panic. At best, Bobby had five minutes of air. We gripped hands tightly and began swimming around in tight little circles, poking away at the trapped air bubbles. My mind raced — no one knew we were at the quarry, especially our parents. They wouldn't find us until next spring or in the summer — long after the ice had melted.

Bobby's eyes grew wide with panic.

I began to cry and kept chanting, "Jesus, save me! Jesus, save me! Jesus, save me!" Bobby yanked the regulator out of my mouth and sucked on it frantically. He took three or four deep breaths. I grabbed for it back and took two deep breaths, then turned it toward him. I knocked his hand away when he grabbed for it and pushed it into his mouth. I signaled "two breaths," then took it back.

I pulled my dive buddy around with me as I hammered away at the ice, crying and pleading for Jesus to save me. I hated diving. I hated the ice. I hated this quarry.

I stuffed my regulator into Bobby's mouth for two quick breaths and yanked it back. I took a breath and felt myself rise up through the ice to the surface. Bobby popped up next to me, choking and coughing. We clung to the edge of the hole and, like Artic seals, pulled ourselves onto the snow-covered ice.

We drove home in terrified silence. I dropped my buddy off at his house. I never dived with Bobby again. I didn't want to be reminded of our time under the ice.

The second incident did not have a happy ending.

I taught an ex-Marine, ex–French Foreign Legion soldier, ex-mercenary (all one person) how to scuba dive. He was a natural and one of my best students. Shortly after I certified George, I hired him to help me recover a forty-ton crane that had slipped off a barge and sunk in about fifty feet of water. Uncle Ricky also signed on for the job.

We worked in zero visibility and worked a two-inch cable bridle fore and aft of the cab so another crane could lift the works out of the water and onto a waiting barge. We succeeded in record time, and George the mercenary did 90 percent of the strenuous underwater work.

The following week, George invited me to join his family, along with our friends Brian and Lisa, for a Fourth of July celebration at Lake Candlewood. I declined but lent him my dive gear.

I was headed out the door on the Fourth when my phone rang.

"Lee, this is George. There's been a diving accident. You need to come up here right away. Lisa's dead!"

I drove the ninety miles to Lake Candlewood's local hospital. George was waiting outside the emergency room when I arrived. He ushered me inside, where a Connecticut state trooper was taking a report from Brian, Lisa's husband.

"Mr. Stanley?" A second trooper signaled from across the room. He was holding my dive regulator. "Does this piece of equipment belong to you?"

Before I could answer, I saw Lisa's petite body laid out on a stainless steel table in the next room. Her lifeless eyes were half closed, and her mouth was open and without expression. Her matted hair was clinging to her pasty-white skin. One arm hung down off the table. Her bathing suit appeared damp. She was all alone.

"Apparently the equipment malfunctioned," the officer explained.

I felt numb and thought I was going to faint. I had never seen a dead person before.

The rest of my diving gear was in the trunk of the patrol car. We went outside with my regulator, and with the trooper's permission, I tested the air pressure in my scuba tank. It read 1,500 psi, or approximately thirty minutes' worth of air. I screwed the single-hose regulator onto the tank valve, turned on the air, and pressed the purge button by the mouthpiece. The regulator worked perfectly.

I turned to George. "Tell me everything that happened out there."

"We rented a rowboat and went a couple hundred feet offshore where I dropped anchor. It was no more than fifteen, twenty feet deep.

"She made a backward entry, and she was underwater for about five minutes when I realized the air bubbles were coming from the same spot. I dove down and found her on the bottom. I guess she had spit out the regulator, and it floated overhead on free-flow. I pulled her topside and tried mouth-to-mouth resuscitation, but she never came to."

What I eventually concluded was that Lisa went overboard and sank like a rock to the bottom. In the process, she panicked and lost the mouthpiece, which floated out of reach and free-flowed air bubbles until George brought her body to the surface.

That was one of the worst days of my life.

■ ■ ■

Word travels fast on the water, and by late afternoon, half of Catalina Island knew that the sailboat "with those prisoners on board" was anchored off Moonstone Bay. Yacht tenders, rowboats, big boats, and rented boats cruised by constantly — including one guy on a boogie board. Some waved, some gawked, and some took pictures, but no one came within a hundred feet of our anchored ketch.

My young crew didn't notice. They were too busy being kids.

"I got another one!"

Billy reeled in his tenth or fiftieth opaleye perch — I'd lost count. Everybody was using green peas as bait, catching fish practically at will and filling up two buckets and the ice chest. For the first time in their young lives, the kids were getting high on something other than booze or drugs.

I don't do drugs. Marijuana makes me sick, but I can smell that stuff a mile away, and the last place I thought I would smell it was on board the chartered ketch.

"Someone's smoking a joint!" I roared.

My eyes raced over the deck, counting juvenile noses. We were sailing back toward Avalon in a fresh breeze. Seven kids were topside, one below.

"Take the helm!" I yelled at Jahn and jumped down the companionway.

The forward stateroom door was shut. I kicked it open and scared a sleeping Devon half to death.

"What?" he asked, dazed and confused.

That was all eight kids accounted for.

I raced back toward the master cabin and saw the bathroom door tightly closed.

"Who's in there?" I bellowed. No answer. "Open up, now!"

I started banging hard on the door. Then it opened and out stepped Darren, the yacht's owner.

"What's the matter, Lee?" he asked with glassy-eyed calm.

He smelled sour, and the small, oval bathroom port light was wide open. I grabbed his wrist and forced open his hand. A crumpled, half-smoked joint fell to the floor. I scooped it up and held it in Darren's face.

"This what you meant when you said you wanted to be part of our project?" I was furious and an inch away from his puffy red face. "Camp kid!" I said with disgust. "Give it to me, all of it!"

"That's all I have. Honest."

I mad-dogged him like a juvenile gangbanger.

Then he did the unexpected. Captain Darren draped his heavy arms over my shoulders and began to cry.

I held him for a long time.

Roy came below. "Everything OK?" he asked with sincere concern.

"Yes," I said.

Roy nodded and went topside.

■ ■ ■

Our fourth and final morning at the island was spent quietly scrubbing the decks and wiping down the brightwork — what sailors call the varnished wood. Roy, Devon, and Darren worked below, squaring up the galley after serving the crew a breakfast of hotcakes, bacon, and freshly squeezed orange juice.

We hauled anchor at eight thirty and motored toward Marina del Rey, some forty miles away. The wind came up at eleven thirty, so we cut the engine and set the sails. Roy cornered Captain Darren and talked about God. Jahn tended to the sails and made Cup-a-Soups and salami sandwiches for lunch. Most of the young crew hung out in small groups on the spacious deck.

Devon was off to the side by himself. "You want to take the helm?" I asked him.

"All right."

He climbed into the cockpit next to me.

"Steers just like a car," I said.

"I know. I been watching."

Devon kept his eye on the compass like an old salt as he slowly worked the ship's wooden spoke wheel. A couple more hours, and we'd be safe and sound back in the harbor. Mission accomplished — all hands accounted for, no gunshots, no stabbings, no mutinies, no one drowned or caught trying to escape. We'd had four carefully structured days at sea with jailed kids who were close to their release time, and no one messed up. I kept them busy and played it safe.

Things would be different for my upcoming film.

That would be ten days at sea with opposing gang members committed to killing one another on the street and with nothing to lose.

But for now, it was smooth sailing.

About a mile from the Marina del Rey breakwater, a handful of powerboats came out to greet us. One of the smaller boats angled in close, and the helmsman yelled out above the roar of his gas engine, "You guys are famous!"

He waved excitedly and took off like a startled antelope for the marina. Overhead an NBC news helicopter appeared and tracked with us down the main channel.

"Hey, Lee," Roy called out from the foredeck, "looks like we got a welcoming committee!"

The Harbor Patrol dock was a quarter mile up ahead. It was crowded with television crews and over one hundred spectators.

"Let's show them who we are, guys," I said. "Sound up!"

"Aye, aye, sir!" the kids cried out in unison.

"Secure the mizzen."

"Yes, sir!"

Two crewmen quickly began dropping the aft sail.

I moved to take the helm from Devon.

"I want to do it," he said, never letting go of the wheel.

"OK," I said and stayed by his side. "Drop the mainsail," I ordered as we followed the natural curve of the main channel and headed up into the wind.

"Dropping the main, sir!" Billy sounded up.

I started the ship's engine. All dockside cameras were aimed in our direction.

"Touch of reverse, Devon, and then put it into neutral when I tell you."

Devon pulled the shift lever back.

"Neutral!"

Devon tapped the lever into neutral.

The strange mix of spectators watched silently as the ketch settled nicely against the dock. They didn't know what to expect.

I patted the helmsman on the back. "Nice job, Devon."

Victor and Billy hopped ashore with dock lines.

"Bow line secure, sir!" Victor reported loudly.

"Stern line secure, sir!" Billy called out, smiling self-consciously.

"Well done, gentlemen," I said.

Judge Moore stepped forward to officially welcome us back. Reporters moved in close, with cameramen hanging over their shoulders.

One reporter singled out Devon.

"What was it like steering the boat to the dock?"

"Wasn't nothing," Devon murmured.

"What did you get out of this trip?" Devon stared at the microphone. The reporter leaned in closer. "Did you learn anything?"

Devon looked over toward me for a moment. His eyes were teary.

"It feels good to know there are people out there who care about you."

Devon climbed back aboard the boat and went below.

I gave Roy a hug and thanked him for his belief in me and for making Wings Foundation's first sailing expedition possible.

"The first of many, brother!" he promised, his warm blue eyes smiling.

The following morning, the *Los Angeles Times* ran a full-page story on our expedition titled "Sailing Straight," and for the first time they featured identifiable photographs of juvenile wards of the court.

We'd gone out, and we'd made it back. And that was only the beginning.

CHAPTER 16

THE PROPER YACHT

I was now known as "that guy with the boat," but I didn't even have a boat!

However, I knew the exact boat I wanted. I fell in love with it about the same time I fell in love with Linda. Eight years earlier, I bought the coffee-table book *The Proper Yacht* simply because of the cover photo of the fifty-eight-foot, black-hulled ketch *Minots Light* under full tanbark sails slicing mightily through the water. I would stare at the color photo while slowly sipping my morning brew and imagine her responding to the slightest touch of her smooth wooden helm.

Designed by the great John G. Alden and brilliantly built in 1951 by Germany's Abeking & Rasmussen, *Minots Light* was exactly how a proper yacht should look.

As with Linda, it was unconditional love at first sight.

"Someday I'm going to own that yacht," I told Linda. I made this bold declaration at a time when I couldn't even afford a rowboat.

Shortly after our maiden voyage to Catalina Island with juvenile inmates, I called yacht brokers in San Francisco, Los Angeles, San Diego, and Washington State. Each one had heard of the beautiful ketch *Minots Light*, and each one assured me they would track her down and get back to me.

Days passed. I got my first call from the San Diego broker. "Mr. Stanley, are you that guy who took prisoners out on the boat a while back?"

"I'm that guy," I confessed.

"Me and my wife saw you on TV," he said excitedly. "I'm afraid I got bad news. That yacht you're interested in sank a few years back off of Honduras, or was it Jamaica? Nope, I think they said Honduras."

Shortly thereafter, San Francisco called to report that *Minots Light* was alive and well in Europe, sailing on the Med.

Then the Washington broker checked in. "I found her!" he declared, sounding like Christopher Columbus must have sounded in 1492. "She is lying in New Zealand. Word has it she's gone to hell in a handbasket."

Tracking her down wasn't going to be easy.

■ ■ ■

Thanksgiving 1985. I squeezed my family of five (oldest son Christopher was ours for the holiday) into our compact Mazda like canned sardines and headed north to celebrate the holiday at Linda's brother Kurt's house in the Bay Area. As we drove across the Golden Gate Bridge, I saw dozens of sailors enjoying the blustery afternoon on San Francisco Bay.

"Want to look at some boats?" I asked the sardines.

Linda responded by inhaling slowly and exhaling with her lips pressed tightly together.

"We've got time," I added.

We drove down to the waterfront town of Sausalito and fought the slow-moving, bumper-to-bumper holiday traffic when suddenly a parking spot opened up right in front of a marina. I grabbed it.

"Providential." I smiled, trying to ease the tension that would require a sledgehammer to crack.

"I'll wait here," Linda said without looking at me.

The three sons sat silently in the backseat. I craned my neck around. "You guys want to walk the dock?"

"No thanks," they murmured.

"I'll go," Shane finally said.

I think he felt sorry for his father. As an overt peace offering, I rolled down the driver's side window so Linda's "half of the family" would not perish and headed for the marina after closing the car door a tad forcefully.

"Happy Thanksgiving!" a lovely woman called from the deck of her classic yacht.

She was peeling a bowl of crisp green apples using a rigger's knife. Shane and I came alongside. I could smell the turkey cooking in the ship's oven.

"Beautiful yacht," I said with admiration.

The sixty-foot wooden boat was probably built in the early thirties. Her chrome and brightwork glistened. All lines were coiled smartly. Her white sails were furled under perfectly fitted covers, and her new teak decks were golden with fresh caulking.

"My husband rebuilt her from the keel up. Took seven years. Nearly murdered each other in the process," she laughed. "Would you like to come aboard?"

I asked a question in return. "Do you have any idea where I might find the sailing vessel *Minots Light*?"

The woman stopped peeling apples and looked at me as if I were daft. "Turn around. She's right behind you."

I turned slowly, as if someone had stuck a gun in my back.

There she was — my proper yacht, *Minots Light*. The faded yellow life ring topped with dried bird droppings confirmed her name. But she wasn't proper at all. My beautiful dream yacht had been painted beige from bow to stern and from waterline to cabin top. *Beige!* The mahogany cap rails were weathered and desperately thirsty for varnish. Her teak decks were soiled, and the sail covers torn and discolored. Lines lay carelessly about, uncoiled with frayed ends. Her worn halyards slapped noisily in the afternoon breeze against her tall Sitka spruce spars. Rust dripped from cracks and crevices.

Every inch of her needed attention or, worse yet, replacement. No wonder I hadn't recognized her.

"Hey, Yuri!" the woman called out. After a few moments, a sleepy-eyed man poked his head out of the companionway of the derelict ketch. He needed a shave, a comb, and some clean clothes. "This gentleman's looking for you!"

Yuri smiled as if expecting a present. I explained my interest in the once beautiful yacht, and he explained, most humbly, that he was not the owner.

"I live aboard free," he said in his thick Polish accent, "in exchange for taking care of boat."

Could have fooled me, Yuri.

I asked permission to inspect below decks. He shrugged and waved us aboard.

It was dark and dirty below and smelled like a mixture of mildew, Old Spice, and diesel fuel. Yuri's soiled sleeping bag lay open in the main salon, along with Yuri's laundry, Polish novels, scuffed shoes, and girlie magazines. He apologetically scooped up his socks from the floor and stuffed them under the sleeping bag.

"Sorry," he said and wandered toward the galley. I knew it was the galley because every surface was covered with long-dirty dishes and frying pans coated with gray-white grease. "You like coffee?" our foreign host asked as he searched the congested countertop.

"Is she for sale?"

Yuri looked at me with his pleasant smile. "Excuse me?"

"The boat. Is *Minots Light* for sale?"

A dark cloud formed over my Polish friend. He turned back to the sink, or at least where I thought the sink should be.

"I don't know," he mumbled.

"Can I contact the owner?" I asked politely.

"I ask him," he said with a touch of irritation.

I left Yuri my card with my home phone number written on the back. I suddenly realized that Yuri would be homeless if the boat were to be sold.

■ ■ ■

We returned late Friday from San Francisco to find a dozen messages on our answering service, half of them from the same person.

"Lee, this is Bob Wallace. I'm a friend of Roy Houston's. Please give me a call as soon as you can."

Bob's first message had come on Thanksgiving. His final message came in later that evening.

Linda found me sitting alone at my desk. I was numb.

"Honey, what is it?"

"Roy was killed."

Old Blue Eyes was riding his stupid motorcycle in broad daylight on the open highway and got stuck in a long line of traffic waiting to get on the freeway. Roy Houston didn't like waiting for anything. Without looking, he pulled a quick U-turn right in front of a speeding car whose driver also refused to wait in line.

Roy died right after they got him to the hospital.

I couldn't sleep that night. I went outside and yelled and screamed at my stubborn old friend for being so careless, so thoughtless, on his stupid bike.

■ ■ ■

Agent Ben Conway mailed out dozens of video copies of our dockside news conference, along with the *Los Angeles Times* article, to Hollywood's movers and shakers. I was confident they would jump at the chance to fund my proposed juvenile-prisoners-at-sea documentary.

True to his word, Judge H. Randolph Moore Jr. allowed Wings Foundation into Los Angeles County's juvenile camps against the silent protest and simmering of Chaplain Torres. My first choice was to go back to that so-called "honor farm" with the twenty-foot-high solid brick wall off of Malibu Canyon—Camp David Gonzales.

"You may have gotten the court's permission to be in my camp," warned the tough, no-nonsense director of Camp Gonzales, "but I will never allow these wards to be released into your custody to go out sailing. Do we understand each other?"

"Yes, sir," I said.

Director Richard Birnbaumer was fifty-six years old, smoked too much, and could read any kid like a book. He trusted no one unless that trust was earned. No exceptions. The boys in his care were some of the most violent juvenile offenders in our nation — and they would make perfect crew members for my planned documentary film.

My agent called. "Lee, I'm afraid we struck out."

"We're not playing baseball here, Ben. What are you talking about?"

"Look, everyone admires what you're doing, but where's the drama, where's the conflict, where's the violence?"

My "play it safe" plan backfired. I had won the trust and confidence of the judicial system and the probation people, but Hollywood wasn't interested.

Since I never heard back from Yuri or the owners of *Minots Light*, I called a Sausalito yacht brokerage and learned that the boat was for sale — for two fifty.

A little over my head.

I called a special meeting of the Wings Foundation board to update everyone on this most "fortuitous opportunity."

"How much?" asked one of my more conservative members.

"Two hundred fifty thousand dollars," I said — and quickly added, "asking." No response. "Do I hear a 'Hallelujah' and 'Amen, brother'?" I added to try to lighten up the gathering.

"How much did that charter cost?" asked Dennis, an associate pastor at a large church in Los Angeles.

"Not $250,000, that's for sure," Mr. Conservative affirmed.

"If we have our own flagship, the kids can work on it and take pride in it, and we won't have to worry about contraband on board," I concluded.

"That's a lot of money we don't need to spend," Mr. Conservative said as he swiveled uncomfortably in his chair.

"Work out a quarterly charter agreement," suggested Pastor Dennis, "without the cost of insurance, slip fees, and ongoing maintenance."

A little rush of the old "me against them" adrenaline jolted my system.

"You know the old adage, Lee," signaled another board member. "The best two days in a boater's life are when he buys a boat and when he sells it."

Now I was feeling a *major* rush of that "me against them" stuff! I rose to my feet. "We cannot allow ourselves to miss the boat, if you'll pardon the pun, because of a corny cliché that is far from the truth or by entertaining an 'it's cheaper to charter' mentality. God does not work that way — at least not through me!"

Linda shot me one of her "easy does it" looks, but I was already out of the gate.

"The best yacht brokers on the West Coast couldn't find *Minots Light*, yet we did, miraculously. The only parking space in Sausalito on one of the busiest days of the year opened up right in front of the dock where she's berthed. Doesn't that tell you something?" I took a breath. "I've had this vision for years, and it's coming full circle — and that boat is the Wings flagship!"

The old "take no prisoners" Lee was back in the saddle, triggered by those subliminal defense buttons that before now I had managed to hide from these wonderful men and women who had given of their time, talents, and resources to partner with me.

"What do you think they would take for *Minots Light*?" asked Dick Archer, breaking the silence.

Dick was trim at age sixty, the distinguished-looking CEO of a major insurance company who was winning his battle against terminal cancer. He had known God for ten years and trusted him without question. He was also one of the most respected executives in the country and fully committed to Wings because, as he explained, "Somebody's got to help you do the work."

Dick usually sat quietly during the first three quarters of any meeting like some schoolboy with his eye on the wall clock patiently waiting for recess. But when the bell rang, people listened to Richard A. Archer.

"If the boat needs a lot of work and they're not using it, they'd probably like to have it off their books."

Dick agreed to meet me in San Francisco on his return business trip from Boston.

"How long has the boat been on the market?" Dick asked the heavyset, middle-aged broker as we walked the wooden docks of Sausalito.

"On and off for a couple of years," he said as we approached *Minots Light*. "She's steel, and a lot of buyers don't want the maintenance of a steel boat. But she's sound—just needs a little work."

"Have you sailed on her?" I asked.

"Yes. Sails great. The owners are friends of mine."

"Would they consider donating it to our foundation?" Dick asked.

The broker had a good chuckle on that one. "I get asked that all the time. Not interested."

Dick pulled a Wings brochure out of his jacket pocket and handed it to the man.

"Maybe you've heard of us. We help troubled youth and take them out on sailing expeditions."

The broker stared at the brochure. "You Christians?"

"Sure!" Dick answered with a smile.

The broker shook his head and handed the brochure back.

"They're Jewish."

"They care about kids, don't they?" Dick asked.

"They are not interested in a donation."

■ ■ ■

"I don't know a damn thing about boats, Lee," Dick Archer said over dinner back at the hotel, "but I would check out any claims that broker made about the yacht."

"Then what?"

"Offer $125,000, with $5,000 down," Dick suggested, "and a balloon of $120,000 in two years. We will restore the boat, increasing her value, and pay the balance when due or give them back the boat. All subject to survey and sea trial."

Dick was smiling.

The sellers were insulted by the offer.

Rather than fire off a counter, I spoke directly by telephone to the two gentlemen who owned the boat. I explained the purpose of Wings Foundation and my plans to produce a television documentary featuring *Minots Light*. I was confident I would be able to promote new electronics, sails, marine paint, lines, and other equipment and services to ensure them that the proper yacht would once again look proper. In addition, I agreed to send them monthly progress reports and photographs of our restoration efforts.

"If we default on the loan," I concluded, "you get your yacht back looking like it did on the cover of my coffee-table book."

The owners agreed.

A sea trial and survey were set for the following week, late September 1985.

Linda and I hit the road long before dawn and drove the four hundred plus miles to Sausalito.

It was a blustery, sunshiny day on San Francisco Bay. Seagulls were gliding effortlessly on the stiff westerly breeze high above confused seas as whitecaps raced toward shore—perfect conditions to test the mettle of *Minots Light*.

"We got a problem," the yacht broker called out as we approached our dream boat with gear bags in hand.

The access hatches in the floor of the pilothouse were wide open, and a uniformed mechanic was standing waist-deep in the engine room.

"What is it?" I asked skeptically as we came alongside.

"Engine's seized," the mechanic reported as he climbed out of the hole wiping his greasy hands on a faded red rag. "Gotta pull the head and check the cylinders."

"How long will that take?"

"Depends on what I find. I can start on her the middle of next week."

We were scheduled for haul-out at day's end, an expensive endeavor that takes place after a potential buyer signs off on the sea trial. Two elderly gentlemen wearing white smocks and holding clipboards appeared from below decks. This was the surveyor team I had hired to thoroughly inspect the yacht, a costly affair that had already commenced.

"The fishing fleet's coming in from Oregon and Washington next week for haul-out," the broker quickly informed us and took a nervous drag off of his hand-cupped cigarette. "You couldn't reschedule until maybe late November, early December."

The last thing I wanted on our sail down to Los Angeles was to get caught in the historic December storms that batter Point Conception.

"Haul it!" I said and ordered a powerboat to tow the once majestic yacht across the harbor.

Silent tears streamed down Linda's beautiful face as she watched a giant, pale blue crane with its eight huge tires and two reinforced slings slowly raise the dripping-wet 64,000-pound *Minots Light* out of the water and place her on dry land at Sausalito's Anderson's Boat Yard. This was not a sad occasion. Linda's eyes fill with tears each and every time one of our yachts is lifted out of the water — and again when it is placed back in the water.

It took boatyard workmen a good hour to clean the heavy marine growth from below *Minots Light*'s waterline, using scraping tools and a high-pressure hose.

I stood back and studied the graceful lines of the mighty ketch, wondering how anyone could allow her to get in such disrepair. I was alarmed to see that the strategically placed sacrificial zincs that protect a yacht's metal components from electrolysis had been eaten away.

"Order an ultrasound," I told the broker.

"They're expensive," he said as if concerned for my pocketbook. "She looks good to me" — and then he turned his back to the wind and fired up a smoke.

Electrolysis is virtually undetectable on a painted surface and, over time, can turn thick plates of steel in the marine environment into fragile metal potato chips. An ultrasound inspection electronically measures metal density and is performed with a small, handheld instrument with a digital display placed much like a stethoscope at random points along the hull.

Minots Light has a steel hull, and steel hulls are very susceptible to electrolysis.

The ultrasound test was scheduled for the following morning.

Linda and I spent that night at Uncle Kurt's home in Novato, a half-hour drive from Sausalito.

"How's it going?" asked Uncle Kurt with a calming smile.

"She'll be back in the water Friday, and after some engine work we'll sail south," I said and casually sipped my coffee.

"What's wrong with the engine?" asked Louise, Kurt's kind and gentle wife.

"They don't know," the practical Linda answered with obvious concern. "The mechanic has to pull the head, whatever that means."

"Oh," responded Kurt without smiling, "that could be expensive."

■ ■ ■

"Mr. Stanley, I need to show you something."

An officious-looking bony, bearded man was standing beneath the yacht holding his electronic "stethoscope" attached to a small, portable ultrasound machine. I noticed dabs of ointment he had applied to get a good ultrasound reading from the hull.

He placed the blade of a large screwdriver against the hull, then hit the handle sharply with the heel of his hand, easily puncturing *Minots Light*'s steel hull. He moved the screwdriver a few inches and repeated the action a half dozen times, chipping a fist-size hole in the boat. At every chalk-marked spot he tapped, the heavy screwdriver punched through the metal hull.

"What's going on, God?" I yelled out frantically as I power-walked along the waterfront and a half mile away from the boat-yard. I was mad, scared, and backed into a corner, all at the same time. "Answer me!"

It is very hard to hear God when you're having a tantrum.

Linda, Kurt, and Louise were standing beneath the wounded yacht when I returned. Kurt was fingering one of the many holes that pierced the side of *Minots Light* (I know — very symbolic spiritually).

"What happened?" Kurt asked.

"We're going home," I told my wife.

During the previous months I had been on a roll. Everything I believed in, prayed for, and claimed had miraculously come to pass. I felt like a spiritual billionaire mounted atop a winged Pegasus, wielding a mighty sword and conquering the enemy, both real and imagined, at every twist and turn of the journey.

Now it felt like the bottom of the ninth, one run down, with two

outs and the bases loaded in the final game of the World Series —
and yours truly had struck out.

The white-smocked survey twins and the ultrasound guru all
assured me they would present written reports of their findings by
the middle of next week. Anderson's Boat Yard would then review
those reports, make their own hands-on inspection of *Minots Light*,
and prepare a written estimate for repairs.

We got home late. Linda went straight to bed. I wandered
around outside the chicken coop, desperately trying to figure out
my next move or, more realistically, how to salvage my last one. I
tried praying to the star-filled heavens, and my voice sounded hollow and disconnected.

Then, in the darkness, those cursed words came echoing back
into my head.

You're a damn bum, and everybody knows you're a damn bum!

Why is it easier to remember the bad things people say about
you? Why is it easier to believe the labels other people give you than
to believe in who you really are?

I went back inside and opened the refrigerator. Staring at an
ice-cold bottle of Chardonnay, I had a quick flashback to when I
was twelve years old and saw my dad sneak a snort straight from the
bottle late one night when I got up to go to the bathroom. I grabbed
the Chardonnay and searched kitchen drawers for a corkscrew.

Instead I found a cassette tape dated six months earlier, April
28, 1985. I stuck the tape into a recorder and pushed Play.

"Very rarely do I do what I'm about to do. And because of the
rarity of what I'm about to do, I feel emboldened to do it."

It was the voice of Dennis Easter, co-pastor of The Church On
The Way, recorded the Sunday he interrupted the worship of three
thousand believers to deliver a profound word from the Lord. Linda
and I were somewhere in the middle of that crowd.

"Lee Stanley, the Holy Spirit is upon you, brother, right now.
There is an anointing on your life that needs to be identified, and

I just need to say it to you: the same Spirit that was upon Christ to release the captive, the Lord says he is giving to you. It's already been upon you, brother, but it is coming upon you in a greater measure than you ever anticipated. Your heart's been after the Lord and it's been for prisoners. But there's an anointing upon you, that the words you speak will always be fulfilled, that when you speak them in the hearing of people who are around you, there will be captives who are set free. There's going to be prisoners released and loosed. Now I know you have a ministry to those who are incarcerated, but I feel the Holy Spirit is settling upon you today something of a *new* anointing, a fresh time — and there's a season you're just coming out of, something that has tried your soul, but the Lord says you are going to go forth in power from this moment on, and the Lord says you are to be excited about what's ahead of you because it's only things of grandeur and just great release that is coming upon you because of an anointing the Holy Spirit has upon your life, brother, and it is really an anointing upon you as a couple. But I just see the Holy Spirit descending upon you, and I just want to identify it today if that's all right. Would you receive that, amen?"

Many consider "a word from the Lord" to be pure bunk. We've all witnessed false "prophecy" in church, on the street corner, or on "hair spray" TV, which had as a goal to manipulate, persuade, get attention, gain authority, or frighten the desperate and undiscerning. False prophecy misdirects the needy, confuses the truth, foils God's intent, and elbows the Holy Spirit out of any gathering.

I disagreed with the church writer who "spoke a word" over Chico, the killer, at the Wings prison meeting because the writer was acting emotionally, drawing attention to himself. He was insensitive to the Holy Spirit and not submitted to the authority of the gathering. In other words, he was "out of order."

It is always the leader's responsibility to affirm or discount any "word" given at a Christian gathering. God anoints submitted leaders, teachers, and preachers to discern such things for the spiritual, emotional, and physical well-being of those gathered in his name.

Pastor Jack allows "a word from the Lord" spoken from the congregation during a service when it is done "in order" and when confirmed in Jack's spirit. He will not affirm or allow any counterfeits and will identify them as such immediately. That takes guts.

The Church On The Way's co-pastor, Dennis Easter, is likeminded and solid as a rock. When Dennis announced to the assembly that he was about to do something he seldom did, I immediately sensed the Lord saying to me, "Here it comes, Lee. Get ready!" I knew the word would be directed at me. I knew the word would be for me, and so did Linda.

I quietly put the unopened bottle of Chardonnay back in the chicken coop's refrigerator and went to bed.

■ ■ ■

Linda and I drove the four hundred miles to San Francisco for our Saturday morning appointment at Anderson's Boat Yard to discuss the fate of the defenseless *Minots Light*.

We arrived a few minutes early and walked in on four men, who stopped talking the moment we entered the room. The yard manager nodded and pointed to a nearby, heavily stained coffeepot and cups surrounded by scattered sugar cubes and an open carton of cream.

"No thanks," I said with a smile.

The mood in the room was tense. The broker asked how the long drive had gone, and without waiting for a response, he introduced us to *Minots Light*'s middle-aged owners. Neither man stood when we shook hands.

"What did I miss?" I asked, closing the door behind me. One of the owners tossed his copy of the bound report on the small, low table that separated us and looked over to his now nervous broker.

"Well, it's no surprise—she needs work," the broker confessed.

I reached for the report and began flipping through the pages. I was stopped cold by the yard's estimate for repairs: $35,000! That did not include lay days (time in the yard), all the gear and equipment that needed replacement, or rebuilding of the yacht's diesel engine.

"Be a good two months in the yard," the manager said. "You got over one hundred square feet of steel that needs to be cut out and replaced, not to mention support frames. It may take three months; we can't really say until we get in there."

"She'll be worth two or three hundred thousand to your ministry when the job's done," added the broker, flashing the God card.

He squeezed his pockets and found a pack of crumpled Winstons. He dug out a cigarette and tossed the empty pack into the trash basket. I kept my eyes locked on the owners. I knew what they had decided but asked anyway.

"Will you cover this?" I asked, referring to the report.

"No," responded the other owner as he stood and poured the last ounce of coffee into his half-filled Styrofoam cup.

Good, I thought, *he thinks we're going to negotiate.*

"We sold you the boat at less than half the asking price," he continued forcefully. "That's as far as we're willing to go."

"Thanks for your time, guys."

I took Linda by the arm and left the office.

We walked down two flights of wooden stairs and cut across the yard toward our Mazda. I avoided looking at the abandoned, pockmarked, once-beautiful *Minots Light* stranded in the steel, landlocked cradle off to my left.

"Mr. Stanley!" The yacht broker came leaping down the wooden stairs and walked quickly over to us, puffing and shining with sweat. "The boys have agreed to meet you halfway."

"All or nothing," I said, "including lay days, less the two I scheduled for haul-out and survey, plus the engine rebuild." The broker started to talk. I held up my hand. "That is the only deal I will agree to."

I helped Linda into our tiny Mazda and walked past the broker to the driver's side.

"OK, already!" whined the broker. "You got a deal."

"What made you think they would agree?" asked Linda as we drove across the Golden Gate Bridge.

"They had to fix her," I said with a smile. "If they put her back in the water with those holes in the hull, *Minots Light* would sink like a rock."

CHAPTER 17

"MORE LIKE A HELLS ANGEL THAN A MAN OF THE CLOTH"

Linda and I hit the northbound traffic every other Friday night headed for Sausalito to work weekends on *our* landlocked yacht. Pastor Jack gave us a letter of introduction to a church in nearby San Bruno, where I was invited to speak about Wings Foundation and *Minots Light*.

"At one time, she was one of the most beautiful yachts on the water," I told the quiet and well-mannered assembly, "built to take her proud owners anywhere in the world. Today she wouldn't be able to make it across the harbor."

I looked out at the two hundred plus people before me. They all seemed so — polite. I concluded by asking for volunteers and explained that *Minots Light* would be at Anderson's Boat Yard until the work was completed.

"We need at least a half dozen volunteers if we're to get back in the water by mid-December," I announced to Linda as I steered for home. "But you saw them," I complained. "They just sat there like bumps on a log."

Linda contacted every manufacturer and wholesaler in the yachting industry that we thought might want to get involved with restoring our fifty-eight-foot ketch. I wrote out a detailed work list and divided it into two categories: (1) work that the boatyard would perform and (2) work to be done by us common folk.

The first thing I did was to hurl Yuri's sleeping bag into a nearby trash bin and open up all hatches, port lights, and the companionway to air out the stink.

Next I started on the cracked toilet, while Linda hunted down a marine hardware store to buy the basics for the work below. After staring at the toilet, I grabbed a handful of tools, reluctantly got down on my knees, and lay across the top of the vinegary-stinking bowl. All the bolts, washers, and nuts were encrusted with — among other things — rust.

On first effort the wrench slipped, and I gouged open my knuckle on the sharp hose clamp that secured the waste hose at the base of the toilet. After I stopped the bleeding, I decided to remove the hose first, which would give me clear access to the hardware. *Whoosh!* As I pulled the hose free, a gallon of waste flushed over my hands and onto the floor. I cursed out loud, identifying the waste.

"Lee!"

My wife was calling from outside.

"What?!" I yelled back in total frustration.

I looked around desperately for a towel or a rag as I plodded my way to the galley, holding both hands before me like a scrubbed neurosurgeon. I grabbed a nearby bottle of 7 Up, twisted off the cap, and poured the carbonated soft drink over my hands.

"What smells?"

Linda was leaning down into the companionway.

"Guess," I growled.

She looked at me. "The bumps on the log are here."

I made my way topside and looked down to see a dozen volunteers from the church, gathered around the base of *Minots Light*. They were all ages, men and women dressed in work clothes. Some of the men were carrying toolboxes or six-packs of soda. A couple of the women were clutching bags of groceries and potato chips.

I suddenly felt embarrassed, ashamed, and grateful, all at the same time. At least I'd gotten my hands cleaned first!

"Thank you for coming," I said.

After a moment, a large, balding man tipped his hat. "Where would you like us to begin?"

For over two months, a minimum of a half dozen volunteers gave us their Saturdays and Sunday afternoons to sand, paint, chip, grind, and throw out tons of rusty, stained, and mildewed junk. They worked quietly and efficiently, as if preparing for the America's Cup, and they never interfered with the boatyard's professionals.

Linda was able to promote new lines, radar, upholstery, paint, and other costly materials, saving us countless thousands of dollars. The local West Marine store gave us wholesale prices on their products, and yard owner Ron Anderson looked the other way when we used his heavy-duty grinders, sanders, and stingers. Often we broke bread with Ron's workers, who gave us welcome tips on how to do our jobs.

Finally, on December 8, 1985, after two and a half months, *Minots Light* was lowered back in the water — and yes, Linda wept. The hull had been painted her famous gloss-black with a three-inch bloodred boot top at the waterline, while a foot below the deck an arrowlike gold stripe ran the length of the hull.

The diesel mechanic continued rebuilding the engine, and a ship's carpenter worked on the cockpit. I wanted *Minots Light* to look exactly like she did on the cover of my coffee-table book when we sailed ever so proudly into Los Angeles, so I started to strip the ugly beige paint from the exterior of the cabins, hatches, and skylights, but the weather turned foul, and I couldn't continue.

"We're casting off on December 15," I told my work crew of churchgoers and paid professionals.

"That's impossible!" declared the ship's carpenter.

"I heard you do the impossible," I said with an encouraging smile.

I put together a crew to sail her down to Marina del Rey in Los Angeles. Since I had never sailed *Minots Light*—or any boat larger than thirty-six feet—I called yacht broker Larry Dudley in Ventura to recommend a captain.

"The *Minots Light?*" Larry asked.

"Yes, sir!" I said proudly.

"*I'll* do it."

Larry Dudley had sailed all over the world and at one time captained Humphrey Bogart's fifty-five-foot yawl, *Santana*. Larry was a class act and had more intimate knowledge of the sea than almost anyone I knew. He also commanded a substantial fee.

"What would you charge?" I asked.

"Just buy my plane ticket up to San Francisco."

"Thank you, Larry. We're set to shove off on December 15 with the afternoon tide."

"It can get pretty nasty off of Point Conception this time of year. You may want to wait a few weeks."

"I can't."

Larry sighed heavily. "I'll bring along another crewman, just in case."

I had witnessed Point Conception from shore. Months earlier, Linda and I drove up to a spot a few miles south of the Point, where the wind was blowing a constant thirty-five knots, gusting to fifty. Offshore, a large sailboat heading south was fighting for her life in twenty- to thirty-foot breaking seas. We watched in horror as a huge wave picked up the modern racing sloop and slammed her down on her beam-ends, her mast lying on the water. After what seemed an eternity, she popped back upright, like a bewildered prizefighter pawing for the ropes.

We prayed that she and her crew would make it to Santa Barbara, the closest port of refuge, forty nautical miles away.

...

Sunday morning, December 15, arrived. I had spent a chilly night in the cockpit, tossing and turning, my mind racing with the anticipation of our voyage. I watched the eastern sky turn light and smiled at the miracle of yet another sunrise. The sweet aroma of freshly brewed coffee found its way topside. My bride was awake.

The ship's carpenter had completed all scheduled work except for some cosmetic work. Linda had provisioned the yacht with fresh fruits, vegetables, beef, chicken, and all the makings for wonderful Italian dinners, exotic salads, and desserts. She had also smuggled aboard one bottle of Dom Pérignon to uncork upon our successful arrival at Marina del Rey.

Our Los Angeles crew was due in at the San Francisco International Airport at 9:00 a.m. Linda borrowed a van to pick them up, while I remained on board to take on fuel and water and do last-minute chores.

"Good morning!"

It was Peter, the ship's carpenter, standing on the dock, toolbox in hand.

"What are you doing here? It's Sunday."

Peter smiled, climbed into the cockpit, laid out his tools, and went straight to work until he had done "the impossible."

Linda arrived an hour later with our crew.

Larry Dudley was first to board *Minots Light*. We shook hands heartily as he scanned the rigging with a twinkle in his eye. He was wearing an old captain's hat and U.S. Navy peacoat.

"Nice coat, Larry," I commented.

"Bogey left it to me. Wear it only on special occasions."

Larry introduced me to his assistant, Phillip, who had raced the last Transpac and won his class. Wings board member and Iron-man competitor Johnny Disterdick was next to board.

"Mr. Lee," as he always called me, "she's beautiful!"

Another man carrying a large seabag on his shoulder and a watch cap pulled down low stepped up behind Johnny.

"Got room for one more?" He grinned.

"You no good bum!" I roared.

It was my brother, Uncle Ricky. "Gotcha!"

We pounded each other on the back as we hugged and laughed. Linda and Uncle Ricky had planned the surprise from the time we took possession of *Minots Light*.

Our church volunteers — now dear friends — arrived to wish us bon voyage and to offer a word of prayer. Their thanksgiving to God for the privilege of helping us restore our yacht humbled me.

When our gear was stowed and bunks and watches assigned, Captain Larry Dudley took the helm. The one 100 horsepower Perkins diesel engine rumbled to life. Our friends cheered and waved as *Minots Light* headed toward the open ocean.

Up ahead, the Golden Gate Bridge appeared as a colossal Erector set before the setting sun. Once we cleared the point past the bridge, we would change course, allowing us to shut down the noisy engine and sail.

"Take the helm, Lee."

Larry went forward, and I took control of *Minots Light*. I held the wheel tightly and stayed the course. I felt proud and successful and as alive as the ship I was steering. We motored under the bridge just as the sun touched the horizon. Linda was smiling. I pulled her close and steered proudly with one hand.

"Thanks for believing in me," I whispered.

"Did I have a choice?"

We both laughed. Life had never felt more promising.

Then our diesel engine sputtered to a stop.

I put the transmission into neutral and pushed the starter button. The engine turned over effortlessly but would not start.

"Raise the sails," Captain Larry ordered and dove down into the engine room.

The crew responded quickly.

"Falling off to starboard," I said as I steered away from the wind. With sails trimmed, *Minots Light* came alive like an awakened giant. Once clear of the point I called out, "Get ready to tack."

"Ready!" the crew yelled back.

"Tacking!"

I turned the large teak wheel hard to port. Sails luffed and snapped loudly, lines whipped in the air as I brought the powerful yacht through the wind and onto her new course.

"Trim as we go," I ordered.

Winches worked, lines tightened, sails filled, and *Minots Light* headed south toward her new home.

The wind was off our starboard quarter now at twelve knots. The sea had turned lumpy with occasional whitecaps. Up forward, the reflections of our red port and green starboard running lights danced merrily along the surface of the black sea. The sky turned dark, and stars appeared overhead.

"Lee, try the engine again."

Captain Larry emerged from the engine room. His hands were shiny with diesel fuel, and he was dripping with sweat from being confined in the close, hot quarters. I turned the key and pressed the starter button.

Nothing.

"Keep it going until I tell you to stop."

Thirty seconds later, Larry signaled to shut it down and disappeared back into the engine room.

At 8:00 p.m. the first watch went below for dinner. I stayed topside with Uncle Ricky. He was tired from his red-eye flight, so I took the helm and he went up on the foredeck. My brother likes to be out in the elements. He bundled up in his foul-weather gear, hooked on his lifeline, and lay down.

"Call if you need me," he said and fell fast asleep.

The crew below settled quietly into their narrow bunks. I

leaned forward and could see Linda in the warm glow of the galley's kerosene lamp, preparing hot, "boat made" soup for the men who would be standing watch throughout the cold night.

I surveyed the horizon. No ship's lights were in sight. San Francisco was a distant glow far astern. The ocean was ours. I lay back on a soft cushion, now wet with dew, and gazed at a trillion twinkling stars. I savored the quiet and thanked God for bringing me into the place he had prepared for me, a promise he made a year earlier in the words of Exodus 23:20:

> *"See, I am sending an angel ahead of you to guard you along the way and to bring you to the place I have prepared."*

■ ■ ■

My faith in God comes from reading his Word, believing his Word, and claiming his Word. "All or nothing" was my deal with him from the very beginning. I also had to learn how to "trust and obey."

After I had known the Lord and Linda for about five months, God made it clear that I was to stop having sex with my girlfriend.

What?! I was an adult, had forsaken all others, and was madly in love with Linda—and she with me. What was the big deal?

God didn't flash any Scriptures before my eyes or threaten a one-way ticket to hell. He spoke to my heart. "You will not understand why," he said, "until after Linda has become your wife."

"This is insane!" said Linda when I told her. "We're in love. I'm thirty-five years old. We're getting married!" Linda paced back and forth in my apartment's small front room. I sat quietly on the couch. I lit a cigarette, gave it to Linda, and fired one up for myself.

My beloved stared out the window. After a very long moment, she snuffed out her cigarette and took a breath of fresh air. "OK. No sex."

A few days later, I was writing the script for an educational film and reached for a cigarette. I was now smoking at least a pack a day — guess why!

"You cannot be in bondage to cigarettes and fulfill your purpose in life."

God again.

I tossed the pack aside.

"No sex. No cigarettes," I said out loud. "Gee, what fun!"

Three days passed before I realized I had stopped smoking.

That was back in October 1976, the same month Linda stopped smoking as well. We married on April 9, 1977, seven months later. The moment the pastor said, "I now pronounce you husband and wife," I understood God's reasons for telling us to stop having sex until we were married. A previously unknown level of discipline was established that no one could ever overturn. We felt clean and new before God and one another. We felt blessed.

It wasn't easy, but Linda and I agree that if we had not obeyed the Lord, we wouldn't be married today.

I explain it like this: Blessings follow obedience.

■ ■ ■

Minots Light's engine would not start.

On our second day at sea, the wind died, and we "ghosted" along toward the dreaded Point Conception, rounding it on the fourth day at a snail's pace over flat seas. By day seven, we were still seventy nautical miles north of Marina del Rey, becalmed and three days shy of Christmas.

All on board agreed to steer for nearby Ventura Harbor, fifteen miles to port. With no wind we put out a radio call for a tow.

It was well past midnight when we arrived in Ventura. Fortunately, no one was awake to see my proper yacht at the end of the towline. I signaled the tug to steer us toward the first vacancy in the marina, an eighty-foot slip. We tied up for the night, and all hands were fast asleep by 3:00 a.m.

"Ahoy, *Minots Light*."

Someone sounding very official was knocking on my hull. I crawled out of my berth and squinted at the ship's clock. It was 7:00 a.m.

"Good morning," I said, shielding my eyes from the low sun.

A large, middle-aged man was standing on the dock looking at me.

"You're in my slip," he said.

I looked around, took a deep breath, and exhaled slowly. "We got in late last night, my crew is exhausted, and your slip was empty," I said, sounding more like a Hells Angel than a man of the cloth.

"Name's John Anderson." He extended his hand. "I own the hotel here and the restaurant on the other side of the harbor. I wanted to see if anyone was aboard before I went into town." We shook hands. "I'm staying on my boat for the holidays."

His boat was a classic sixty-five-foot Chris-Craft in a nearby slip, in perfect condition, and named, of all things, *Arc Angel*.

"Our engine's not working, and we ran out of wind," I said, trying to justify my initial sour attitude. "So I had to get a tow. We were headed for Marina del Rey." John just smiled peacefully back at me. "What are your rates here, anyway?" I asked, still feeling like a brat.

"No charge." He looked at his watch. "Need anything in town?"

"A good diesel mechanic."

"I'll have my guy come down."

He looked up at *Minots Light*'s rigging and followed the lines of her black hull.

"She's lovely," he said and walked up the dock.

His guy showed up at noon and had the engine purring in less than an hour.

My crew departed before sundown. Uncle Ricky, Linda, and I stayed on board. John stopped by and was pleased that our engine was fixed. Later we joined him and his wife at nearby Anderson's

Restaurant. He was greeted warmly and didn't act like the owner and spoke respectfully to his hostess. When she offered to seat us before others who were waiting, John waved her off and headed for the bar. He wouldn't even let me pay for a bottle of wine.

John Anderson became a close friend and a member of Wings Foundation's board of directors until his health failed him.

Walking back from Anderson's Restaurant along the waterfront that evening, I wondered how many potential friendships I had stomped on over the years because of my defensive attitude.

■ ■ ■

1986. The New Year. Wings Foundation had a yacht, an office, financial support, and a core group of dedicated volunteers. Wings was making a tremendous difference in the lives of LA County's violent juvenile offenders. Ninety-five percent of our kids stayed out of jail. Our scant recidivism rate was the key factor in getting financial support.

Finally a boat slip opened up in Marina del Rey, and I planned to make our arrival at "The Biggest Small Boat Harbor in the World" a promotional extravaganza for Wings Foundation. I hand-picked my prisoner crew, secured a court order for identifiable photographs, and scheduled a press conference/reception to take place on Sunday morning at the harbormaster's dock.

We left Ventura at sunset, sailed through the night, and arrived at Marina del Rey at 10:00 a.m. More than two hundred people showed up for our arrival, including county supervisors, the chief probation officer, judges, law enforcement agencies, Wings volunteers, dozens of reporters, and TV news crews.

The following morning, the *Los Angeles Times* newspaper headlines blared:

SAILORS JUST MISS COLLISION
Fog Nearly Sinks Youth Program

The teenage crew and skipper of a sailboat used to reha-bilitate juvenile delinquents got some unexpected excite-ment Sunday when their newly purchased vessel plunged into dense fog and had a close encounter with a merchant ship.

What started out as a carefully planned promotional event to bring attention to the unparalleled success of Wings Founda-tion turned into a desperate at-sea battle for survival. None of the reporters dockside got the full story. That's because I asked our teen crew and volunteers to minimize the drama and report the encoun-ter as nothing more than two ships "too close for comfort" passing in the night.

■ ■ ■

The weather report for our sail south to Marina del Rey prom-ised fair winds and moderate seas. On board were three prison kids temporarily released into my custody for the voyage and three Wings kids. Andrews (nicknamed "Baby Huey") was the first kid in Wings Foundation and living proof of our success. He was articu-late, cheerful, and one hundred pounds overweight, with blond hair and piercing blue eyes. Another shipmate was the aforementioned Dee, "the Governor" as he was called while locked up in Camp Miller. My son Shane, then fourteen, was also on board, along with Wings volunteers Skip Cook, Andy Cotte, and Jahn Rokicki.

Our first few hours at sea were uneventful. The sky turned black, stars appeared, and the wind held out of the northwest at ten knots, pushing us quietly along at six knots. *Minots Light* felt strong and responsive under full sail. I was anxious to get to Marina del Rey, although disappointed her topsides were still beige and her varnish cracked and peeling.

The evening meal was served at 7:00 p.m. By eight thirty the galley was secured. Our teen crew stayed below in the main saloon, swapping stories, while Jahn Rokicki, Shane, and I went up to the pilothouse to monitor systems and keep our eye on the radar screen. Andy Cotte was outside at the helm.

About an hour had passed when volunteer Skip Cook came up from the main saloon.

"I think you need to go down there," he said, gesturing over his shoulder.

His voice sounded concerned.

"What's the problem?" I asked.

"Dee is mocking you, and the other kids are loving it."

"You didn't join in, did you?" I asked with a smile, trying to ease Skip's concern.

"He's also mocking God."

A burst of laughter erupted from the main saloon. I stepped below to find Dee holding court with the five other kids gathered tightly around him. They sobered quickly as I entered the room.

"What's going on?" I asked, staring right at the Governor.

"Nothing," he said, avoiding eye contact.

"You don't mock God on my ship!" I was mad and didn't care if they knew it. "Is that clear?" No response. *"Is that clear?"* A few nodded and murmured. "Now break it up!"

The kids slowly pushed away from the table and wandered up into the pilothouse. Dee faked a yawn and stretched. I kept my eyes fixed on him as he went forward to his quarters.

At 2:00 a.m. I made a last check of the radar and, under the glowing red overhead light, marked our position on the chart, and then I turned the ship over to Jahn.

Just before 4:00 a.m., someone knocking on my cabin top awakened me. I pulled on some clothes and went topside. Jahn was at the helm wearing his parka with the hood up, smoking a cigarette. We were in a dense fog bank.

"Got a large ship on the radar twelve miles off our starboard bow," Jahn reported.

I have standing orders that whenever a "blip" appears on the radar, I am to be awakened. I looked around. The fog was so dense I could barely see the bow of our ship.

"When did the fog roll in?"

"Ten minutes ago. Wind's holding — makes it kind of nice."

"At least the fog's keeping the seas down."

Jahn looked at the speed indicator. "Seven knots. What a sweet boat."

"You remember the first time I showed you my book with *Minots Light* on the cover?"

"Yeah," he replied, working the helm ever so gently.

"You said if I ever ended up owning her, you'd become a believer."

"Did I say that?"

"Yes, you did.

"You sure that was me?" he asked with a knowing smile.

I affirmed most definitely that he was the one and stepped back inside the pilothouse. Jahn had marked the blip on the radar screen and noted our DR (dead reckoning) position on the chart three minutes earlier. We were five nautical miles offshore and clear of the shipping lanes.

"She's moving pretty fast," I called out, watching the blip. "What do you think she is?"

"Looks like a supertanker, but I've never seen one out here."

I tracked the blip's progress.

"Whatever it is," I said, "it's closing on us pretty fast. Jahn, turn ten degrees to port."

"Ten degrees port. How far off is she?"

"Seven miles," I called out. "Hold this course."

Shane entered the pilothouse, along with a couple of Wings kids. Jahn flicked his barely smoked cigarette overboard.

"What's happening, Dad?"

Shane sensed my apprehension.

"We've got company."

I studied the blip.

"You can't see where we're going in this fog," someone said nervously.

"We have radar." I repositioned the marker over the blip. "Jahn, give me another ten degrees to port."

"Ten degrees to port. Lee, can I have someone help with the sails?"

Volunteer Skip Cook pulled on his jacket and went outside. Andy came up from the galley with fresh coffee.

"It's like he's tracking us, Dad."

Shane was studying the radar.

"Andy, wake up the rest of the kids." My voice sounded anxious. "Jahn, twenty degrees to port."

The massive ship now appeared less than three miles away and was heading right for us. Dee came into the pilothouse wrapped in a blanket.

"I want everybody in life jackets!" I ordered.

"Why we need life jackets?" Dee asked, wide-eyed.

"Andy, free the lifeboat."

My crew scrambled silently for life jackets.

No matter which way we turned, we could not get that monster off our tail.

"Everyone stay in the pilothouse!"

All eyes nervously watched the radar screen.

I grabbed the ship's radio/telephone microphone. "Northbound vessel, northbound vessel — this is the sailing vessel *Minots Light*. Do you copy? Over!"

No response. The radar showed it closing, now less than a mile away.

I spoke more firmly into the microphone. "Northbound vessel — this is *Minots Light*. Do you copy? Over!"

The blip was now a quarter mile away.

"The guy's asleep at the helm. Jahn, forty-five degrees to port!"

"Forty-five degrees to port. Lee, I can hear him. He's headed our way."

"What are we going to do, Lee?" Dee was visibly shaking. "What are you—"

"Shut up!" When I get scared, I get angry. I could hear the distant rumbling of the approaching ship.

Dee started to lose it. "Oh, Jesus, please help us, Jesus. Please, Jesus, save us!"

"Shane! Handle him!"

Shane grabbed Dee's hands and yanked him to his knees.

"Pray!" Shane barked.

Dee cried hysterically, pleading with his Maker. The other kids were now visibly frightened, and their wide-open eyes darted back and forth from me to the radar screen.

"Skipper hailing northbound vessel, come in. Over."

A thick voice crackled over the ship's radio.

"Captain," I shouted into the radio mic, "you're headed straight for us."

"I have you on radar," he responded helplessly. "I cannot turn."

"Stay the course," I yelled into the radio. "I'll turn to port. Jahn, forty-five degrees to port—hurry!"

The rumble of the fast-moving ship grew louder and louder.

Jahn called from the cockpit, "Lee, we're heading into the wind. We're going to stall out."

"Fire up the engine!"

I could hear the hiss of the tanker's massive, unseen bow wave somewhere nearby. On the radar it was still plowing straight for us.

Dee panicked.

"Shut him up!" I ordered, my eyes locked on the radar.

Shane grabbed the six-foot Dee and held him tight. A bellowing ship's horn blasted overhead.

"Hang on!" I cried out. "He's going to hit us."

We all grabbed on to each other. I watched the large blip on the radar intercept us dead-center. Suddenly, *Minots Light* was caught in a torrential downpour. Kids were wailing and hanging on to each other. The downpour continued relentlessly. After what seemed like an eternity, the downpour stopped.

I stared at the radar screen and grabbed for the radio microphone, my hands shaking. "Captain, this is the sailing vessel *Minots Light*. Do you copy?"

"Go ahead, skipper."

His voice sounded strange.

"Sir, I — read you to port. Over."

I watched as the large blip on our radar screen slowly distanced itself from *Minots Light*.

"Skipper, I read you astern." He was short of breath. "Are you all right?"

"Yes, sir." I took a long beat. "We're fine."

We both signed off. All eyes were on me.

"Dad, what happened?"

Shane was relieved but shaken. Jahn appeared in the companionway, drenched.

"You OK?" I asked.

"Yeah," Jahn said thoughtfully. "That was kind of close."

"I kept waiting for his huge bow wave," Andy Cotte said with an anxious smile.

Dee looked ashamed. "Lee, I'm sorry." He stared at the floor, shaking his head. "I didn't mean the things I said down there," he confessed. "I didn't."

"You know all that rain?" Everyone turned to Jahn, who was still in wet clothes. "This is weird," he said, "but it was salt water."

"It can't rain salt water," one of the kids stated and looked over to me for confirmation.

"That's right," I said.

"So what happened?"

Good question.

Everyone on board (except Jahn, who had been at the helm) witnessed the huge blip on the radar screen cut right through the center of *Minots Light*. But instead of a horrific collision, a torrential downpour of salt water hammered us.

The merchant ship hadn't swerved around us — it couldn't move that fast. Where had the bow wave gone? Why hadn't it swamped us? And the ship's captain reported that immediately after the "visual impact," he saw our boat directly astern, perpendicular to his.

It certainly didn't go beneath us.

"Did you ever see it?" one of the kids asked Jahn.

"Not through the fog. Besides, it was raining too hard to see anything!"

"But it wasn't rain," Shane said, quieting the pilothouse. "It was salt water."

Jahn shook his head and looked over to me.

I smiled back at him.

"Oh, come on, Lee," Jahn warned. I held my smile. "It couldn't have gone *over* us — that's impossible!"

■ ■ ■

At dawn, the kids returned to their bunks. Jahn had put on dry clothes and was fast asleep. I poured a fresh cup of coffee, pulled on my fleece-lined jacket, and climbed topside. The fog was still thick, and the wind was holding out of the northwest at ten knots. I trimmed the sails for course 065° magnetic, which would take us right to the entrance of Marina del Rey. Andy stayed in the pilothouse, reading his Bible and every so often checking the radar screen.

By 9:00 a.m., the yacht was shipshape and all crew members were dressed in their red Wings Foundation shirts and blue baseball caps. Outside the marina entrance we fired up the engine and dropped sail. All hands came topside as I took the helm and steered *Minots Light* down the main channel.

Up ahead, the large crowd waiting at the harbormaster's dock and the TV satellite dishes began to take shape through the fog.

I checked my watch. It was almost ten o'clock.

At last we were home.

CHAPTER 18

"I JUST KILLED SOMEBODY"

"Dave Adams was right," I called out as I pushed open the front door of the chicken coop and tossed my car keys into the large wooden bowl on the kitchen counter.

"About what?" Linda asked as she greeted me.

It was late afternoon.

I walked over to the sink, turned on the hot water, and squirted liquid Joy into my left hand. I rubbed my hands together quickly until the yellow-white suds covered them and then ran both hands under the water. I always washed my hands as soon as I got home from a detention camp.

"Dave warned me not to brag about Wings Foundation's success rate." I pointed at my wife. "*You* warned me — but I didn't listen!"

I grabbed a towel from the cupboard door and stared out across the valley. An elderly man was mowing his lawn with an old push-type mower. I could hear a horse trotting around a dusty exercise ring nearby, to the crack of a trainer's whip. The horse smelled like it was sweating, or maybe it was my imagination.

"What happened?"

"Tony — Baby Huey — he's in jail!" I put the towel back on the towel ring and closed the cupboard door. "Our Wings poster child's been out robbing people and stabbing people between guest appearances on Christian television." I stared at the floor and shook my head. "Thank God none of the victims called in while he was giving his on-air testimony—or better yet, while I was bragging about our 95 percent success rate."

I walked over to the window and watched the dust from the nearby stables float by in the afternoon breeze.

"I knew there was something about Huey's demeanor over the past couple weeks I should have addressed." I turned to Linda. "But I couldn't lose Wings' mascot, right? So I let it slide."

There are many community-based organizations dedicated to turning ex-cons and probated youth into productive, law-abiding citizens. In order to get funding and survive, a foundation like Wings has to come up with statistics—impressive "beat the odds" statistics—or it will fold. People usually need proof that what you claim you are doing works *before* they send their money!

The only true measuring stick in the world of ex-delinquents is court records. That's how we validated our success rate. If the ex-delinquent has not been rearrested or sent back to jail, he or she is deemed a productive, law-abiding citizen.

But what about the dude in your program who doesn't get *caught* while smoking a joint, snorting coke, robbing a bank, shooting people, or violating probation? What do you call him?

I called him "Baby Huey."

How many more "Baby Hueys" were living a double life?

Realistically, there was no way for me to find out, so I left that problem with God.

"If a Wings kid is breaking the law—nail him, Lord!" That was my prayer.

Wings Foundation stopped posting statistics, and I stopped taking interviews and appearing on talk shows.

Of the thousand troubled young lives Wings Foundation was directly involved with, today I can honestly say that only 15 percent became productive, law-abiding citizens.

Was it worth the time, effort, and money?

You decide, because this is one area where statistics don't tell the whole story.

If your effort stops one killer from killing, one drug dealer from dealing, one prostitute from hooking, or just one gangbanger from banging, you have made a tremendous impact toward reducing crime.

Remember earlier when "Governor" Dee from Camp Miller told me that most criminal kids and adults commit a crime a day — "like taking vitamins"? Let's be kind here and say they commit only two crimes a week, or 104 crimes a year, and they are on the street for ten years.

That's 1,040 crimes committed by one person.

Get my point?

And what about the lives that were saved and changed, or the potential victims who were passed over because that criminal was no longer out there plying his trade?

God bless every person, organization, foundation, or group that is committed to turning thugs into citizens. Support them, encourage them, and applaud them.

Your life or the life of a loved one may depend on their efforts.

■ ■ ■

We finally outgrew the chicken coop and rented a five-bedroom, abandoned log home hidden way up in the Santa Monica Mountains on forty acres, a mile away from civilization and an hour's drive from the marina. The two-story home was built three years earlier on a plateau overlooking Malibu Lake and had never been occupied.

I tracked down the black, inner-city medical doctor who owned the property.

"This was a dream project I built to surprise my wife," he explained as we stood on the porch that fronted the house. "I surprised her, all right. Once I drove her out here, she wouldn't even get out of the car."

We rented the good doctor's deserted dream for $1,200 a month, which included a freshwater well and a small gas generator on the back side of the hill that provided minimal electricity. Most often, however, we used kerosene lanterns for light. Heat came from the various fireplaces throughout the house.

Since there were no phone lines, I acquired a portable telephone that was the size of a lunch pail and weighed ten pounds. Shane and I built our own motocross racetrack, and I bought Linda a four-wheel-drive Suzuki Samurai to conquer the steep, winding dirt road that led up the mountain to our romantic hideaway. We lived like pioneers, and I loved it.

One time when Shane was alone, a couple of druggies approached the property. Shane grabbed a rifle and sent them running with a warning shot. Another time while I was out at sea, Linda was awakened in the middle of the night by the sound of someone walking around on the front porch. Scared to death and clutching a pistol, she snuck downstairs to find a five-point buck nibbling on the potted plant next to the front door.

During our two years at "the log," as we called it, seven kids fresh out of prison camp and with no place to go lived under our roof. They worked hard and played hard and learned what it was like to be part of a God-fearing family.

There were no "behavioral problems," as the clinics like to call "conscious disobedience," but we did experience a tragedy.

Blond-haired, blue-eyed eighteen-year-old Jay Marks had lived at "the log" for nine months after his release from Camp Gonzales because his mother and stepfather did not want him in their lives. Jay was working full-time and liked helping Linda prepare meals. To acknowledge his success, Wings Foundation restored a donated car, painted it robin egg blue (Jay's favorite color), and presented him with the keys.

"Lee, may I cook dinner for my mom and stepfather on board *Minots Light?*"

"Yes," I said, and added jokingly, "just don't take them out sailing."

Linda helped Jay shop for all the fixings of a gourmet meal. The morning of the big day, Jay got up early, ironed a dress shirt, polished his Top-Siders, washed "the Blue Jay" (his Oldsmobile), and loaded up the station wagon with an ice chest and a picnic basket with tablecloth, napkins, and three of the finest place settings the Stanley household could provide.

"Have fun," I said, handing Jay my 35mm still camera.

"Don't burn the dinner," Shane chided as he swatted Jay on the arm.

The kid just stood there next to the open car door with tears in his eyes.

"I really love you guys," he said and climbed into the car and drove off.

An hour later, I got the devastating phone call.

"I just killed somebody."

Jay's voice was trembling over the telephone.

"Jay, tell me what happened."

I could barely understand him because he was so upset.

"It was an accident, Lee. I swear to God I wasn't doing anything wrong. It was an accident!" he sobbed.

Jay took the Pacific Coast Highway route down to the boat because he did not like driving on California's dangerous freeways. Traveling southbound with the flow of traffic, the police report stated, a man riding a bicycle on the right side of the road suddenly swerved to avoid a drain grate — and turned right in front of the driver's robin egg blue station wagon.

The victim bounced off the hood, smashed the front windshield of the vehicle, and was thrown to the pavement. The victim, who was not wearing a helmet, suffered severe head trauma.

At the hospital, the bicyclist was pronounced dead. No charges were filed against Jay or the Wings Foundation. But the damage was done, and the boy couldn't forgive himself for taking another life.

Jay never got to cook a gourmet meal for his parents, and shortly thereafter he enlisted in the U.S. Army.

I never heard from Jay again.

Lee and Linda Stanley aboard their trawler, *Stanhaven III*, in the Pacific Northwest. (Photo by Sheila Hall.)

Lee (right), with brother, Ricky, before taking off after prep school for parts unknown. (Photo courtesy of Stanley Trust.)

Lee Stanley, certified SCUBA instructor, at the quarry where he was trapped underneath the ice while diving. (Photo by Ric Stanley.)

Lee's father, renowned artist Frederic Stanley, with his portrait of Colonel H. Nelson Jackson. (Photo courtesy of Stanley Trust.)

Ice Station Zebra, starring Rock Hudson, with Lee Stanley (in center, below Rock Hudson) at the controls of the submarine. (Photo courtesy of MGM.)

Stars of Lee's first documentary, *On the Line* (L-R): J. N. Roberts, Mentor Williams, and Lee Stanley. (Photo by Ric Stanley.)

David Abrahamson, the oversized blond Viking,
and crew, restoring *Minots Light* at no charge.
(Photo by Lee Stanley.)

Father and son, Lee and Shane, bring home
the Emmy gold for *Desperate Passage*.
(Photo courtesy of Stanhaven Productions.)

Lee directs Michael Landon, host of the multi-Emmy
Award–winning documentary *Desperate Passage*.
(Photo courtesy of Stanhaven Productions.)

A billboard on the famous Sunset Strip in Hollywood
promoting Lee's first TV special, *Desperate Passage*.
(Photo courtesy of Stanhaven Productions.)

Actor Paul Newman, deeply moved by *Desperate Passage*,
spends the afternoon with Lee and Linda.
(Photo courtesy of Stanhaven Productions.)

Lee dances with
daughter Quinn
after performing her
wedding ceremony.
(Photo courtesy of
Stanley Trust.)

Our kids (L–R): Brett, Quinn, Shane, and Chris.
(Photo by Lee Stanley.)

Lee with Big Mike (standing left) and his posse on the
streets of L.A. (Photo courtesy of Stanhaven Productions.)

Shane, Dwayne Johnson, and Lee.
(Photo by Linda Stanley.)

Linda and Lee aboard their sailboat.
(Photo by Shane Stanley.)

Rick Leavenworth, adventurer and friend featured in Lee's award-winning documentary, *Mountain Tops*. (Photo courtesy of Stanhaven Productions.)

Juvenile inmates released into Lee's custody for a four-day sailing adventure; first-time-ever identifiable photographs of juvenile wards of the court. (Photo courtesy of Stanhaven Productions.)

Minots Light, the fifty-eight-foot ketch on the hard in Sausalito, California. (Photo by Lee Stanley.)

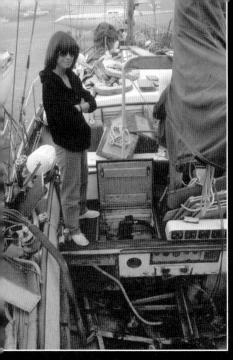

Linda aboard the completely torn-apart *Minots Light*. (Photo by Lee Stanley.)

Minots Light underway with juvenile inmates, before new sails and varnished topsides. (Photo courtesy of Stanhaven Productions.)

Lee at the helm of his dream yacht, *Minots Light*. (Photo courtesy of Stanhaven Productions.)

Lee (standing right) with his brother, "Unca Ricky." (Photo by Linda Stanley.)

Dockside press conference in Marina del Rey after
near fatal at-sea encounter aboard *Minots Light*.
(Photo courtesy of Stanhaven Productions.)

Lee filming underwater sequence of one of his television specials.
(Photo by Shane Stanley.)

During filming of *Desperate Passage*, Lee confronts his inmate crew while anchored off Santa Barbara Island. (Photo courtesy of Stanhaven Productions.)

Academy Award–winning host of *Gridiron Gang*,
Louis Gossett Jr., with the film's writer, producer, and director
Lee Stanley. (Photo courtesy of Stanhaven Productions.)

PART 4

CHAPTER 19

INMATES BELONG IN JAIL, NOT ON BOAT RIDES

"Ahoy, *Minots Light!*" a voice called out.

We were docked temporarily at the Marina del Rey transient docks on the main channel, and often yacht skippers called out a greeting as they motored by.

I came up from below decks to see a robust man at the helm of a thirty-two-foot classic Wells ketch standing off a dozen yards from our starboard quarter. He looked like an oversized Viking, with long blond hair, mustache, chiseled chin, and broad shoulders under a black cable-knit sweater, wearing a Greek fishing cap pulled down low over one eye.

"That's really *Minots Light*, huh?" he bellowed and laughed a hardy laugh that echoed across the channel — and I'm sure far inland as well.

I waved back but was at a loss for words. His classic black-hulled ketch was in bristle condition — and an exact mini-replica of the *Minots Light* pictured on the cover of my coffee-table book, only twenty-six feet shorter in length. Her hull was shiny black and accented with a gold cove stripe and red boot top. Her Sitka spruce masts were bright with varnish, and crisp tanbark sails were furled smartly against the booms and head stay. The four brass Dorade air vents were polished to a mirror finish, and her beautiful mahogany cabin sides, hatches, and cap rails were varnished to perfection.

"You're helping the camp kids."

"Yes. My name's Lee." There was an awkward silence as he stared at the ugly beige paint covering the topsides of *Minots Light*. "Your yacht's beautiful!" I said.

"How long you here for?"

"We're waiting for our slip to open up in A-Basin." He laughed warmly and started off. "What's your name?"

"David Abrahamson. I'm over in E-Basin."

He laughed again and motored away, revealing the perfectly carved name of his boat, *Nightingale*, in gold leaf on a varnished plaque affixed to the transom.

This encounter only confirmed to me that *Minots Light* should be in bristle condition and look like *Nightingale* before being featured in our planned at-sea documentary, but like everything else in yachting, that would take money—about $7,000 to $10,000.

The media coverage of our arrival in the marina generated a small increase in donations, but not enough to support our sailing program. I also began to hear murmurings from a few skeptics that convicted violent juvenile offenders were getting treated to boat rides when the place they really belonged was inside a prison.

■ ■ ■

Presiding Judge of the Juvenile Justice System H. Randolph Moore Jr. retired and was replaced by the Honorable Judge Gabriel "Gabe" Gutierrez. I gave the new judge one month to settle in before waging war for a court order that would allow me to take kids out of prison for my documentary film.

"Why do you want to meet with Judge Gutierrez?" asked the secretary over the telephone from the twelfth floor of the Los Angeles Criminal Courts Building.

"What happened to Judge Moore's secretary?"

"How can I help you, Mr. Lee?"

I felt like I was starting all over again.

"I want to discuss Wings Foundation's plans for rehabilitating juvenile wards of the court." No response. "And my name is Lee Stanley, not Mr. Lee."

"How can we reach you, sir?"

I gave her my number. "What is your name?"

"Miss Fink."

I hung up the phone and turned to Linda, who was about to leave for work.

My wife wasn't smiling.

"She was cross-examining me!" I said defensively.

Linda collected her leather briefcase from the kitchen chair. "You can't talk to people like that and expect them to want to help you."

"She was rude."

"You were looking for a fight."

"She had no idea who I was."

"She does now!"

Linda kissed me good-bye and was gone.

I hadn't been down to the marina in over a week, so I drove south. There was a slight breeze — a perfect day for sailing. I grabbed a Big Mac at the McDonald's drive-thru on Pacific Coast Highway and saved it for when I was on board *Minots Light*. I thought about pulling over and calling Miss Fink from a pay phone to apologize for being rude. I kept thinking about it all the way to the marina, but I didn't make the call, so I asked God to forgive me instead.

When I pulled into the parking lot, I could see a half dozen people climbing around on *Minots Light*. No one had permission to be on board.

I bailed out of my Mazda and stomped down the ramp.

"What's going on?" I bellowed as I hit the dock — only to see David Abrahamson, the blond Viking, standing at the helm of my boat.

He waved and laughed that hearty laugh as I came alongside. Three men on board were stripping the beige paint off the cabin sides. Two others were smooth sanding the stripped areas. David was hand rubbing mahogany oil stain into *Minots Light*'s exposed raw wood.

"Hey, guys," David called out to his workers, "this is Lee Stanley. This is his boat!"

The men, in their twenties and thirties, nodded a greeting and continued working as hard as they were before the owner showed up.

"How do I help?" I asked.

"These are my guys. They don't need any help." David laughed again.

I moved closer without climbing aboard my own boat. I didn't want to intrude.

"What's this going to cost, David?" I asked with a hollow smile.

"Lee, that's not why we're doing it, OK?" He laughed again.

By profession, David Abrahamson was a contractor who built beautifully designed and crafted custom homes in Beverly Hills — a self-made man who took tremendous pride in the things he did without the ungodly curse of being prideful. He feared God, loved the sea and the boats that sailed on it, and could trim a tanbark sail better than most people can comb their hair. He had a work ethic and character traits that made you want to spend time with him.

It took David and his talented crew a couple hundred man-hours and ten straight days to restore *Minots Light* to her original glory.

The following week, we secured a permanent slip in A-Basin, directly across from the Marina del Rey Harbor Patrol Station. That same week, I called Miss Fink and apologized for my mouth and got a meeting with the new presiding judge.

■ ■ ■

The Honorable Gabriel "Gabe" Gutierrez was a hefty, middle-aged Hispanic man with a large face, white toothy smile, and thick salt-and-pepper hair highlighted by a short white stripe in the front. Unlike his predecessor, the judge had allowed his desk to overflow with files, newspaper clippings, phone messages, reports, framed photos, and a large open leather briefcase with scuffed edges.

He stood up from the clutter as I entered his chambers and then shook my hand firmly.

"I remember seeing that press conference down at the marina on TV," he said and pointed to an armchair off to his right. "You and those boys almost got run down by a supertanker."

No schmoozing this heavyweight. He led with a quick jab followed by a right cross, looking for a first-round knockout.

I sat quietly without throwing a punch.

A light rap on the judge's open door signaled the end of round one. The ring girl, Miss Fink, stepped in, carrying a wooden tray with two coffee cups, a serving of cream, and small sugar cubes wrapped tightly in paper. We both watched in silence as the pleasant and tight-lipped Miss Fink placed our in-between-rounds refreshments in front of us and stepped out of the ring.

"Cream?" the judge asked as he raised the small pitcher in my direction.

"Thank you."

The coffee was soothing and smelled fresh. I held the warm cup with both hands and waited for the bell.

"Why did you want to see me, Lee?"

Round two.

"I want your permission to film one of my sailing expeditions with camp kids for a television documentary."

Gabe rubbed his eyes, turned his swivel chair, and stared out the window. He turned back in my direction.

"Do you have a proposal I can look at?"

I handed the judge my neatly bound presentation with the pen and ink sketch on the cover showing a teenage boy gripping the helm of a sailboat, the wind whipping his hair.

"This has never been done before," the judge said, reviewing the proposal — "filming this sort of outing with hard-core gang kids with the supervision of only one adult. These kids are used to acting out in a violent way." He continued scanning the report and got stuck on the last page. "No police, no probation officers, no counselors?"

"I don't want to treat them like prisoners. They will be crew members who will have to work together to run the ship."

"Where do you want to pull the kids from?" he asked as he scanned the pages.

"Camp Gonzales."

"Have you talked to the director — Birnbaumer?"

"Not yet."

"When do you want to do this?"

"As soon as I get funding."

My budget for the documentary was $250,000. Dave and Lynn Adams were true to their word and presented me with a check for $25,000.

The next four months passed with minimal donations to Wings Foundation, and not one dime earmarked for the production. Agent Ben Conway suggested we try again to get one of the networks to fund the project.

"They want creative control," I complained, walking back to the car after a very frustrating pitch to some studio flack in a Brooks Brothers suit. The guy was neat as a pin, cleared his throat in between sniffs, and said with furrowed brow, "This could be interesting," three times before abruptly ending our chat. "Give me a week to see if the team gets behind this puppy."

"Lee, *whoever* funds it will want creative control," Ben explained. The late afternoon sun was in our eyes as we drove the winding part of Sunset Strip. "At least it will get on the air."

"I don't want it to just get on the air. I want it done right, Ben — which means I get creative control!"

The networks either refused me outright or insisted on "ammo" — such as preplanned shipboard fights, a list of horrific crimes committed by my delinquent crew (which we would reenact), and a detailed account of their gang activity. They insisted on "beats," as they like to call story points, outlining all potential conflicts and how the filmmaker could force certain confrontations or dramatic arcs to detonate. And they would require final "casting" approval on my juvenile crew members.

"Who do you see directing this?" I was asked.

"Me," I said with conviction.

"I thought you were going to drive the boat," Mr. Network Exec said with obvious concern.

"I am."

"How can you direct the film and drive the boat at the same time?"

"Well," interrupted my agent, Ben, "we might consider another director if —"

"Ben, I direct," I said with finality. "And there will be no stars, no doctors, no social workers, or anyone else on board unless I agree to it."

"Lee, you're being unreasonable," Ben said as we rode the elevator down to the parking lot. "You can't do everything."

I was feeling claustrophobic and tried to keep my mouth shut but didn't. "I am going to captain the yacht. I will keep the kids from going AWOL and from killing each other or me, and I know exactly how I am going to direct my camera crew." The elevator doors opened, and I stepped out ahead of Ben. "This is a documentary and there will be no staging, no phony gimmicks, and no Hollywood 'beats.'"

"Without the networks' support, I'm concerned you won't get on the air."

"Ben," I said respectfully, "God gave me a vision for *Desperate Passage*, and I'm going to do it his way."

The afternoon traffic was heavy and irritating. We drove in awkward silence. I thought we would stop for lunch at our regular spot, but Ben passed by Cock 'n Bull and turned into his underground parking structure.

Ben Conway had been my agent ever since he brokered my first acting job some twenty years earlier. I knew Ben, and Ben knew me — the good, the bad, and the forgiven. He waived his agency commissions when I first started out as an actor and made me feel like I was his greatest asset. I taught him how to scuba dive and dance on the tables at The Daisy nightclub, and I dined with his family at Thanksgiving. We played touch football with our pals at Beverly Glen Park off Sunset Boulevard, and he was on the pit crew at one of my desert motorcycle races.

His beautiful green-eyed daughter Kathy was my son Shane's first babysitter, and Ben and I held each other and cried for a long time at Kathy's memorial service after she was swept out to sea in Maui.

Ben was more than an agent; he was my friend.

"Lee, I don't think I can help you anymore," Ben said as we stood in the enclosed underground parking area of his building.

"I understand," I said, feeling numb.

"If you change your mind — " Ben started to say, but he knew better.

He gave me a hug and disappeared up the stairwell.

■ ■ ■

"We need to find Christians or Christian businesses that will support your vision."

Ironman athlete and Wings board member John Disterdick was sitting across from me at Denny's Restaurant one early September afternoon. Johnny D had become a man of tremendous faith after being swept off his high horse of fast cars, faster women, millions of dollars, and two failed marriages—and he knew the power of the media.

"Christians want godly programming," he concluded. "This is a tremendous opportunity to help provide it."

Johnny D gave me some qualified leads, as did Wings board chairman Dick Archer. By the end of the month, I had pitched the financial requirements and spiritual virtues of *Desperate Passage* to over a dozen Christian groups and prominent Christian businessmen. They were receptive and promised to take my financial needs to prayer.

Like their television network counterparts, not one got behind the project.

I knew in my spirit ("heart," for those of you whose toes just curled) that *Desperate Passage* was to begin production before the holidays, now a mere seven weeks away. *Minots Light* was ready to go to sea. With only 10 percent of our quarter-million-dollar budget in the bank, I decided to commit to a production schedule and met with Judge Gabe Gutierrez.

"I would like a court order for five days of unrestricted filming in Camp Gonzales," I explained to the judge, "and seven boys released into my custody for ten days at sea."

I gave him my detailed float plan, along with backup plans for any emergency. This time I would notify the Harbor Patrol, the U.S. Coast Guard, and local law enforcement officials at Catalina Island, where we would spend part of our trip.

"I will need signed release forms from the boys and their parents," Gabe instructed, "and the names of the seven boys you want to take out of camp." He stared at the float plan. "We're taking a huge risk here, Lee." I said nothing. Gabe continued, "Is Barry behind this?"

Barry Nidorf was Los Angeles County's chief probation officer.

"He deferred to whatever you decide."

"What about Birnbaumer?"

"We haven't discussed the film yet," I said.

That was an understatement. Richard Birnbaumer was the one who had informed me in no uncertain terms that he would *never* allow kids in his camp to be released into my custody to go out sailing.

I concluded my business with Gabe and headed straight for Camp Gonzales.

"I need to speak with Mr. Birnbaumer," I told the camp's secretary.

She punched in an extension and informed Mr. Birnbaumer of my request.

"I'm sorry, Lee," she said after hanging up. "He's not available."

"I just came from a meeting with the presiding judge," I pleaded. "Judge Gutierrez asked that I speak with him right away."

I had never seen the Camp Gonzales director's office before. It was small and congested, with hospital-green cinder block walls and only one small window up near the back that was the perch for the director's personal air-conditioning unit. Across from the large metal desk was an overstuffed couch, with nonmatching and worn armchairs at each end. There were no pictures on the wall. The desk was covered with active files, and there were framed family photographs of the Birnbaumer clan, featuring children who appeared to be smiling because they were happy.

Birnbaumer was on the telephone, sitting at the desk. He did not acknowledge my presence until after he hung up. He remained seated.

"You needed to see me?" he asked without a hint of a smile.

I gave him a copy of my *Desperate Passage* proposal and watched his expression harden as I reviewed its contents. I concluded by telling him of the presiding judge's pending court order. His eyes narrowed as he looked back at me for a long, uncomfortable moment.

I had done an end run around him, and we both knew there was nothing he could do to stop me.

"Do you have any questions or concerns?" I asked.

"I've got a lot of concerns," he said tersely and closed the proposal.

"Mr. Birnbaumer, nothing in this film will misrepresent or discredit you, Camp Gonzales, or the department."

He remained tight-lipped.

"You have my word, sir," I said, and then I left.

■ ■ ■

A week later I was down at the marina working on *Minots Light* when a man stopped by. He had seen the yacht sailing on San Francisco Bay and was visibly delighted to see that she had been restored properly. He introduced himself as Carl Himmelman, a news cameraman who had come to Los Angeles to find work in the motion picture and television industry.

I told him about my planned documentary.

"If you give me a screen credit, I'll shoot camera for free."

"I need a cameraman for two solid weeks, 24/7, with no breaks — and we'll be at sea for ten of those days."

"That's OK. Could you use a second cameraman?"

"Yes."

"I'll ask a guy who covered news with me in San Francisco. Do you have a camera boat to shoot from while filming the *Minots Light*?"

"No."

"My wife and I live on our forty-eight-foot sailboat. If you pay for fuel and expenses, you can use our boat, and the film crew can stay on board."

Carl phoned me later that night to tell me his partner from San Francisco agreed to work for free with a screen credit, and Carl's wife would do all the cooking on their boat for the film crew.

A week later, Johnny D secured all the camera equipment from the Production Group's general manager, Duke Gallagher—two video cameras, sun guns (lights), radio mics, tripods, two complete sets of everything—at no cost.

I spent the following week selecting the juvenile crew to be featured in the documentary, along with two alternates. I cast opposing gang members, killers, drug addicts, and burglars—two blacks, two whites, two Hispanics, and one kid of mixed race—between the ages of sixteen and eighteen.

Most of the parents or guardians were grateful and signed release forms. One mother balked and asked how much I was going to pay her to sign the release.

"Why would I pay you?" I asked, sitting at her kitchen table cluttered with the remnants of last night's fast-food offering and empty beer cans for ashtrays.

"Well, you want him in your movie, right?"

"I think it would be a great experience for your son," I said.

Her burly live-in boyfriend leaned over to study the release form.

"Damn," he snorted, staring at the form, "you gonna be making the money?" Mama fired up a cigarette and smiled.

"We don't have a budget to pay anybody, including me," I said. "If the film does make money, it will go to Wings Foundation."

The boyfriend tossed the release form back on the table. Mama stared at it as she carefully tapped her cigarette on the pop-top opening of a crushed can of Bud Lite.

"He don't know how to swim. He ain't ever been to the ocean." She rested her head in her hand, deep in thought. She dropped the cigarette into the beer can, and it hissed just for a moment.

"We never took him nowhere. Always promised him, but—we never did." She shook her head as if trying to erase the truth. "You got a pen?"

I dug my ballpoint out of the folder and handed it to her.

She signed the release.

"Thank you," I said and took the form and put it away. She had tears in her eyes. "You OK?" I asked.

She nodded silently and reached for another smoke.

■ ■ ■

Three days before filming was to begin, one of my juvenile crew members got tossed in the box for punching out a teacher. Both alternates begged to go in his place, but I had met another prisoner named Gary Neal Brown, and I wanted him on the boat.

"Do not take that kid out of camp!"

I was in probation officer Mike's tiny office.

"Lee, to put it mildly, the boy's screwed up. He's been in and out of institutions most of his life and will fight you just as soon as look at you." He pushed a thick packet across his desk. "Take a look at his file."

"He's been coming to Wings the last couple of meetings, and I think he needs a chance," I explained.

"And he loves Jesus, right?" Mike said with a derisive smile. "I think you're making a big mistake."

Gary Brown did not trust anyone — not even God. He lied when it was cheaper to tell the truth and was known to take a swing at you before you could duck. He showed up at a Wings meeting one night and sat in the back, brooding. He was six foot one, 170 pounds, with pasty-white skin and dark hair. He looked constantly menacing.

I chose Gary for the voyage.

CHAPTER 20

DESPERATE PASSAGE

The first four days of filming at Camp Gonzales went well. We shot every square foot of that prison, including the enraged inmates in solitary confinement. My two cameramen were obviously out of their element and didn't dare move without a nod, a gesture, or specific direction from me. A couple of fights broke out, but no one on our crew got hit.

I direct my documentaries in a specific way. Before cameras roll, I have a clear vision of why I am making the film, what I hope to capture in front of the camera, how I will do it, and, most important, why. I pray specifically for God to reveal the one he has chosen to work on the project. I give specific direction to my subjects in front of the camera and to all of those behind the camera. My paramount goal is to create an atmosphere that will allow God's purposes to be realized.

That is why total creative control is so important to me.

Before filming begins, I try to win the trust and confidence of my subjects by listening carefully to them. I want to understand their hopes, their fears, their needs, their circumstances, their goblins, their egos, their enemies — their true "selves" — allowing me to discover those unique qualities that make viewers interested in their stories. I instruct my subjects never to look into the cameras — and I warn that if they do, that part of the film will be cut.

Conversely, my camera crew is never allowed to speak with the subjects. Cameramen are briefed before filming begins to watch me out of the corners of their eyes. No camera is to roll without my signal, and no camera is to "cut" without my order — unless they run out of film or fall off a cliff.

I shoot my documentaries as if they were three-act plays, with a beginning, middle, and end. During filming, I study those in front of the camera as their "character arc" develops, which will eventually become my story arc.

I produced *Desperate Passage* because I wanted viewers to decide for themselves if there was a kid left inside today's juvenile criminal. In other words, who are these hooligans — and are they worth saving?

More important, *can* they be saved?

On the morning of our fifth and final day of filming at Camp David Gonzales, I loaded up my seven juvenile prisoners and drove them to the Marina del Rey sheriff station. The media had not been notified of our expedition. There were no police or reporters. Only the Harbor Patrol and the Coast Guard were aware of our float plan.

Linda and a couple of Wings volunteers were already at the sheriff station.

As we arrived at the marina, a sheriff helicopter appeared overhead and tracked us to the parking lot. I climbed out of the van and escorted my seven juvenile prisoners down to our yacht. Carl's forty-eight-foot sloop was tied to the dock in front of *Minots Light* and weighed down to the waterline with supplies and production gear. Carl's attractive wife, Kathy, was standing in the cockpit, smiling. I signaled for her to get out of the shot, and then my criminal crew and I proceeded to climb aboard *Minots Light*.

One crewman, Russell Logan Lawrence, watched a boat sail by, heeled way over. "Is this thing going to tip over too?" he asked with obvious concern.

"Not too much," I said with a reassuring smile. "Come on aboard."

Russell Logan Lawrence was five foot ten, with olive-colored skin, and was a member of the Paramount Stoners street gang. He had served ten months of a possible four-year term, on four counts of assault with a deadly weapon.

I liked Russell right from the start.

The others climbed below and joined us in *Minots Light*'s main saloon.

Seventeen-year-old Tony Vasquez looked around without saying a word.

"You approve?" I asked the mild-mannered Mexican.

"Yeah," Tony murmured.

Tony was locked up for dealing drugs, carrying a concealed weapon, and being under the influence of the drug PCP. Most of what he knew about life he learned from gangs.

"Can I sleep upstairs?" Tony asked with a slight gesture.

"I'll assign quarters after we stow your gear."

Tony was mellow and seldom spoke. He was also a hard-core gang member who lived by the sword. A rival gang member stabbed and killed one of Tony's brothers. At the funeral, the same gang shotgunned his other brother in the face and blinded him.

"That's my bunk," Big Mike said with finality, pointing to the large settee on the port side.

Big Mike White, eighteen, was six foot five, 320 pounds, and locked up for two armed robberies and two assaults with a deadly weapon — a sawed-off shotgun. He had four previous arrests for the same offense. Big Mike was the leader of 113th Street Block Crips, a particularly vicious gang from Los Angeles.

"Big Mike, you can sleep anywhere you want," I said, trying to lighten the moment.

The others laughed — all but Raymond Gulley.

"How come he gets to sleep where he wants?" Raymond asked with a surly attitude.

Gulley was black, muscular, and a member of the Bloods, archenemy of the Crips. He was locked up for drug dealing and strong-arm robbery. This was Raymond's first taste of freedom in over two years.

"Where would you like to sleep, Mr. Gulley?"

"Back there," he said, pointing to my stateroom aft, and smiled.

I assigned each crew member his bunk and did not separate opposing gang members, reminding them they would have to become a team in order to run the ship.

One crewman, John Spurling, was an unusual seventeen-year-old delinquent. John was white, six foot tall, 190 pounds, with short blond hair, and wanted to become a preacher. To help pay the family bills, John robbed a health food store of $150 with a deadly weapon and wound up in detention for fourteen months. John's habit of smiling when he was nervous, plus the fact that he often read the Bible, made him "different" in Camp Gonzales, where conformity is law and acting tough is standard behavior.

Henry Lee Wilkes was the sixth crew member. Henry was eighteen, with thirteen prior arrests for burglary, drug abuse, and violation of probation.

The seventh crew member was seventeen-year-old Gary Brown. He had two previous arrests for burglary, drinking in public, receiving stolen goods, and violation of probation. He had served five months of a possible seven-year sentence.

The last crew member was forty-four-year-old ex-gangbanger and friend, Andy Cotte. Andy had helped out on Wings Foundation's first sail with the eight kids from Camp Miller and Camp Kilpatrick.

We spent the first night on board *Minots Light* tied up at the sheriff dock. Presiding Judge Gabe Gutierrez came down to meet my crew and stayed for dinner. Gabe had met Big Mike before, when he sentenced him to Camp David Gonzales. Gabe spoke to my crew as if they were young men, not criminals, and even helped in the galley.

"They're experts at disguise, Lee," Gabe said with concern as we walked up to the parking lot together. "They will do and say anything to get what they want." There was a cool breeze out of the northwest, and stars were appearing overhead. "It's going to be difficult to see the boy underneath the deceptive camouflage."

"I know," I said. "And I've got ten days to find out who they really are."

The following morning, *Minots Light* set sail for Catalina Island, thirty-two miles away. Each crewman took his turn as helmsman, boatswain, lookout, steward, and cook. None of them had ever been on a boat.

Most of them got seasick.

It was late November and cold for Southern California.

We arrived at the island after dark and moored at the protective Cherry Cove. The only other boat around was our camera boat. After a shipboard dinner of homemade ravioli (pre-prepared by Linda, as were most of the dinners), the boys wrote in their diaries — something I required at the end of each day — took turns using the head, and by 9:00 p.m. were zipped into their sleeping bags.

Both cameramen motored back to their sailboat after agreeing to leave their inflatable dinghy in the water "ready to go" and to monitor channel 68 on their VHF radio in case something "went down" during the night.

I went forward to adjust the wick on *Minots Light*'s kerosene anchor lantern and looked off toward the mainland. The night was clear, and I could see lights twinkling to the north, low on the horizon, twenty-six miles away.

I checked on my juvenile crew. No one moved. Someone was snoring, so I assumed they were fast asleep. I sat down at the navigation station and listened to a weather report, and then I called Linda on my ship-to-shore telephone.

"How's it going?" my wife asked. "Over."

"We had an uneventful crossing." I spoke quietly into the hand-held microphone. "So far, everyone's on their best behavior. Over."

"What's the plan for tomorrow?"

"Teach them how to skin-dive."

"Do they know how to swim?"

"They all said they did. None of them have ever been skin diving before."

A long pause. Finally Linda broke the silence. "Lee, be patient. Over."

I knew exactly what Linda meant. After four years of claiming the word from the Lord, of hope deferred, prayers uttered, money raised, dead ends, court orders, release forms, float plans, an army of support and encouragement from family and friends; after taking a self-possessed stance against television networks, common sense, and the counsel of a dear friend and agent, I finally got the green light to do *Desperate Passage* "my way."

"My way" was supposed to be God's way. But when my motley crew was behaving like a bunch of Cub Scouts, I couldn't help but wonder if I'd made a huge error in judgment.

Maybe — just maybe — the networks were right. Maybe I did need "beats" and choreographed fights and pissing contests, and a big handsome television star at the helm decked out in a turtleneck sweater and reading off of cue cards scribbled on by the networks' "approved" onboard writer.

Maybe this thing never would get on the air. Maybe.

"Honey?" Linda's voice came over the ship's radio. "Are you still there? Over."

"This was not my idea," I said. "It was God's. I'm going to let happen whatever he wants to have happen."

A huge weight had just been removed from my shoulders. We completed our call, and I went topside for a breath of island air. There were no sounds except for the small wavelets spending themselves on the pebble beach a hundred yards astern. Overhead the stars were brilliant and more numerous than I can ever remember seeing.

"It's all yours, Lord," I said in a soft voice.

The next day, I taught skin diving. Raymond refused to go in the water, and while at anchor, Big Mike fell overboard. He was more embarrassed than angry, losing his baggy pants down to his knees and some of the gangster image he had worked so hard to maintain.

So far, there had been no breakthrough. My juvenile crew were still wearing masks, hiding their real feelings from me and each other.

As the days passed, some of the crew became irritable. Gary Brown complained because I wouldn't allow him to listen to heavy metal on the ship's radio. This was primarily for personal, spiritual reasons — but I couldn't have *any* music playing, even "Amazing Grace," during filming. Ambient sounds are recorded during filming, and we needed clean backgrounds that would allow us to edit scenes without abruptly cutting into any music that was playing during filming.

Regardless of the logic, Gary Brown was upset. The newness of our adventure had worn thin, and I sensed a wave of change in the boys' attitudes.

Each night after my crew was asleep, I would call Linda with the same report: "We don't have our film yet."

On day six, we set sail for uninhabited Santa Barbara Island, forty-two miles off the coast of Los Angeles. During a hike on the island, Raymond and Gary Brown had an altercation. I was able to intercede before a fistfight broke out, and — for the first time in front of his peers — Raymond Gulley cried.

"I don't know," he explained to me later. "It just came out. I started crying for no reason, ya know. I was taught if you cry, you're a punk — but I don't know."

The following day, we sailed to Cat Harbor on the back side of

Catalina for a prearranged bike tour of the island. But my crew was less than excited. Some had begun to take their adventure and their freedom for granted. Their disguises were wearing thin, and the real boys were beginning to show through. They became petty and irritable. Gary was annoyed because he had to wear a helmet. Only Preacher John, our Bible-based crewman, seemed to truly appreciate his temporary freedom.

Day eight was Thanksgiving. Linda stocked two turkeys on board *Minots Light* for the celebration. They were served with mashed potatoes, gravy, yams, green beans, and cranberry sauce. No sooner had the first turkey been polished off when Russell Logan Lawrence blurted out his displeasure.

"I don't like being told what to do," he announced. "You're like a counselor. You keep telling us what to do."

"Instead of asking," added Gary.

Earlier that morning, I had permitted Russell, Henry, and Gary to take the ship's dinghy off to go fishing. My one request was that they did not go ashore at the vacant campgrounds. That was private property, and posted signs — NO TRESPASSING — made it very clear.

The first thing my juvenile shore party did was row over to the campgrounds, tie up the dinghy, and head for the boarded-up cabins. I blew the ship's air horn, which startled everyone, and ordered the Sea Scouts back to the yacht.

"You make us feel like we're back in jail," uttered Henry.

"You make us do stuff we don't want to do," complained Russell, munching on a third turkey leg.

"Like what?" I asked for clarity.

"Making us keep the boat clean and rolling up our sleeping bags every day — not letting us do what we want to do."

"I don't know," mumbled Gary. "It's like we don't have any choices."

Big Mike poked at what was left of the second turkey and cut into some of Linda's homemade pumpkin pie. Gary helped himself to the last piece of mincemeat pie.

"Would you like me to warm that up for you?" I asked.

Gary shook his head, apparently still reflecting on having to roll up his sleeping bag each morning. He took one bite of pie, then yawned and stretched, letting his arms drop heavily to his sides.

"I don't know," he concluded. "You still feel like you're caged up."

■ ■ ■

Day nine. The crew played a dispirited game of touch football on the beach. The joy was gone, and, once again, the boys seemed to be "doing time," waiting for their release date from camp.

I rowed the dinghy back to *Minots Light*.

Suddenly, for no apparent reason, the boys began to argue. No punches were thrown, but cruel words cut deep, and emotionally Gary was sliced up pretty bad. Nobody liked him, he was told. As a matter of fact, nobody could stand him. The boy staggered, clenched his fists, shouted, and spat out hateful words until — finally — his verbal arsenal had been exhausted. Seventeen-year-old Gary Neal Brown began to sob — at first silently and then uncontrollably. Tears came rushing down his face, and out poured seventeen years of suppressed rage, fear, loneliness, heartache, and pain.

For twenty minutes, Gary downloaded his tormented soul, astonishing his adversaries and causing them to brush back tears of their own. Russell handed Gary a towel, and he pressed it hard against his tearstained face. He lowered the towel and stared at his trembling hands.

"I want to be loved." He sighed and wiped his eyes. "I just want to be normal."

Russell stepped forward and took Gary's hand in his.

"I'm sorry," Russell said.

Henry came over and wrapped his arms around Gary and sat back down.

"I don't know about the rest of you," I said quietly, "but I need to pray."

"So do I," someone murmured.

"If you want to join me, just bow your head."

Everyone did.

Late that evening, I called my wife by ship-to-shore telephone.

"Honey, we've got our movie!"

■ ■ ■

The morning of our tenth and final day at sea, we set sail for Marina del Rey, where we were greeted dockside by my family, Presiding Judge Gabe Gutierrez, and a county van with bars on the back and side windows.

We returned to Camp Gonzales, where my juvenile crew shared their at-sea experiences with the rest of the prison population. Crew members' parents were also in attendance. It was a powerful time, with tears of release shed by those of all ages. When the evening was over, camp director Richard Birnbaumer walked over, batted back a tear, and took my hand in both of his.

"Good job, Lee. Thank you."

CHAPTER 21

"LAY OFF THE JESUS BIT"

My wise friend Dan Matthews once told me, "You never really know someone until you have summered and wintered together."

During *Desperate Passage*, I "summered and wintered" with my wife.

Linda did most of the behind-the-scenes work and handled the logistical trials and tribulations of a small film company and Wings Foundation. What no production handbook prepared us for was the day my fifteen-year-old son, Shane, announced that his biological mom, Carol, was diagnosed with terminal pancreatic cancer and was given three months to live.

Carol never remarried. She was a nonpracticing Jew who spent a short season going to temple with Shane once I became born again.

"Whatever you need, we are here for you," we told her. "You know you have our prayers," I added.

"I don't want your damn Jesus!" she retorted. "If you really want to help," Carol pleaded, "find me someone to cook, clean, and run errands until I have to go to a hospice. Just lay off the Jesus bit."

What about God's promise to Shane? I thought to myself.

Eight years earlier, when Shane was seven, we attended a prayer service at The Church On The Way.

Pastor Jack asked the congregation, "If you feel the Lord is speaking to you right now, raise your hand."

Shane raised his hand. "God just told me my mom's going to accept Jesus as her Lord and Savior."

Pastor Jack stared back at Shane for a quiet moment, then responded, "I agree with you."

"You agree with him?" I said, almost out loud. "Pastor, you don't know his mother."

Carol was a beautiful and shapely twenty-two-year-old transplant from New York City. We met at a supermarket in West Hollywood during the summer of 1966. I was working on *Ice Station Zebra*, an MGM epic starring Rock Hudson. Carol had just arrived on the West Coast after burying her adoring mother and fleeing from her controlling yet soft-spoken attorney father. All of this surfaced in the frozen-food section during our first few minutes together.

"What do you do?"

"I'm an actor," I said, my voice taking on a new, rich quality.

"Have I seen you in anything?"

I gave her my full list of credits, fudging on a few and capping the verbal résumé with *Ice Station Zebra*, starring Rock Hudson.

"Oh my God! Rock Hudson," she cried. "I have his autographed picture in my bedroom back in New York. I love Rock Hudson!"

Carol and I married in the fall of 1968, believing in our hearts that I would become the man she dreamed of and she would become the woman I needed. Bell-bottom pants, open-necked frilly shirts, and puka shells began to edge out steel-toed motorcycle boots, crash helmets, and racing leathers. Transportation priorities faded from my blue Greeves 250 Challenger to an oversized silver, gas-guzzling convertible.

I found myself competing in a world where I didn't belong and where I no longer cared about grabbing its imitation brass ring.

After five years of marriage, the last two indifferent, we were granted an easy divorce in 1974, due to "irreconcilable differences."

Now, twelve years later, at age forty-two, Carol was dying of cancer.

Linda and I called every contact we knew for a nurse or some qualified individual to care for Carol. Surprisingly, no one was available.

"Come on, God, this is getting ridiculous. Help us find someone."

It was late at night, and I was driving home alone from an edit session in Hollywood.

You and Linda are to care for Carol.

God's message came through loud and clear, and it was the last word I wanted to hear.

I snorted and shook my head. *"You* tell Linda!"

Over the years, Carol and Linda had had their disagreements and had settled on a polite, "arm's-length" relationship.

I got home, and my wife was in bed, wide-awake.

"You know why we can't find anyone for Carol?" Linda asked.

"Why?"

"You and I are supposed to care for her."

That morning I called Carol and told her we had found someone.

"How much?" she asked.

"We will bring them over this afternoon. If you approve, we can negotiate."

We drove over to Carol's house. She opened the door and cried out.

"No! Oh no, you can't."

She began to cry.

"The price is right," I said with a smile.

"What are you trying to do to me?"

Linda did the housework, laundry, and shopping, and she prepared meals for nine weeks and stayed the night whenever Carol was having an especially difficult time. I drove her to the hospital for treatments but spent the majority of my days editing *Desperate Passage*.

Toward the middle of September, Carol's father and his wife came out from New York. Linda asked if she could do anything special when her parents arrived.

"I would like to celebrate Thanksgiving" was Carol's only request.

Linda cooked a fourteen-pound turkey, along with all the trimmings. It was truly a festive celebration. Two days later, Carol was admitted to Cedars-Sinai Medical Center.

We respected Carol's demand to "lay off the Jesus bit," so we prayed fervently in our home for the Lord to reveal himself to her. I also remembered that prophetic evening at The Church On The Way when Carol's salvation was promised to our son, Shane, and affirmed by Pastor Jack.

"I need to pray for you."

Carol was alone in her room and on a morphine drip to offset the intense pain. Earlier that evening, the Lord had prompted me to drive over to the hospital and pray for her in Jesus' name.

I pulled up a chair next to the bed and took Carol's limp hand in mine. Every time I mentioned the name of Christ, Carol would smile and whisper, "Yes, oh yes." I changed the cadence of my prayer. Again, whenever I mentioned "the name that is above every name," she responded.

The next morning, Carol died.

The following Thursday, Linda and our collective kids, along with Carol's parents and her brother and his wife, boarded *Minots Light* to take Carol's ashes out to sea. The ship's flag was set at half-mast. The ocean was calm, and the sky accented with soft, puffy clouds. We motored out the required three miles, then drifted quietly in the one-knot current. We prayed and then Shane cracked open the urn and released his mother's ashes into the sea.

A month later, Shane and I were driving along Pacific Coast Highway down to the marina. He looked out toward the ocean, and his eyes filled with tears. I pulled over to the side of the road and put my arm around my son.

"You OK?" I asked.

He nodded with a big smile.

"The Lord just told me that Mom is with him."

CHAPTER 22

"YOU MAY WANT TO DUMP THE PRAYER"

Every television network and major cable station rejected our completed documentary film. No talent agency found *Desperate Passage* worthy of representation, and no sponsors would step up to pay for airtime.

"What's up, God?" I cried out. "I did what you put on my heart. I didn't compromise. Why doesn't anybody want my movie? Correction—why doesn't anybody want *your* movie?"

I was gripping a returned VHS of *Desperate Passage* in one hand and staring at the last and final network's form letter of rejection in the other. What made it worse was that I could tell just by looking at the VHS that they had watched only the first few minutes and hadn't even taken the time to do a cover-up rewind.

I was told how to make it "better." *In television, you've got to grab them in the first couple of minutes, or they'll switch to another channel. The pacing is too slow.* And my personal favorite: *You may want to dump the prayer—you don't really need it.*

"What are you doing?" Linda asked as she walked into the edit bay.

"I'm seeing where I can tighten up a few scenes," I replied, scanning different segments of *Desperate Passage*.

"Leave it alone," she said and walked out.

I quickly followed after her. "Linda, nobody wants it. Do you have any idea what that feels like? I created it."

"No, you *didn't* create it."

"I produced it and directed it; I shot camera; I appear in it; I'm the ship's captain, counselor, mediator—" I started swearing and crying, all at the same time. "I believed in it."

"I still do," Linda said without yelling back. "Just don't ruin it."

"Nobody wants it!" I bawled. *"Nobody!"*

■ ■ ■

"What are you guys, Moonies?"

Linda and I were sitting across from Steve Bell, KTLA Television's general manager. Steve was trim, good-looking, and impeccably dressed—a Harvard graduate, going on fifty, with a childlike sense of wonder.

Two tumultuous and frustrating years had passed without getting a broadcast commitment for *Desperate Passage.*

Steve pointed toward the corner of his huge, hand-carved mahogany desk.

"Your video's been sitting there for three months. I had a meeting canceled, so I watched your film. It's a masterpiece. I cried. I laughed. I love it! Tell me what you want to do with it."

"What do you *want* to do with it?" I asked.

Steve became even more animated. "Make it the biggest television event of the year. This is the kind of programming I can get behind!"

We were all smiling.

"Steve," I said, "we're not Moonies. We're Christians."

"OK, I'm Jewish. Do you think you could get someone like Michael Landon to host it?"

"I don't know Michael Landon," I said with a fast-fading smile, "and I am not changing one frame of this film."

"I don't want to change anything. That's your baby. We just

bought the reruns of his *Highway to Heaven*, and I thought it might be a nice tie-in."

Everyone in television wanted Michael Landon for something. I called his office, and after telling his secretary I was "in the neighborhood," personally delivered an eight-minute promo for *Desperate Passage*.

"Would you like to see it?" I asked Mr. Landon's kind, longtime secretary.

She pushed the cassette into the machine and hit Play. The first time her telephone rang, she turned off the phone.

"Wow!" she said, wiping her eyes when it was over. "Wow!"

A week later she called.

"Michael would like to host *Desperate Passage*."

"Wow!" was all I could say. We both laughed.

We filmed Michael Landon's segment on a hill overlooking Camp David Gonzales. It was an honor and a pleasure to work with him. After filming, Michael stayed for a couple more hours to learn about my family and our work. I commended him for the quality of programming he consistently brought to television.

"It was always an uphill battle, Lee," Michael said with a reflective smile. "But if you know something is right and good, then you have to stand your ground."

■ ■ ■

Desperate Passage aired on Los Angeles television station KTLA on Wednesday, August 31, at 8:00 p.m. All Southern California counties declared the week of August 29 "'A Cry for Help' Week for Our Youth" in support of *Desperate Passage*. Pastor Jack Hayford piped in the broadcast for The Church On The Way's Wednesday night service.

"There are swearwords in the film," I warned Pastor Jack before the broadcast. "KTLA has elected not to censor them out."

"It's time the body of Christ grew up" was all he said.

Nielson gave *Desperate Passage* number one in the prime-time ratings for the entire two-hour time slot, beating out all the networks and cable stations.

The following morning, I received a phone call from a Hollywood agent.

"Mr. Stanley, my name is Dan Atwater. I have a client who would like to meet you."

"Who's that?" I asked the agent, who sounded strangely like Uncle Ricky.

"Paul Newman."

"Really?" I said, playing along. "Have him call me tomorrow around three o'clock. We'll set something up."

The next day the phone rang at three.

"This is Dan Atwater. I have Mr. Newman for you."

"Go ahead."

After a moment, another voice came on the line.

"Lee Stanley, you are one hell of a filmmaker!"

It was Paul Newman. He was deeply moved by *Desperate Passage* and explained that he lost his only son, Scott Newman, to drugs and wanted to get together just to talk. The following afternoon, Linda and I had lunch with Mr. Newman and later walked the boardwalk together at Venice Beach. He asked for understanding on how we were able to win the hearts of our delinquent crew when highly paid professionals couldn't help his son.

"We only have one thing to offer," I said. "Hope in Christ."

That same year, *Desperate Passage* was nominated for four Emmy Awards. My mother and my brother and his wife flew out from Florida to join the West Coast Stanleys for the awards ceremony.

The first category of the evening was for "Best Documentary." I was nervous and anxious and started wishing that my mom and Uncle Ricky hadn't taken the time or spent the money to watch me go home empty-handed.

"And the winner is: Lee Stanley for *Desperate Passage.*"

I can hear those wonderful words even now. I let out a deep sigh and hugged my wife and my sons and started to stand when Uncle Ricky pulled me in for a hug.

"Way to go, bro!"

Tears were streaming down his face. My mom was crying too. A half hour later, I made another emotional trip to the stage for "Best Film Crew" with my son Shane by my side. Shane had done production sound for the six-month update segment and the filming of our host/narrator Michael Landon. David, Carl, and I received Emmys for our camera work.

God kept his promise. *Desperate Passage* inspired millions of viewers across our nation. Lives were changed, relationships were restored, and the heart cry of today's troubled youth was heard — and responded to by individuals, churches, businesses, institutions, and government agencies.

PART 5

CHAPTER 23

A BOXFUL OF EMMYS

"We've prayed and given it a lot of thought, but Jane and I are going to pass on financing your film."

"Why?" I asked, trying to hide the hint of panic in my voice.

I was talking to Bert Boeckmann, a big bear of a man and the owner/president of Galpin Motors, the number one Ford dealer in the whole wide world.

Bert laughed. "No one ever asked me why before."

Bert listed his reasons for passing on *Maiden Voyage*, our next project, in which Linda and I were planning to take seven girl prisoners out to sea.

"I've been involved with the film business before," Bert concluded. "Most of them are deceptive, and you end up with a project you'd be ashamed to have your name on."

"May I respond?"

I carefully countered Bert's concerns and promised, if given the opportunity, that I would produce a film that would make all of us proud.

"Call me in a week." Mr. Boeckmann hung up.

The reason I was feeling a tad panicky was because we had sold *Minots Light* and had just purchased a beautiful classic sailing yacht after I persuaded a sponsor to pay cash for the new boat in exchange for flying a burgee bearing his company logo from the starboard spreader during our next production.

"What's your plan if the Boeckmanns don't fund *Maiden Voyage?*" my wife asked with logical concern.

"Give back the boat?"

Linda was not amused.

As requested, I called Mr. Boeckmann the following week.

"Can you and Linda stop by the house this afternoon?" Bert asked.

"Yes. It will have to be early because we have to be in Pasadena by four o'clock for the Emmy Awards."

He certainly wouldn't ask us to stop by the house if the answer were no. Then again, Bert and Jane Boeckmann care about people and love the Lord, and maybe they just want to fellowship.

No. Bert's a no-nonsense guy. Business is business.

Linda and I arrived at Bert and Jane Boeckmann's San Fernando Valley Mediterranean mansion around two o'clock in the afternoon dressed in our formal Emmy attire.

"Come on in!" Bert said as he extended his huge hand to me and kissed Linda on the cheek.

He was dressed in khaki shorts and a Hawaiian shirt and was barefoot.

I was in a rented tux and felt like a starched penguin.

"You sure you can do your film for $250,000?" he asked before closing the heavy mahogany front door.

"Yes, sir!"

Off to my right a brass elevator lowered from overhead and settled silently on the main level. The gate parted and out stepped Bert's lovely and petite wife, Jane, who looked like she had just descended from her own heavenly beauty salon. We exchanged warm greetings.

"You're not one of those Christians who doesn't drink, are you?" Bert asked with a chuckle.

"No, sir."

Bert ushered me downstairs to the bar where the men could tilt back a couple. He uncorked a bottle of vintage red wine, poured out two glasses, and handed one to me.

"Call Alan, my attorney, tomorrow," Bert instructed. "Have him draw up an agreement."

That was it? No cross-examination, no sitting up begging with hands pawing the air, no making me crawl across the parquet floor on my belly?

"Thank you," I said. "You have my word that I will bring the film in on time, on budget, and as promised."

"I expect you to. If you start having any problems, let me know."

"Yes, sir." I felt my heart rate accelerate, and I took a deep breath. "Mr. Boeckmann, I have to have creative control."

"I sure as hell don't want it!"

We clicked glasses and drank.

Maiden Voyage (hosted by Sharon Gless) was the first of six documentary films funded by Bert and Jane Boeckmann. Through *Maiden Voyage*, viewers experienced how God's love can soften the most calloused of hearts.

Our next production was *A Step Apart* (featuring blended families and hosted by Marlo Thomas). The strong ratings and positive reviews declared, "This film reveals the one underlying emotion that can bring blended families together — their hunger to be loved."

A Time for Life (which I hosted) followed, where we went to sea with three terminally ill kids and three hard-core prisoners, with the hope that the sick kids would pass on the joy of life to those who never had it. Again, strong ratings and reviews: "Exceptional filmmaking redeems much of the worst that television has produced. Parents and children who watch this together may literally find their lives transformed."

Father/Son (hosted by Edward James Olmos) was our most challenging project, in which three boys and their fathers, who had been separated by the courts and unable to hear each other's lonely cries for help, were reunited on our sailboat for ten days at sea. All relationships were healed and restored. The reviews reflected the impact *Father/Son* had on our audience: "A gripping television special — one can only regret that this kind of magnificent therapy is not available to everyone."

In *Good Cop, Bad Kid* (again hosted by Olmos), I partnered a male juvenile gang member and female juvenile drug dealer with their worst enemies — a male anti-gang unit cop and a female K-9 narcotics agent. Each kid lived with the cops' families for seventy-two hours. As reviews reflected, the impact and camaraderie were compelling and inspirational — for both the kids and the cops.

The films were released on prime-time commercial television. There was no preaching, no overt testimonies slipped in for the unsuspecting, no Bible verses to confirm or amplify what was taking place on the screen. Yet each production touched hearts and changed lives — on God's terms.

The presiding judge granted permission for each production to have wards of the court released into our custody — with no restrictions.

Members of the probation department became our greatest supporters as they consistently cooperated with us while we filmed inside the detention centers.

Colleges, probation departments, and children's services nationwide have used our productions to give revealing insight into the world of troubled youth and the impactful roles (both good and bad) that authority figures play.

Our most financially successful production, *Gridiron Gang*, was the only one I did not want to produce.

All six productions received strong, positive reviews, changed thousands of lives, and won a boxful of Emmys.

CHAPTER 24

GRIDIRON GANG

"You've got to make a documentary about this!"

The year was 1990, and Linda was reading an article in the *Los Angeles Times* about Camp Vernon Kilpatrick's juvenile prison football team.

"They go out and play straight schools," she stated.

"No more prison-kid films, and I'm done with documentaries."

My goal now was to make scripted feature films financed by studios. Our television specials had established me as a respected filmmaker, and I felt I now had enough "juice" to direct my own scripts and maintain some say over creative control.

Linda cut out the article and left it on my desk. After three weeks of her gentle nudging, I called LA County's chief probation officer, Barry Nidorf, announcing that I would like to produce a documentary on Camp Kilpatrick's Mustangs football team.

"Lee, we're requiring everyone to present a written proposal on how they would produce the picture, including specific benefits to the department and to the juveniles," Barry explained.

"What do you mean, 'everyone'?"

"The article got a big response from Hollywood. I have to tell you, we've kind of already reached an agreement with"—he named a well-known star.

"What are the deal points?" I asked, now desperately wanting what I just might not get.

"Fifteen thousand dollars option against fifty thousand upon start of production."

I spent the next three days writing out a detailed proposal, and I hand-delivered it to Probation's headquarters in Downey, an hour's drive from our home in Agoura.

A week later, I received a form letter, thanking me for my interest and announcing that the Camp Kilpatrick Mustangs' football film rights had been awarded to the well-known star.

"You're going to get screwed, Barry," I told the chief over the phone. "We have funding from the Boeckmanns, and we're ready to produce the film."

I had grown deeply passionate about the project and knew exactly how I would bring the Mustangs football story to the screen.

"I'm sorry, Lee. Maybe we could get you on as a consultant."

I was crushed.

Football practice started in mid-August, and I stayed clear of Camp Kilpatrick because I couldn't bear watching another filmmaker attempt to capture the spirit of those throwaway kids.

I say "attempt" because over the past couple of years I had turned down *Movie of the Week* offers from well-established network producers. Hollywood's concept of capturing the heart and soul of my television specials required mutiny, escape, fistfights, no God talk, and no praying.

The third week of August, I learned through the grapevine that the "well-known star" lost interest in the Camp Kilpatrick football story and, as they say, "moved on." He also never paid Probation the agreed-on $15,000 option fee.

I called Chief Barry, and he kindly granted me the exclusive rights.

The Mustangs had completed their first two weeks of practice when we started filming. From the moment we rolled out our cameras, I felt blatant resistance from the deputy probation officer/football coach, Sean Porter.

"What's the problem?" I asked Sean.

"You'll get in the way of what I'm trying to accomplish," he retorted, trying unsuccessfully to suppress his contempt for me.

I had just requested a private meeting with Sean and his three assistant coaches, Malcolm Moore, Glenn Bell, and Alex Williams.

"I'm not going to get in your way," I said with shortness of breath, my heart pounding against my T-shirt.

Sean's a big guy with a short fuse, and his face was turning bright red.

"I'm not going to be under your microscope. Don't know what else to tell you, pal."

He started to leave.

"Sean, we're making the film with or without your cooperation." He paused at the door. "My vision for all of this is much greater than just making a documentary. I understand what you are trying to do here, and I admire you for it. But right now, you're coming off like a jerk, and that's not going to help either of us reach our goals."

Sean looked at the other coaches, who remained seated. He took a breath.

"What do you want?" Sean asked, with no hint of submission.

"Let me do my job."

■ ■ ■

Since we had missed the important first two weeks of football practice, I asked Sean to re-create two important scenes — the first time he told his delinquent players what it took to become a Mustang, and the first day of practice.

Those two scenes in the completed documentary set up the entire film and were repeated almost verbatim a dozen years later in the scripted feature film *Gridiron Gang* for Sony Pictures.

Our four weeks of filming went smoothly and were uneventful as far as production challenges were concerned. The Mustangs lost their opener against Boron High School, 31 to 0. For the first time in their lives, these untamed, dangerous street kids committed to a program and lost. The little gangbangers-turned-football-players actually believed they could win, and when they didn't, they cried.

Great story. Great filmmaking.

■ ■ ■

It took close to a year to complete the postproduction phase of *Gridiron Gang*. Academy Award winner Louis Gossett Jr. signed on as host/narrator. Once the film was in the can, I screened it for Dan Atwater, the agent who introduced us to Paul Newman, and his associates at CAA, the "hottest" agency in the business.

"That's a nice little documentary, Lee," Dan said after the screening.

The entertainment industry gurus didn't cheer. They didn't laugh, and they didn't cry. They just sat there void of emotion and endured my eighteen-month labor of love.

"Dan, *Gridiron Gang* would make a great feature film."

Dan smiled politely. "I don't think so. Studio pictures demand a bigger canvas," he explained. "This is great television."

"I wouldn't call it great television," corrected the senior suit as he stood to leave, "but it is good television."

Dan looked at his watch. "There's another screening scheduled here at five."

Dan shook my hand, as did the others, leaving me alone in the room.

I felt deflated, confused, and frustrated. I walked back to the projection room. The balding, middle-aged projectionist handed over my videocassette.

"Congratulations!" he said, wiping the tears from his eyes. "That's one of the best films I've ever seen."

■ ■ ■

Three months later, *Gridiron Gang* aired in prime time on LA's KTLA. The following is a sampling of *The Hollywood Reporter* trade magazine's review:

> *Gridiron Gang* has the best elements of great drama. It would be difficult to imagine anyone who would not be choked up to watch these young men go through wild rides of gut frustrations with life and defeat and joy, but for this brief period, their tears communicate great hope for us all. Especially when you consider that this was accomplished with less than a network-size budget, there are laudable technical credits.

After the broadcast, every major studio rep, along with a half dozen actors, writers, and producers, wanted the feature film rights to *Gridiron Gang*.

I drove around Hollywood to meet with studio heads and their producers.

The youngest guy we interviewed had little "juice," came all the way out from Los Angeles to Agoura, and had produced only one feature film, called *Juice*, starring the late rapper-thug Tupac Shakur and the then unknown thespian Samuel L. Jackson.

Neal Moritz was thirty-four years old, above average height and build, and dressed like one of the studio's messengers. We talked for an hour. Neal was more interested in what we had to say than telling us all about himself. It was also obvious that he was passionate about *Gridiron Gang*.

"Neal, I want to direct."

"That's not my decision," he said. "Whoever puts up the money has the final say on who directs."

After our meeting in Agoura, Neal called almost every day.

Over the next couple of weeks, I met with a few more studio heads, and then I took the matter to prayer.

Linda and I came up with the same response: Neal Moritz.

CHAPTER 25

"WE HAVE A BLUEPRINT—YOUR DOCUMENTARY"

"You have a meeting tomorrow at three o'clock with the head of Columbia Pictures."

"Will you be there?" I asked Neal Moritz.

"I don't need to be. You have to approve our partnering with the studio to finance and distribute *Gridiron Gang*."

As an actor, I usually got to the set around sunrise, half waved to the guard at the gate (if my part was big enough for a "drive-on"), and went straight to a dark, cold sound stage, searching for coffee and donuts before flopping down half asleep into a makeup chair. Now I was a producer, and producers went to the Thalberg Building, a huge, white, three-story monolith named after Hollywood's first "wonder boy," producer Irving Thalberg.

"Good afternoon, Mr. Stanley," said the polite, uniformed guard at the well-protected front gate of Columbia Pictures. He tipped his hat as he opened the electronic gate, and I drove onto the hallowed grounds of Columbia Pictures. I parked in the "producer area" and walked the short distance to the Thalberg Building, where another uniformed guard in the main entrance greeted me with a welcoming smile.

"Would you sign in here, please, sir?"

The large room was decorated with a dozen Academy Awards—

Oscars, if you will—honoring some of the greatest motion pictures ever produced.

"Take the elevator to the third floor and then turn to your left."

I rode the elevator in anxious silence. At the third floor the doors parted. I turned and walked down a long corridor lined with glass-encased movie posters of some of Columbia Pictures' famous movies. A jog to the right, and I found myself in the executive suite's outer office, where I exchanged greetings with a pleasant-looking woman.

"Mr. Canton will see you now," she said.

Mark Canton, the head of Columbia Pictures, was—not tall, OK. His hair was dark brown and curly (kind of like Charlie Chaplin). His office was big and airy and adorned with all the appropriate photographs, salutations, awards, and souvenirs.

Mr. Canton stared at me with a most sincere smile.

"I just loved your documentary," he said.

"Thank you."

"We want to make your picture," he said with self-conscious enthusiasm.

"That's wonderful, Mark."

"We'll get a writer we can agree on, and once we approve the script, we'll bring on a director."

I stared back at Mark. After an awkward moment, he raised a manicured finger and pointed with a knowing smile. "*You* want to direct."

"Right," I said with a nod.

"We'll have to get approval from the star, of course. Stars always have director approval."

"Mark, it's important to me that *Gridiron Gang* doesn't turn into just another phony Hollywood movie. The kids in my film trusted me with their lives. They opened up, and the film worked. That's why everybody wants it." Mark listened carefully. "I don't want the studio's *Gridiron Gang* to misrepresent them."

"Can't happen," he said with a smile. "We have a blueprint — your documentary. All we have to do is stay with the documentary and stick good actors in front of the camera."

The first order of business was to hire a writer. Fortunately, everyone on the studio's team voted for Jeff Maguire. Jeff had written Clint Eastwood's just-released smash hit, *In the Line of Fire*, and had volunteered a few years back at Camp Kilpatrick Juvenile Detention Center. Most important, he was deeply impacted by the documentary and wanted to honor its story line and emotional thread.

Jeff and I spent many hours and days together, interviewing the kids in lockup at Camp Kilpatrick and going over story points, dialogue, and characters. The first draft of the script took about three months.

Shortly thereafter, I received a telephone call from KTLA's general manager, Steve Bell.

"Congratulations, Lee!" Steve was excited. "You've been nominated for a National Prime-time Emmy for directing *Gridiron Gang*. That should guarantee that you'll direct the feature."

After a dozen meetings, it was decided by the "studio brass" that Jeff Maguire had been wrung out pretty tight and that it was time to bring in another writer to do a "script polish" on Jeff's not-so-shiny final pass.

Numerous drafts of the script for *Gridiron Gang* came and went — with each draft further and further removed from the spirit and story line of my documentary.

A couple of months later, Linda and I made the long drive to Pasadena for the Emmy Awards.

I gripped my wife's hands tightly as clips from the five nominated films in our category were projected overhead. The house lights came up.

"And the winner is . . ."

Actor and presenter Larry Fishburne opened the "hermetically" sealed envelope: "Lee Stanley, director of *Gridiron Gang*."

■ ■ ■

Finally, after four nonproductive years of trying to get my project off the ground, Columbia Pictures put *Gridiron Gang* "into turnaround," which means in reality, "We have no further interest in your project."

Bert and Jane Boeckmann were, to say the least, disappointed with Columbia and elected not to fund future projects.

To keep my name in the hat, I rewrote old scripts and modernized concepts for television series I had created years earlier.

Nothing sold.

Wings Foundation virtually evaporated because Linda and I no longer had the resources to support the work. Over the next many months, I grew frustrated and showed little consideration for my wife's feelings or fears. Too often I was rude and spoke harshly to Linda as if she had no idea of what "the artist" was going through.

To save our marriage, Linda stopped working with me and became a real estate agent. Fortunately, she was good at it.

CHAPTER 26

"WHEN'S MY DINNER WITH THE ROCK?"

"Dad, call Neal," Shane suggested.

In the nearly twelve years since Neal Moritz came out to Agoura and won our hearts and the rights to *Gridiron Gang*, he had become one of the most successful and respected producers in Hollywood. I hadn't seen or spoken to Neal in years.

"Neal, do you want to do *Gridiron Gang*?" I asked over the phone.

"Yes," he said. "Let's get together next week."

We met the following Tuesday.

"Who do you see starring in *Gridiron Gang*?" Neal asked.

"The Rock," Shane said, having seen his biography on A&E the night before.

Neal yelled out to his assistant in the outer room. "When's my dinner with The Rock?"

"Monday night," a young woman's voice answered.

"I want to go back to Maguire's original script," Neal said. "What about a director?"

"I would like to produce with you and have Shane executive produce. I already directed *Gridiron Gang*, Neal. Get someone you're comfortable with. And I want to shoot it at the actual juvenile prison — at Camp Kilpatrick."

"Will they let us do that?" Neal asked. "We'll have two or three hundred people on the set."

"I'll get permission."

Neal had his dinner with The Rock.

Instead of giving him a copy of the original *Gridiron Gang* script, he gave The Rock a DVD of our documentary. A few weeks later, The Rock (aka Dwayne Johnson) agreed to visit Camp Kilpatrick Juvenile Detention Center.

I arrived early at Canyon Café, where I was to meet Dwayne and drive up the mountain to the prison. He was already there, surrounded by a dozen locals, fielding their questions, posing for pictures, and signing autographs.

I waited a few minutes before introducing myself.

"Mr. Stanley, what an honor to meet you!" the six-foot-five Dwayne said as he stood and extended his muscular, tribal-tattooed arm, hand wide open. "I loved your documentary. I cheered and cried through the whole thing."

Here I was, shaking hands with one of the world's most sought-after movie stars, a seven-time world champion wrestler, "the People's Champion," "the Brahma Bull," "the Great One," if you will — and what came across was that Dwayne Johnson is a gentleman.

That first impression has never changed.

I had briefed the Kilpatrick staff that The Rock would be arriving around midmorning. Before we walked into the prison, Dwayne pulled me aside.

"Lee, how should I act with these kids?"

"Just be yourself. They can smell a phony a mile away."

We spent nearly two hours inside Camp Kilpatrick, and most of that time Dwayne spent talking with the kids.

They loved him.

We were reunited with friend and Oscar-nominated writer Jeff

Maguire and met with Neal Moritz's first choice for director—forty-two-year-old Phil Joanou.

We exchanged pleasantries, and Phil quickly took over the conversation. At first blush, I couldn't image this featherweight, non–football playing USC film school graduate wrangling beefy stuntmen, snarling prison kids, or me—let alone Dwayne Johnson.

"We have to stick to your documentary, Lee. You nailed it. My biggest concern is that I won't live up to your original."

Neal's studio of choice to fund and distribute *Gridiron Gang* was Sony Pictures.

The studio also signed rapper and host of MTV's *Pimp My Ride* Xzibit, a class act who cares about kids and seemingly everyone he meets.

"Lee, you told Neal we could make the picture at the actual juvenile prison?" asked Sony's president of production, Matt Tolmach. "That is what you said, isn't it?"

"Yes," I replied without blinking.

"Good, because I just signed The Rock to a 'play or pay' deal, and I can't afford to make this picture unless we can film at Camp Kilpatrick."

A "play or pay" deal means that whether or not the picture is produced, Dwayne Johnson still gets his hefty acting fee.

After that first gathering of eagles, I quickly called the Los Angeles County Probation Department's acting chief, Paul Higa. Paul was the director of Camp Kilpatrick when we made our documentary and appeared briefly in the film. Over the past many years, Paul had quietly earned his way up the corporate ladder and was now head of the second largest probation department in the world, awaiting the county supervisors' confirmation as chief (which was soon to come).

I had not seen or spoken with Paul in a dozen years. Correction: You do not speak *with* Paul. Paul is a man of very few words—a careful listener and extremely private. You speak *to* Paul and wait a few beats or days for his simple yet thoughtful response.

Paul agreed to have lunch the following week, which allowed me sufficient time to prepare a knockout presentation to convince Mr. Higa to green-light our request to virtually take over his juvenile jail for six weeks.

Paul looked the same as the last time we were together, except for a few more gray hairs and some added pounds to his five-foot-six frame. I was moved that this man with tremendous responsibility and authority set a personal tone for our time together. Once lunch was served, I steered the conversation around to *Gridiron Gang*.

"Paul, I need your help."

I opened my six-page proposal and read it aloud. Paul did not respond during my ten-minute recital. I closed the document and placed it on his side of the table. He dabbed his mouth with a napkin.

"How will the kids in camp benefit?" he asked.

"Shane and I will teach a class on filmmaking one night a week so the kids will be able to understand what it takes to produce a film, and during the day bring small groups of the camp kids out to the set to watch. We'll also make efforts to provide entry-level jobs for those kids who show an interest in production once they leave camp."

Paul paged through my proposal.

"Any questions or concerns?" I asked, breaking the two-minute silence.

"No."

"May we film at the camp?" I finally asked, my heart ricocheting around my rib cage.

"Yes."

We completed our lunch together with minimal conversation. Paul picked up the check on his own personal credit card.

"Give my best to your family," he said.

We shook hands and parted.

"God bless you, Paul Higa," I said as I watched this giant of a man drive off in his Toyota pickup.

A few months later, fifty-three-year-old Paul Higa succumbed to a stroke and died.

He never did get to see our movie.

■ ■ ■

"Quiet, please. Roll cameras!"

"Action!"

And so began the filming of *Gridiron Gang* inside Camp Vernon Kilpatrick on my birthday, May 23, 2005, twelve years after the documentary first appeared on television.

Thanks to Paul Higa, the camp staff acclimated to our fourteen-hour days, supported our needs, and made every effort to make our experience at Kilpatrick a success. We taught our one-hour film class after work every Tuesday night to our "captive audience," with a different guest speaker at each class. Dwayne spoke for ninety spellbinding minutes about his life as a juvenile delinquent (arrested seven times), football player, wrestler, and movie star.

I'm not sure who got more out of the evening — Dwayne, the camp kids, or me.

I demanded tight security on both sides of the Camp Kilpatrick wall and required all production personnel to wear identification badges whenever entering or exiting the facility.

We ran a very tight ship — and had no problems.

After six intense weeks of filming inside a remote, "working" juvenile prison, we moved our traveling circus onto city streets. The studio was pleased, so far. The "dailies" (footage shot and developed for viewing each day) looked good, and edited scenes played well.

We were all feeling confident and sure of ourselves when tragedy struck.

The call came in on Sunday morning, July 17, from our writer and dear friend Jeff Maguire. Jeff's twenty-year-old son, Danny, was bicycling home from a friend's house the night before and was struck by a hit-and-run drunk driver.

"The doctors said there is no hope for survival," Jeff said with gut-wrenching emotion. "They told us we should let him go."

I cried and prayed with Jeff for a miracle.

Monday, July 18, was one of our biggest days for *Gridiron Gang*. We were staging a football game at a local college and had three hundred plus actors and extras, along with more than a hundred crew members on the scene. Shane and I arrived at the set at six thirty in the morning and told production assistants and department heads that everyone had to be on the football field at 7:00 a.m., no exceptions.

"There has been a tragedy that struck one of our own," I called out, fighting back my emotions.

I scanned the four hundred plus faces surrounding me. No one moved. I caught The Rock's eye and knew by his expression that he was aware of what I was about to announce.

"Danny Maguire, Jeff's son, was struck by a hit-and-run driver last night. Right now, Danny is in a coma and fighting for his life." I could hear some gasping and others beginning to weep. "I'm going to pray for Danny and his family. If you want to join me, then take the hand of the person next to you."

I waited as all joined hands.

I prayed out loud and boldly asked for God's almighty grace to be poured out on Danny and the entire Maguire family. I concluded with the Lord's Prayer. Others joined in. By the second verse, the entire *Gridiron Gang* "family" was praying.

"In honor of the Maguires," I said, "let's make this the best day we've ever had."

Danny Maguire never recovered. Three years after the accident, Danny passed away.

CHAPTER 27

"THIS IS RARE AIR"

Gridiron Gang was produced on time, on budget, and as promised.

Four months later, the "first cut" of the film was completed. Sony Pictures (through the Nielson National Research Group) set up a recruited audience survey screening at the Bridge: Cinema de Lux in Los Angeles. The audience consisted of 279 moviegoers between the ages of fifteen and thirty-four.

"At this initial screening," the Nielson written report stated, "*Gridiron Gang* played to enthusiastic 'excellent' ratings and well above average 'definitely recommend' scores overall. The movie played very well, regardless of gender or age."

"This is rare air we're breathing," responded a very pleased Amy Pascal, chairman of Columbia Pictures. "These are the highest scores we've had for a movie in nearly ten years."

Two more survey screenings with different demographics and at a different theater reported the same results with the exception of one category, which scored even higher.

Upon completion of production, I received a Mustangs football, signed by all cast members, and a letter that read as follows:

Dear Lee,

I am glad to finally be able to live up to the promise I made you almost thirteen years ago. This is a dream come true for me, and it wouldn't have been possible without all your hard work, commitment, and passion. You are an inspiration to me in life, and I am proud to be able to call you my friend.

Respectfully,
Neal Moritz

And from our star:

Hey, Brother!

It was an honor to make *Gridiron Gang*. I'm so proud of our movie and so proud for you and your family to finally see your dream come to fruition.

Peace and continued blessings,
DJ (Dwayne Johnson)

■ ■ ■

Attending a major motion picture world premier is pretty heady stuff. Searchlights pierce the evening skies, and sawhorses and whistle-blowing policemen keep the "common folk" in place as movie stars and power people roll up in shiny stretch limos. Photographers and TV cameras take aim, and from the backseat out pop Mr. and/or Ms. Important, all smiles, smelling good and looking perfect. Unless it's a famous actor, the crowd wonders, "Who's that? Must be somebody—he's walking on the red carpet!"

I had the privilege of walking the red carpet with Linda by my side for the world premier of *Gridiron Gang* at Hollywood's Grauman's Chinese Theatre. I was living the dream—a dream that took shape out of a desperate need to capture the heart cry of today's troubled youth—and my own heart cry to learn how to become a man, a husband, and a father.

Reporters and movie fans elbowed their way through the anxious overflow crowd to get a shot, a comment from me about the movie. I wasn't feeling important or prideful. I was feeling blessed, and I thought back to that day with Michael Landon when I commended him for his good work.

"It was always an uphill battle, Lee," Michael said with a smile. "But if you know something is right and good, then you have to stand your ground."

We need more Michael Landons in the world of entertainment and more individuals like Bert and Jane Boeckmann, who have the heart and compassion to finance productions that allow people who know their craft to deliver products that impact audiences — on God's terms — without scaring off or, worse, condemning viewers who need to be inspired.

■ ■ ■

Gridiron Gang opened on September 15, 2006, in more than 3,500 theaters nationwide. Commercials appeared on network and cable television promoting our movie, along with billboards and one-sheets on city buses throughout Los Angeles and across the country. Newspapers ran full-page ads, and one building in Beverly Hills displayed a nine-story blowup of the movie poster.

We hosted private screenings for city and county leaders, as well as a private screening at Camp Kilpatrick for the kids and staff in appreciation for their cooperation and support.

All that media hype and promotion, fueled by millions of Sony Pictures dollars, paid off. After the opening weekend, *Gridiron Gang* was the number one movie at the box office.

PART 6

CHAPTER 28

WHAT ARE WE AFRAID OF?

Today's most financially successful films are rated G or PG, yet the trigger pullers, the industry decision makers, pump out R-rated (or worse) films and television productions. They keep pushing the envelope, and we keep lining up or flopping down on the couch to absorb their latest interpretation of life according to crap.

As long as we buy the tickets or watch their channels, they will continue to make productions that rattle our brains and stomp on good morals, values, and ethics.

We must create quality entertainment that reflects life as it can be — or should have been — without hitting people over the head with the gospel.

Where's the balance?

Over the past couple of years I have learned a simple truth: some of the projects I have acquired or written are either too "religious" (aka "Christian") for the secular world or too secular for the Christian world.

Why is it that when we work under the banner of "Christian," we are often forced to dilute the truth and power of the pen or the camera by creating characters who do not exist in real life?

Christian films have the unbridled reputation of being artificial, manipulative, and predictable, with watered-down, one-dimensional characters and unbelievable (notice I did not say *supernatural*) story lines. We preach; we point; we judge; and we prance around our blatant theme to *suspecting* audiences for what purpose—to lead them to Christ?

Too often we are doing more earthly damage than kingdom good.

What are we afraid of?

I am not saying we shouldn't tell Christian stories. One of the biggest box office successes in history is *The Passion of the Christ*.

There is a great example—*and* it was as Christian as you can get. But more important, it was well produced, brilliantly acted, and brutally honest.

Gridiron Gang is a story about juvenile prisoners—those who are among the most violent of street criminals—who are taught the game of football so they can take on "straight schools" and learn what can happen when they commit themselves 100 percent. A well-known Christian billionaire wanted to fund the production if—and only if—it contained no swearwords.

Fortunately, the studio turned him down for that reason alone.

Remember earlier when Pastor Jack Hayford screened my TV special, *Desperate Passage*, for the congregation as it was broadcast? That documentary had a dozen cusswords in it and featured real kids who killed people. Those same killers dropped their thug facade and cried out for help.

Hearts were touched; lives were transformed—and no one complained.

Am I advocating that we cuss and curse or give somebody the finger every five minutes in our films or books?

Absolutely not!

What I am saying is this: I believe it is our responsibility as artists to create characters, circumstances, and settings as they really are—as long as those incidents are justifiable and are not used for shock value alone or as a short-circuiting of the creative process.

If a character in my films or books encounters the person who just brutally murdered his loved one, I promise you he will not say, "Gosh darn you."

He will cry out from his gut, from his soul — so I, you, we, will believe him.

The majority of my television specials featured violent juvenile offenders. I depicted them as they really are because I wanted my audience (especially those who prided themselves on being "badass") to drop their facade and experience the transforming power of Christ's love played out right before their "mad-dogging" eyes.

If we set up watered-down, artificial, phony characters in the beginning of our films or books, audiences will not believe, or even come to realize, the magnitude of their transformation or experience God's power, forgiveness, and unconditional love.

Christians who watch our films know in their guts that the filmmaker is a born-again Christian.

Nonbelievers consistently ask, "What is it about your productions that are so different, so life changing?"

I always give the same answer. "You experienced the love and presence of Jesus Christ. Imagine what he can do in your life, if you will only let him."

I was once introduced on a television talk show as a "Christian filmmaker." I respectfully corrected the host and said, "I am a Christian who happens to be a filmmaker."

Christ made that very clear to me the first time I picked up a camera after becoming born again.

"I died for everyone," he reminded me. *"Your work needs to be for everyone I died for."*

EPILOGUE

I've had no formal training in dealing with troubled youth — or troubled anybodies — except for my personal experiences with trouble, confusion, hopelessness, fear, and pain in my own life.

What healed me was the fervent prayer of caring, committed believers, my surrendering to the Lord, and God's unconditional love.

That's all I have to offer. Many juveniles accepted it, and today are model citizens who would make any parent, spouse, or child beam with pride. They are grateful to God and grateful that someone took the time to share God's love.

Others went back to the streets or are back in jail — or are dead.

What I have learned is that we must never give up on anybody.

The kids I worked with in the past are now adults. I enjoy their occasional phone calls from all over the country. It seems as though they are as surprised to hear my voice as I am theirs.

Last week I had lunch with "Baby Huey" — you remember, he was the Wings "poster boy" — along with his wife. Five years ago, I officiated at their wedding. Baby Huey now works in the film industry and owns his own home.

Russell Lawrence (featured in *Desperate Passage*) and I break bread together annually. Russell is the manager of a highly respected lighting company on the West Coast and the father of four. I performed his wedding ceremony as well.

Thirty-eight-year-old Kay was featured in *Maiden Voyage*. Linda and I were there for Kay when her infant child was murdered, and we have stayed available to her for the past twenty years. She remarried, has a twelve-year-old daughter, and is a certified notary public and employed in the auto industry.

Bartow, whom we tried to help years ago when he was in Camp Gonzales, got sentenced to twenty years for attempted murder. While he was locked up in an Arkansas federal prison, we paid for his education and wrote him often.

He called after he was released two years ago. "Thanks for being there for me, Lee," Bartow said as we sat down for our first meal together outside of prison walls. He is now working in his family's business, is married, and has one child.

Leslie was making a thousand dollars a day selling drugs before getting locked up. After ten days at sea, she turned her life around. Linda and I had not seen Leslie since the premier of *Maiden Voyage* twenty years ago. Recently over lunch, we met her three children. Leslie owns a number of successful restaurants.

When *Gridiron Gang* hit the theaters, we heard from dozens of Wings kids with whom we had lost contact or who were just going about their lives. Some came out for the premier, where we had the opportunity to give them a hug and meet their spouses and families.

■ ■ ■

And what about our own kids?

Years ago, the Lord gave me a promise for Linda's oldest son, Christopher, who turned his back on God and me at the age of fifteen.

Linda and I held on to God's promise for twenty-five years, as we have held on to other promises you have read about in this book. Seven years ago, our fervent prayers were answered, and Christopher welcomed the Lord back into his life. Today he is a public insurance claims adjuster, husband, and father of two daughters.

Five years ago, Christopher announced he was getting baptized at his church and asked if his mother and I could be present.

"Of course," I told him.

"Thank you," he said. "Lee, I want you to baptize me."

Middle son Brett continues to live in God's promise of "total victory."

Daughter Quinn and her husband have adopted four children and established a foundation called Open Arms, supporting birth moms and dads who find that they are unable to parent their new-born babies.

Shane is married and producing, directing, and writing. Occasionally we work on film projects together.

Recently, I have had a chance to reflect, renew, and do some writing. I like writing and want to write books that inspire people to believe in themselves — but more important, to believe in the Lord.

I want to continue making independent, "honest to God" films that reinforce God's principles.

I enjoy speaking to a handful — or to thousands — of people about the practical Lord I know and how he will give you an abundant life.

I want to support organizations that are off the radar screen but are consistently doing what God has put on their hearts.

I want to have the guts to walk away when I get the slightest whiff that a business deal is not right. Even the wildest of animals or fish know to boogie when they sense the slightest bit of danger or threat. Looking back, I know I could have saved thousands of hours and dollars if I had acted on those subtle promptings telling me that the deal or the person stank.

I want more patience. I do not like it when things I pray for, hope for, and work for take so long to come to fruition.

I want to live aboard a yacht, something Linda and I have always promised we would do, and sail to different ports to experience and write about the quiet majority — those who love America and are living life on God's terms.

As you can imagine, I had no idea what direction my life would take after that first encounter back in 1981 at Camp David Gonzales. I also had no idea that I would walk down a path that would take me to the red carpet at Grauman's Chinese Theatre.

Over the past three decades, and in the most alarming and miraculous ways imaginable, I have learned that Jesus Christ is *exactly* who the Bible claims he is.

The one thing I did not expect was that in the process Jesus Christ would reveal *exactly* who Lee Stanley really was, and that in order for me to fulfill my God-ordained purpose on earth, I would have to change—a change that only God Almighty himself could bring about.

It didn't all happen overnight. But it all happened—his way.

ACKNOWLEDGMENTS

Many friends and family members have given their time, encouragement, and expertise to help me write my memoir. Without their support I don't think I would have been able to complete it, let alone get it published. I'm sure I have left out a few, but these deserve special recognition.

My grateful appreciation to Dave and Lynn Adams; Jed Allan; Victor Anderson; Rick Bee; Stephen Blount; Andy and Nelda Cotte; Daniel Bernstein; Dudley Delffs; Sheila Ett; Jac Flanders; Dr. Jack W. Hayford; Dwayne Johnson; Pastor David Loveless; bestselling author Bill Myers; Sean Porter; Zondervan executive editor John Sloan; Stacy Jenel Smith; my daughter-in-law, Val Stanley; the world's greatest brother, Ric Stanley Jr. Esq.; my son Shane Stanley, who encouraged me on an almost daily basis to write my memoir; and my forever loving and inspirational wife, Linda, who kept me on track — no matter the cost.

ABOUT THE AUTHOR

Lee Stanley is a writer, producer, director, and licensed Protestant minister who has been nominated for ten Emmy Awards and has won five. He is the recipient of numerous national and international filmmaking awards, a two-time winner of the CINE Golden Eagle Award, winner of awards at the WorldFest-Houston International Film Festival, and the winner of the prestigious Christopher Award for the positive impact his films have on the American family. Lee's work has won him the respect and endorsement of the White House, the U.S. Department of Justice, and civic leaders nationwide. He has been honored with a Certificate of Appreciation from the U.S. attorney general and has been the guest speaker at the National Conference for Attorney Generals.

Lee produced the number one box office hit *Gridiron Gang*, starring Dwayne Johnson, for Sony Pictures, based on his Emmy Award–winning documentary special of the same title.

Lee is best known for the *Desperate Passage* documentary series where violent juvenile prisoners were released solely into his custody for ten-day, at-sea expeditions aboard the filmmaker's fifty-eight-foot sailboat. This documentary series was nominated for thirty-three individual Emmys and won thirteen.

This book is Lee's profoundly moving, brutally transparent journey through life both before and after he was broadsided by an unexpected encounter with God.

"If you are not exactly who you claim to be," Stanley cried out, "then I will drop you like a bad habit!" Lee took on the motion picture and television industry, the judicial system, the world's largest probation department, the public school system, social workers, counselors, and child psychologists and discovered, after a roller-coaster ride of trials and tribulations and miraculous victories, that the heavenly Father keeps his word—*when* you have the guts to trust in him.

Lee is the president of his own production company, Stanhaven Productions, and was the founder of Wings Foundation, a nonprofit organization that served Los Angeles County's probated youth. Lee is an accomplished yachtsman, certified scuba diving instructor, skier, and photographer, and he currently enjoys his weekly boxing matches. Lee and his wife, Linda, have been married for thirty-three years. They have three sons and one daughter and reside in Southern California when not cruising in various oceans aboard their long-range motor yacht, *Stanhaven III*.

AUDIO-VISUAL RESOURCES

Author/filmmaker Lee Stanley's award-winning productions are available for your DVD library at www.stanhavenmedia.com.

TITLES AVAILABLE ON DVD

Gridiron Gang. The Emmy Award–winning documentary that launched the number one box office hit for Sony Pictures. Losers in the game of life, these juvenile prisoners are taught the game of football and learn that when they're willing to commit themselves 100 percent, they can be winners. 90 minutes.

> *"Filmmaker Lee Stanley takes us through a quite amazing transformation. It is difficult to imagine anyone who would not be choked up to watch these young men."*
>
> The Hollywood Reporter

Desperate Passage. Multiple Emmy Award–winning documentary. Seven juvenile prisoners are released into Lee Stanley's custody for ten days at sea aboard Lee's fifty-eight-foot sailboat. 94 minutes.

> *"Lee Stanley is to be praised for his knowing view. A stark revelation—when the mind thinks with the heart."*
>
> The Hollywood Reporter

Maiden Voyage. Emmy Award–winning documentary in which Lee and his wife, Linda, take six girls — prisoners of a maximum-security detention facility — on a ten-day sailing voyage to confront nature and each other so they can experience a side of life not filled with gangs, violence, and drugs. 54 minutes.

> *"The girls had a chance to see how a normal family functions and to taste what love is — and to have an opportunity to hear God."*
>
> Valley Magazine

A Step Apart. Some experts say the American family isn't working anymore. In this documentary special, seven stepfamilies drop their defenses, bare all, and tell all on what it takes to make a stepfamily work. 94 minutes.

> *"Stanley's camera reveals the one underlying emotion that can bring them together — their hunger to be loved."*
>
> Los Angeles Times

A Time for Life. Six kids — three hard-core prisoners with no hope nor any value for human life, and three who are full of love and full of life yet suffer from terminally ill diseases — share their lives together for one week at sea. Hosted by Lee Stanley. 94 minutes.

> *"Exceptional filmmaking redeems much of the worst that television has produced. Parents and children who watch this together may literally find their lives transformed."*
>
> The Hollywood Reporter

Father/Son. Lost in a wave of blame, three boys and their fathers who have been separated by the courts and unable to hear each other's lonely cries for help are united on Lee's fifty-eight-foot sailboat where, despite the close quarters, they have the room to change their minds and their lives. 94 minutes.

"A gripping television special — one can only regret that this kind of magnificent therapy is not available to everyone."
                                                    The Hollywood Reporter

Good Cop, Bad Kid. In this powerful one-hour special, a juvenile gang member prisoner is released into the custody of an anti-gang unit cop, and a drug-dealing imprisoned girl is released into the custody of a K-9 narcotics agent. Each youth lives, eats, and stays together with the cop's family for seventy-two hours. The impact and camaraderie are compelling and inspirational — for both the kids and the cops. 54 minutes.

On the Line. Lee's first documentary film is an intimate look at the men (Lee Stanley featured) who race the Mojave Desert in one of the most grueling motorcycle races of all time — and the women who wait. 90 minutes.

Mountain Tops. Paraplegic Rick Leavenworth's solo assault on Red Slate Mountain, a 13,163-foot peak in the High Sierra. An inspirational story of courage and faith against the greatest of odds. 30 minutes.

Street Pirates. Seven juvenile inmate are temporarily released into Lee's custody to train and race in one of the largest sailboat regattas on the West Coast. No one could have imagined the outcome. 60 minutes.

Share Your Thoughts

With the Author: Your comments will be forwarded to the author when you send them to *zauthor@zondervan.com*.

With Zondervan: Submit your review of this book by writing to *zreview@zondervan.com*.

Free Online Resources at
www.zondervan.com

Zondervan AuthorTracker: Be notified whenever your favorite authors publish new books, go on tour, or post an update about what's happening in their lives at www.zondervan.com/authortracker.

Daily Bible Verses and Devotions: Enrich your life with daily Bible verses or devotions that help you start every morning focused on God. Visit www.zondervan.com/newsletters.

Free Email Publications: Sign up for newsletters on Christian living, academic resources, church ministry, fiction, children's resources, and more. Visit www.zondervan.com/newsletters.

Zondervan Bible Search: Find and compare Bible passages in a variety of translations at www.zondervanbiblesearch.com.

Other Benefits: Register yourself to receive online benefits like coupons and special offers, or to participate in research.

ZONDERVAN®

ZONDERVAN.com/
AUTHORTRACKER
follow your favorite authors